THE

CHALLENGE

OF THE

MAHATMAS

Martin Green

Basic Books, Inc., Publishers   New York

Library of Congress Cataloging in Publication Data

Green, Martin Burgess, 1927–
    The challenge of the Mahatmas.

    (His The lust for power ; v. 1)
    Based on a series of seven talks given at Tufts
University.
    Includes index.
        1.   Gandhi, Mohandas Karamchand, 1869–1948—Ad-
dresses, essays, lectures.   2.   Tolstoy, Lev Nikolaevich,
graf, 1828–1910—Addresses, essays, lectures.
3.   Civilization, Modern—20th century—Addresses,
essays, lectures.   I.   Title.   II.   Series.
DS481.G3G73   954'.035'0924   [B]   77–75245
ISBN: 0–465–00904–2

For John and Susan Swan,

fellow-seekers

The Challenge of the Mahatmas,
volume one of *The Lust for Power*

When Mahatma Gandhi was killed in January, 1948, one of the world leaders' regrets ran, "The process of mass application of force to resolve contentious issues is fundamentally not only wrong, but contains within itself the germs of self-destruction. . . . If civilization is to survive, men cannot fail eventually to adopt Gandhi's belief. . . ." This gem of top-level jargon came in the name of General Douglas MacArthur, Supreme Allied Commander in Japan.

CONTENTS

Contents

Preface:

On the Whole Project

OUR AGE'S MAHATMA, our Great Soul, was Gandhi, but in my title I associate Tolstoy with him and call both of them equally Mahatmas. I do so because both stood for one overwhelming idea, which was the same in both cases, and made standing for it into a whole life. The association in title is not too eccentric, for Gandhians have sometimes given Tolstoy a similar Hindu honorific, Rishi, or Saint, and in other ways have linked his name with Gandhi's, because Tolstoy was their master's great master. I mean, of course, the Tolstoy of his last years, after his conversion, not the Tolstoy of his great novels. And the "challenge" of my title is in some ways more acute in Tolstoy, just because this Mahatma had been a great novelist and then turned away from art as being inadequate or worse. This makes his a sharper challenge from this book's point of view. A Mahatma's call is to all of us, whatever we are doing, to turn from it and follow him, but I shall describe it from the perspective of those like me, teachers of literature, men of letters.

To be a challenge, a man's example must offer a lot that is attractive and inspiriting, as well as much that is grim, dismaying, overawing. The attractive things I will group around three main themes: war, empire, and the spirit. The dismaying things will emerge of themselves.

Tolstoy and Gandhi seem to me to have thought more seriously than anybody else about war. I mean "thought," obviously, in a very existentialist and unphilosophic sense. They were more appalled by it, refused more resolutely to accept it, and told us more authoritatively not to do so. And those others of us who cannot accept it, now that they have aroused our attention, are called to follow their example. That I chose to be a man of letters meant in itself that I always shrank from violence, retreated to the social corners farthest from it. But as long as we remain a part of our society, however passively and reluctantly, violence pursues us, both morally, in the form of responsibility for what our government does, and literally, in the form of retribution—by now a retribution that may this time really destroy our civilization.

"Empire" is a word whose ordinary meanings I want to extend in two ways. First, I want it to cover what Immanuel Wallerstein calls, in his book of that title, "the modern world system." This is the international economic-cum-political structure that began to emerge in the sixteenth century, and that made the interests of the rest of the world subservient to those of Northwest Europe; the system that has—while opposing itself to the empires of the older kind —yet regulated the exploitation of the world's resources, human and nonhuman, ever since. Second, I want "empire" or imperialism to mean the character of the art and science and thought of those countries, even in the moments when that thought has been hostile to the political and military activity of their governments.

I am concerned with the lust for power built into our imagination more effectively than into that of others, built into our radicalism as well as into our conservatism. To treat imperialism this way is to psychologize it, but I am concerned with cultural psychology, not individual. Indeed, seen in terms of individual psychology, Tolstoy and Gandhi, rather than their enemies, are likely to seem prime examples of the lust for power within radicalism that I was diagnosing as our hidden sickness. But from the point of view of cultural psychology, they used power—they *were* hugely powerful psyches—against itself, against all the truly sinister manifestations of that lust. It is indeed just this fact—that they alone performed this paradox—that makes them our Mahatmas.

By the "spirit" I mean what is often called religion, or one kind of religion. I take Tolstoy and Gandhi to be the men who could bring Christianity, and other such religions, to life again today. "Spirit" or "spirituality" are convenient words because they illuminate those aspects of religion, aspects of upward striving and moral transcendence, of asceticism, of soul fighting body, that distinguish this kind of religion—aspects that the adherents of religion today minimize. Indeed, even the adherents of Gandhi in the West, those who follow his teachings in civil disobedience, apologize for this strain in him. But I believe it is precisely that asceticism that makes him and Tolstoy our Mahatmas. One of the seminal ideas of our time has been the intellectual crusade that Norman O. Brown called "Life Against Death." His book gives a post-Freudian account of a struggle within both personality and culture of the body against the soul, in which the body is identified with life, the soul with death. That is what we have come to believe, but we have not taken account—because it is such a huge account—of how completely this theory undercuts the best as well as the worst achievements of civilized culture. We have been convinced—at the level of sensibility—that our cult of mind has led us into our present suicidal situation, and that we should put our energies into curbing it. But Tolstoy and Gandhi tell us that it is the cult of appetite— the appetites of the body as well as the ego—that has been our sin. They are the only men willing to tell us, and able to convince us, that the soul lives by denial of the body, but that it must be chosen and cherished for doing that—that the *soul* is to be identified with life.

They are then our Mahatmas by virtue of those three themes they develop, which trouble us all, though some of us more than others. Above all, they are my Mahatmas, by virtue of three of my characters; as a man of letters, and so incomplete contemplative, would-be man of peace; as a citizen of England, the supreme imperialist power, now suffering the corruptions of imperial decay; and as, in some vestigial sense, a Christian.

So I am planning to write three books about them, with the general title of *The Lust for Power*. All three bear down upon the same point—their unity of focus is quite painful in intensity—but their material and type are unlike one another. The third will be a joint biography of the two men, measuring the one against the other, with the theme of being a Mahatma; a biography in the same sense that *The Von Richthofen Sisters* was a biography of Max Weber and D. H. Lawrence. The second will be a study of how imperialism, war, and so on, have shaped our culture's imagination by means of fiction; it will take the form of a study of the adventure novel—primarily of Defoe, Scott, and Kipling —with reflections on the relations between this fiction and the kind we call "serious." This first volume, as I have said, describes the challenge of the Mahatmas to men whose imaginations have been shaped that way.

The book is built around a series of seven talks I gave at Tufts University after my trip to India in November 1975, when the image of Gandhi was fresh in my mind. They were in effect one long talk, with six intermissions, full of the idea I had come back with, and bristling with its ramifications. Those talks still seem to make the points I want to make here, but the conditions of reading a book are somewhat different from those of listening in a group of twenty to thirty in Tufts' Laminan Lounge every Tuesday afternoon. I wanted to include considerably more information, in order to give my argument more authority, and—with the same motive—to be more personal and auto-biographical in places. This new material goes into the chapters that are inserted before, after, and between the talks, though I have also similarly stiffened, or starched, the talks themselves in places. But formally it is interesting, I think, to preserve the talks, in amber as it were, as a more natural, more spontaneous, form still seen within the more premeditated.

The Challenge of

the Mahatmas

I

Introducing Tolstoy and Gandhi

LYOF NIKOLAEVICH TOLSTOY was born in 1828 and died in 1910. Mohandas Karamchand Gandhi was born in 1869 and died in 1948. In their unregenerate days they were very different from each other as social types, though after their conversions they became, in their difference from us, essentially identical. Each was the youngest of several brothers, but the Tolstoys were Russian nobility, soldiers and landlords and serf-owners, men of pride and power by calling, rulers, through the class they belonged to, of a great and growing empire. The Gandhis were Indian merchants and administrators in a very small and backward princely state, one among many on the subcontinent dominated by England. Manhood presented itself to the two boys under very different aspects.

But to identify the two by family, class, or country would be too large a task to undertake in a brief introduction like this. All I can hope to do is to give some account of each one's physical or biological personality, including how that varied at different stages of his life. This will, I hope, give more color to the schematic account of their development as Mahatmas which follows.

Gandhi was always physically slight and frail, with big ears and a small chin and jaw. The bottom of his face was disproportionately small, with a big-lipped mouth that lost all its teeth and fell in. He was generally considered ugly when past his youth and, even when young, physically insignificant. He is said to have been active and vivacious as a child, and to have assumed some favorite's privileges, precedences over others, within the family. But the major anecdotes, from his schooldays on, are of shyness, aversion to fighting and boisterousness, and an unusual moral intensity—a care for his moral reputation, a will to sacrifice himself, a competitiveness in good deeds. When a worldly schoolfriend persuaded him to cultivate worldly strengths and virtues—by means of eating meat, visiting brothels, and so on—Gandhi suffered lurid hallucinations of reproach. At the same time he was a very possessive, jealous, would-be dominating husband, from the age of eleven.

His was clearly a very powerful though uneasy ego, which forbade itself certain sorts of gratification only to reach for larger kinds. He was also keenly curious and adventurous of mind, though not a star performer intellectually. He broke with religious rules and family precedent by determining at eighteen to go to England to study law. He left his wife behind, glad, one guesses, to be free from the quarrels and tensions that were frequent between them—quarrels one biographer relates to Gandhi's biological inferiority in his wife's eyes, Kasturba being a beautiful and vigorous woman, and Mohandas not a handsome or commanding husband. It seems that Kasturba was never sexually responsive to him, so that the sexual act between them remained all his responsibility, his appetite, his animalism. To feel that was a great burden and depressant to him.

It was, then, a meek young man, in superficial but also in profound senses of meekness, who went to England as a student in 1888. He suffered, then and later, from both headaches and constipation. He was also a heavy eater, and Erik Erikson has analyzed him as an oral and anal-retentive type. Indeed, his imagination and moral sense do seem to be dominated, or characterized, by strong feelings—mostly negative—about alimentation and elimination. Certainly his years in England deepened his concern with diet and with various kinds of ascetic religion.

His career as a lawyer began inauspiciously, perhaps because of his acute shyness and nervousness when he had to speak in public. He could not remember what he had to say, and he could not make himself heard. His voice was never to be loud or rich, his speeches were never to be high flights of oratory, but he was, later, unfailingly efficient and collected, and indeed a spell-binding speaker in an anti-rhetorical style. So it seems equally likely that this early shyness was a result as much as a cause of his uneasiness with his profession. His beliefs and feelings ran strongly against the irreligious Westernism of the law in India, and against the clothes, manners, work habits, and huge fees that a lawyer had to accept. So we may read as deeply revealing the fact that he sometimes fell asleep in the courtroom, in the days when he had everything to learn there—a failing inconceivable in the later Gandhi.

It was not until he had found another identity, as reformer and protector of the Indian community in Natal, that Gandhi became the confident and commanding man of law we see in an early photograph, the alert and vigorous executive in the elegant English suit. But this was a brief phase, for that persona was almost a by-product of his

5

process of self-discovery and self-realization; the latter drove him quickly past all such self-manifestations, to brahma-charya (asceticism) and mahatmahood, past the English suit to the dhoti and the loincloth, past the executive's vigor to the pilgrim's patience. He experimented in the care of his body ever more boldly as he grew older—turning from orthodox medicine to sunbaths, mudpacks, diet experiments —and achieved an extraordinary control of his bodily functions.

Indeed, by a significant paradox, it was in Gandhi's last phases that his body became a triumphant manifestation of his will—supple-waisted, quick-legged, young-fleshed. In his last years he was notably stronger and abler than his contemporaries, instead of feebler and frailer, notably young or ageless, a vivid physical presence and hero of carnality. And the development of his personality ran parallel. Though those last years brought him the terrible disappointments and insoluble problems of Pakistan's split away from India, brought him angry criticism and reproach from many sides, still none denied that Gandhi had achieved an extraordinary self, had built up a spiritual body of incomparable force.

Tolstoy was a highly emotional child and boy, a frequent weeper, easily fascinated by others. His mother died when he was two, and all his older siblings were boys, so he grew up in a very male-oriented household and fixed very strong feelings upon his father, his brothers, and later his friends. He longed intensely to have one brother's handsomeness, another's serenity, another's integrity. Of course we don't know whether similar things were true of Gandhi, because the latter's mode of self-awareness and his habits of self-description were so different. Tolstoy was educated by the great literary classics of self-consciousness, Sterne, Rousseau, Byron, and so on. And it seems clear that he experienced himself, for much of his early life, as an inchoate entity buffeted by fixed personalities. He was of course determined

by certain objective measures. He was physically strong—
and Tolstoy experienced his physical selfhood with phenomenal vividness—and, like Gandhi, he was notably
unhandsome. He had small deepset eyes, a shapeless nose,
and in photographs there is a rough harsh texture to his
expression that speaks of alternations of advance and re-
treat, ambition, suspicion, and resentment by the self
within.

Intellectually, he seems not to have accepted measure-
ment by public standards or to have reacted against his
acceptance of them, and wiped it out. He knew himself
instead as a succession of enthusiasms and boredoms,
certainties and self-doubts, which so completely described
his intellectual life that he didn't know if he was "clever"
or not. He never, as it were, stood still long enough to be
measured. And in more ordinary terms of self-image, psychological or sociological, the young Tolstoy was a succession
of impersonations: as the man about town, the intellectual,
the poet, the child of Nature, and so on. This is what one
sees—one impersonation or another—in the group photographs of him with his brothers, or with the writers of
Nekrassov's group, or alone, as an imperious young officer.

What gradually emerged from beneath this turmoil of
impersonations was a residual identity as ever-potential self,
a man who could not actualize any of his ambitions in
particular because he must actualize all of them in general,
and in rapid succession; the identity that finds a convenient
social label as "the artist-type," though it is in fact one kind
of deliberate naif. Tolstoy presents characters who represent
himself in fiction as characterized by blushing and stammer-
ing and awkward silence, by gaucheries of frankness and
sullenness, enthusiasm and criticalness, disconcerting their
acquaintances, making large claims on their friends' feelings,
and then retreating or disappearing when the latter open
themselves in response. Then in his mid-thirties Tolstoy fell

in love with a family whose children as a group embodied an ego very like his own—an ego of inflammable responsiveness, only lightly circumscribed and limited by the label "girl." (It was the daughters he was most concerned with.) Sonya Behrs was a little more than half Tolstoy's age, and she possessed a forcefulness of naiveté equal to his. They reinforced each other's self-images and ambitions—his to become a great novelist, hers to become a great mother, both in the largest sense of those concepts—and for several years that was enough.

Those were the years in which he wrote *War and Peace* and *Anna Karenina,* and she bore thirteen children. But it seems she always felt herself, sexually, as a girl violated by a man of her father's age and, like Kasturba Gandhi, she never enjoyed the sexual act itself. However, both Tolstoys flourished physically, and flaunted their carnal exuberance in the faces of others, Sonya while pregnant running and jumping across the garden toward visitors, Lyof hanging upside down from parallel bars while discussing estate matters with his bailiff. But of course this naive openness had to resolve itself into something more determined: either consciously and purposefully, a movement onward into risk, as in his case; or unconsciously and unintentionally, a conservative concentration on what one *has,* as in hers. Tolstoy's urge for self-fulfilment drove him, even as he wrote novels, to explore other modes of being beyond the novelist's—for instance, Platon Karataev's mode—and to find the best of those superior to his own. Hers led her more and more to concentrate her behavior and to some extent her sympathies in limited and conventional modes of wifehood and motherhood.

Finally Tolstoy wanted to cease being a count and a novelist, even to cease being a husband and a father. He wanted to follow the path that led toward Mahatmahood. This cost him many terrible scenes with Sonya, since both had chosen to be passionate people. (The terrible scenes between the Gandhis came early in their lives together, and neither of them had chosen passion in the same sense.) Tolstoy took to wearing a Russian peasant's smock and boots and to growing his beard long. With his terribly wrinkled brow and small, rough-featured face, he came to look like, he became, a manifestation of the Russian soil, of the rocks and roots of the immemorial Russian forest. Over that knotted and gnarled root still played, of course, the light of intelligence and will, but Tolstoy had eliminated, as it were, that intermediary "cultural" self, that "modern" ego, all sensibility and self-consciousness, that he had cultivated in his youth, and out of which his great novels had grown and flowered. His physical personality was less vivid at the last than it had been before, and less carnal—more an idea of agedness—than Gandhi's.

These, then, were the two men—what one might have seen of the two Mahatmas had one lived alongside them. But in this book I am concerned only with their Mahatmahood, and the challenge that offers to liberal humanists. So an introduction must rehearse the major facts about the two men relating to their religious training, their conversions, and their vocations as Mahatmas. (Because Tolstoy was a European and a Christian, in this matter his case must be easier to understand than Gandhi's, so less need be said about him.) Then must come something about their treatment of the three great themes, war, empire, and the spirit. And finally the contact between the two, the handing over from one to the other, the moment of tradition and initiation, and the manner of their respective defeats and deaths.

Gandhi was born in Gujerat in the modh bania subcaste of the Vaisyas, the merchant caste. His family was vaishnava by religious affiliation, which means they made a cult of Vishnu, the Preserver, and probably had their own guru in

the local temple. But his mother, Putlibai, whom he regarded as a saint and who was much more his life-model
than his father was, had been raised in the pranami sect,
noted for the religious influence they accepted from Islam.
More than other Hindus, the pranamis sang hymns, revered
their book of Faith, and insisted on celibacy in their gurus.
It was, however, maryada, another of the four ways of Hindu
devotion, that required above all restraint of the passions
from its devotees, and some scholars have thought that
Putlibai must have been a maryada, since that restraint was
so marked in her and in her son.

Moreover, the Gandhi house was visited by Jain monks,
who believed in the confession of sins and in *anekantavada*
—the possibility of reaching a truth by several different
routes, or perhaps the term is better translated as the multi-
form character of truth. It was one such monk, Becharji
Swami, who persuaded Putlibai to let Mohandas go to
England to study in 1888, a journey that offended orthodox
Hindu piety. So he was surrounded from his earliest days
by a variety of religious influences and by the teaching of
variety and suppleness as themselves religious virtues,
though at no expense to fervor.

Gujerat was preeminently a land of caste distinctions,
and the Vaisyas were important among the other castes,
though they formed only 5 percent of the total population,
and the modh banias were only 6 percent of the Vaisyas.
The caste virtues of the merchants were prudence and
sobriety, and the strict ones were vegetarians and teetotal-
ers. In matters of devotion, it seems that Putlibai made a
cult of Rama rather than of Krishna (the two main avatars
of Vishnu), and Gandhi in his later life followed her. He
always recommended chanting the formula "Ramanama"
as a specific against moral and spiritual evils, and reading
the Ramayana legends. The cult of Rama was populist and
ascetic, hostile to the caste hierarchy, and devoted to

Tulsida's *Ramayana* poem. That of Krishna was more ritualistic and caste dominated, more sentimental and sensual in its devotional style. One may say, then, using Christian terms, that Gandhi was brought up a Protestant among Hindus. And he retained that style. One of the Gujerati poems he most often quoted was Sharmal Bhatt's "For a bowl of water, give a goodly meal," which is very like the versified texts and morals in *Pilgrim's Progress*. And he was always, from long before his conversion, a deeply pious boy and man.

But Gandhi was often described as being as much a Jain as a Hindu, which implies a rationalist and revisionist piety. Jainism was an offshoot from, rather than of, Hinduism; by now it is, at least in its more intellectual formulations, like post-Kantian or post-Unitarian Christianity. In 1884 the Jains outnumbered the Vaishnavas among the Vaisyas of Gujerat as a whole, and of that part where Gandhi was born, the Kathiawad peninsula, by three to two; Jains and Vaishnavas interdined and sometimes intermarried.

Moreover, Gandhi felt the influence of Jain ideas long after he had left Gujerat. When he was living in South Africa and looking for a religion to commit himself to, he sent a series of questions by mail to various people, and got the only answers to satisfy him from a young Jain, Raychand Mehta. Gandhi had met Raychand in Bombay, where the latter worked as a jeweler, and had been much impressed by him. He regarded him as a religious genius. Raychand himself was from Kathiawad; his mother was a Jain, his father a Vaishnava.

In his letters to Gandhi he defined the soul as a discrete, indestructible, living substance whose true nature is achieved in perfect knowledge, and in passionlessness, bliss, and freedom. It seeks liberation from the passions, which subdue it to matter. At death it does not melt back into Brahman, as Hinduism often teaches; indeed, there is no

Brahman, in the sense of a Creator or Supreme Being. God is another name for the soul, and its highest realization is achieved in self-knowledge. (It would seem that Emerson's thought could be called Jain, and one sees why Gandhi found Emerson and Thoreau such congenial spirits when he read them in England and South Africa.)

At the level of social practice, the Jains have been called the Quakers of India, being noted for both their pacifism and their prosperity. For instance, Ahmedabad, an industrial city of Gujerat dominated by Jain families, had the most modern welfare institutions in India. Erik Erikson has called Ahmedabad India's Pittsburgh, because it is so highly industrialized and unionized, and financed by local investment. It is dominated by a few families of this type, with a strong sense of paternal responsibility to their employees. It was just outside Ahmedabad that Gandhi founded his first ashram, and it was in the city that he conducted his first industrial strike, in which he had the help of the principal owner's sister. Gujerat was Gandhi's home country, not so much by accident of birth as because of those Vaisya families. By contrast, in Rajputana, dominated by Kshattriyas (the warrior caste), Gandhi was not at home, and Gandhism seemed a very strange doctrine. The same is true of Maharashtra, intellectually dominated by the Chitpavan brahmins, a fiercely orthodox branch of the Brahmin caste who have a tradition of political power. Unlike those Indians, the Jain Vaisyas understood Gandhi from the beginning. Nevertheless, he said that a Jain could not be a complete satyagrahi,* presumably meaning that their mode of religion was too purely contemplative.

In England, Gandhi came in contact, through the

---

* "Satyagraha," usually translated "firmness in truth," is Gandhi's name for his kind of peaceful militancy. A satyagrahi is one who practices that militancy.

Theosophists and the Vegetarian Society he joined, with a whole range of experiments in socialism, religion, and the simple life. He read the New Testament, responded particularly to the Sermon on the Mount, and in general was strongly attracted to Christianity. But it was Tolstoy's *The Kingdom of God Is Within You*, which he read in 1894, that gave him his decisive conversion experience. Writing about that book in 1928, for Tolstoy's centenary, he said, "I was at that time a believer in violence. Reading it cured me of my scepticism and made me a firm believer in Ahimsa." Ahimsa, or nonviolence, was the faith in which he led his first, South African, campaigns of resistance, and he advanced along that path step by step until he became a Mahatma.

Tolstoy was born into what he called the warrior caste in Russia. He was, of course, taught Christian ideals as a child, and saw pilgrims who were on their way to the holy places of Russia. Such pilgrims were given a meal in the Yasnaya Polyana kitchens, and some members of his family followed the religious life at monasteries. In those days— more exactly when he was five—he and his brothers even invented a game of Christian goodness; they called it "The Ant-Brothers," because the Russian word for ant, *muravey*, got confused in their heads with "Moravian," the evangelical sect that inspired the idea. They sat together under an improvised tent, and said and did nothing but kind and loving things to each other. This was, he said when looking back, the moment of greatest truth in his life. (Gandhi, too, said that he had been wisest when he was seven, and that Jesus was wisest as a boy, when he argued against the doctors—"Then and then alone uninhibited truth must have come out.") Nikolai Tolstoy told his younger brothers that he had written the secret of human happiness, which was Christian love, on a green stick that he had buried near a ravine on the Yasnaya Polyana estate; when he came to the point of death nearly eighty years later, Tolstoy asked to be buried in that spot.

But as he reached puberty, he says, he was taught quite other truths—those appropriate to his caste—by his brothers, who took him to a brothel; by his friends, who took him gambling and to the gypsies; and even by his good and loving aunt, Tatiana, whose dream for him was that he should form a liaison with a married woman, become adjutant to the emperor, and then marry a rich girl who owned lots of serfs.

"I cannot recall those years without dread, loathing, and anguish of heart," he wrote after his conversion. "In my writing I did the same as in my life." That is, he glorified the ideals of his caste, concealed and ridiculed his own "best strivings." He lived, internally as well as externally, according to his caste code, and not according to spirituality. His first novel, *The Cossacks*, and the associated stories are about the experience of war and of imperialism, and they explore the excitements and the rewards of both experiences.

He wrote in those days as an aristocrat. In a discarded preface to *War and Peace*, he wrote:

I am not a bourgeois, as Pushkin boldly said, and I boldly say that I am an aristocrat by birth, by habits and by position. I am an aristocrat because I am not only not ashamed, but positively glad to remember my ancestors—fathers, grandfathers, and great-grandfathers. I am an aristocrat because I was brought up from childhood in love and respect for the highest orders of society and in love for the refined as expressed not only in Homer, Bach, and Raphael, but also in all the small things of life. . . . I am an aristocrat because I cannot believe in the high intellect, the refined taste, or the absolute honesty of a man who picks his nose and whose soul converses with God.

In his two major novels, of course, it is not aristocratic adventure, military or imperialist, that is celebrated, but

prevailed. In a dozen ways he cleared the air of the recrimination and suspicion that generally, but particularly in
India, poison the atmosphere of politics.

He did so partly by maintaining a truly remarkable openness about everything to do with himself, manifested week
by week in his newspaper articles. From 1924 I pick this,
written after he had had an operation for appendicitis:

> I am free to confess that daily I am obliged to expend a great
> amount of mental energy in acquiring control over my thoughts.
> When I have succeeded, if I ever do, think what a storehouse of
> energy would be set free for service. As I hold that appendicitis was
> a result of infirmity of thought or mind, so do I concede that my
> submission to the surgical operation was infirmity of thought. If I
> was absolutely free of egoism, I would have resigned myself to the
> inevitable; but I wanted to live in the present body. Complete
> detachment is not a mechanical process. One has to grow to it by
> patient toil and constant prayer.

And this reference to growth and imperfection may serve
as a cue to describe his own attitude to being a Mahatma,
which may be helpful to readers first approaching this
phenomenon and finding themselves put off. By and large
he detested the title, though he could not deny its appro-
priateness. How else could one describe what he was doing?
He detested it because of all the trappings of the religious
circus that in Indian culture go with it: the crowds, the
hysteria, the superstition, the sentimentality, the legends,
the charms, the shouting, the people pressing near to touch
him or to gaze upon him—all of which were repellent to
Gandhi, who was a very private man.

"I went to a place where everybody was busy shouting
'Mahatma Gandhi, kijai'* and everyone was trying to fall at
my feet but no one was willing to listen to me," he wrote in
1921. "I was feeling disgusted with myself and disgusted

---

* Victory to Mahatma Gandhi.

with all around me. When I hear the cries of 'Mahatma Gandhi, kijai,' every sound of the phrase pierces my heart like an arrow. . . . How I wish they would instead light up a funeral pyre for me and that I might leap into it, and once and for all extinguish the fire that is scorching up my heart." One must take such talk of death and fire very literally from the Mahatma; the fire in his heart was a passion of disgust for all things human.

Even as used in private, the title offended him, because it treated as achieved an enterprise that must, in his eyes, be something he was only achieving—or not achieving. But that quotation will remind us of the functions of anger in Gandhi's moral economy, his use of anger against himself and against his followers, to purify the nonviolent movement itself of violence. Thus he (and Tolstoy) discovered the only true "moral equivalent of war"; they developed a force of will equal to that of the great warriors, but directed against all organized aggression.

When we turn to the theme of asceticism or spirituality, we might begin by remarking on the preoccupation of both men with death. Thus Tolstoy writes:

"Throughout the centuries, the *best*, that is, the *real* people, always thought about *it*. *It* is 'how it will all end.' . . . . Death, death, death awaits you every second. Your life is accomplished with death in view . . . inevitable ruin, that is, senseless life and senseless death, awaits him [man] if he does not find that one thing which he needs for the true life." (*My Religion*, 1884) . . . "Frequently I think well, but I think without death—and this is a frivolous and empty thought. Frequently I live well, but I live without the expectation of death—and this is a frivolous and empty life" (*Two Letters on Henry George*, 1893).

Gandhi, as the last quotation from him hinted, thought about death even more actively, in terms of the martyrdom he must be ready to embrace at a moment's notice. He had more reason (every reason, as events proved) to expect assassination, though Tolstoy also thought, and not un-realistically, that he would be killed for his beliefs. But we can omit examples from Gandhi, and note the way Tolstoy established this constant reference to death as a literary convention—one quite unlike most of the conventions of twentieth-century literature. Thus he begins *The Law of Love and the Law of Violence* (1908), "The only reason I am writing this is because, knowing the one means of salvation for Christian humanity from its physical suffering as well as from the moral corruption in which it is sunk, I, who am on the edge of the grave, cannot be silent." And he ends it, "That is what I have wanted to say to you, my brothers. Before I died."

Their asceticism proper can be examined in relation to eating and to sex, though it has, of course, many other ramifications, and all related ultimately to the theme of nonviolence. For it is our possession of a body, Gandhi said, that by its appetites necessitates our violence. And in *The First Step* (1892) Tolstoy says, "To be good without fasting is as impossible as it is to walk without standing up." What is the chief interest of most men, he asks, and his answer is, eating. Spiritually must direct itself against that appetite as much as against any other. The Christianity of beefsteaks, he declares, is a contradiction in terms, which is what Gandhi thought when, as a boy, he first came across Christians—men who ate beef and drank beer and yet claimed to be religious.

Both men saw this question of eating also in historical and political terms, saw the increasing richness of our diet as a phenemenon of the spread of empire, our third theme. Men are taught to want more, and nowadays this wanting is taken to be a virtue. In *On Life* Tolstoy says, "We believe the masses *should* have as many needs as possible and gratify them." He and Gandhi, on the other hand, condemned this eager multiplication and intensification of appetites, which is the modern world system's motor. A striking case of this in diet is meat eating, to which they opposed their vegetarianism. (And in fact man's diet *was* essentially vegetarian before 1800, as Fernand Braudel shows in *Capitalism and Materialism Life*. Asia could not have supported anything like its actual population if they had been carnivorous. Europe alone ate quantities of meat, because Europe was half-empty. And historically, too, the meat eaters have been the warmakers of the nations.) Tolstoy in *The First Step* reports his butcher telling of the moral struggle he went through before he could kill his first animals, though "now" he does it without a second thought. Tolstoy claims that most Russians still cannot kill an animal, but wonders how much longer that will remain true.

The Mahatmas' asceticism in the matter of sex is notorious. They insisted that chastity was better than sexual fulfillment, and denied that erotic love was a value, denied the monogamous and domestic kinds of love as well as the promiscuous and luxurious. "A man whose activities are wholly consecrated to the realization of Truth, which requires utter selflessness, can have no time for the selfish begetting of children and running a household," said Gandhi. And it was a monogamous and domestic love that Tolstoy depicted in *The Kreutzer Sonata*, and just such another that ruined his own happiness.

Asceticism is the root of all life for them, including political life. "I saw that nations, like individuals, could only be made through the agony of the Cross and in no other way," said Gandhi. That was the path to nationhood along which he drove India. (Tolstoy, once he became a Mahatma, was not concerned for his nation's greatness.) "Joy comes not out of infliction of pain on others but out of pain voluntarily borne by oneself." And indeed that idea should be familiar to us from Christianity, as Gandhi's phrasing reminds us. What is unfamiliar is, of course, the application of such an idea to politics—or should we not say, the application of such an idea to life?

But these are hard sayings, and it is time to remind ourselves of the other, more humanly comfortable, sides of the Mahatma. I won't refer to Gandhi's gentleness, his sweetness, his humor, his cleverness, though all these qualities were his. A more interesting profile is illuminated by G. D. Birla's remark, "A saint is not very difficult for the world to produce, and political leaders are put forth in plenty, but real men are not to be found in abundance on this earth. Gandhiji was a man among men—a rare specimen not produced by the world even once in a century." What Birla means is perhaps what was made more explicit by Zakir Husain, who described his first impressions of Gandhi as being—to his own surprise—of a level realism. And this was not merely a matter of Gandhi's making objective judgments. "His thought and speech expressed his whole personality, and his personality was not an accident of nature, or a product of inherited culture; it had been fashioned by himself, in accordance with a moral design."

This firmness and fullness of self—which dozens of witnesses confirm—should reassure us against our fears that we may be confronting the ineffably innocent or the totally sweet. Gandhi had made rough choices, had forced himself, and he offered us everything he was with a consciousness— which we were expected to share—of those processes of choice, self-cruelty, and psychic self-mortgage. But he presented himself also with perfect self-confidence, perfectly unashamed, or at least with no shame, no self-concealment, to cramp his relation to us. And though it is less surprising that Tolstoy should have seemed "a man among men," still we should be struck by the testimony of men like Chekhov and Gorky, both of whom felt large reservations and resentments against Tolstoy, that they nevertheless also felt "as long as this man lives, I am not an orphan on the earth."

Introducing Tolstoy and Gandhi

Turning now to the theme of empire, we find that some Marxists, especially Indian Marxists, have detected and defined what is for us the crucial political resemblance between Tolstoy and Gandhi. "It was the convergence of two souls wracked with the problem of the transition to modernity of essentially medieval and Asiatic societies. This transition involved the problem of the maintenance or resurrection of identity. It involved, further, the critical appraisal of where some other countries had been led by such a transition," says Mohit Sen, of the Communist party of India (C.P.I.). He points out that Lenin long ago described Tolstoy's Russia in terms that apply perfectly to Gandhi's India—as a patriarchal country, only recently emancipated from serfdom, and literally given over to the capitalist and the tax collector, to be fleeced and plundered. In Tolstoy's lifetime, as Lenin said, the ancient foundations of Russian economy and peasant culture, foundations that had held for centuries, were broken up for scrap with extraordinary rapidity. "Most of the peasantry wept and prayed, moralized and dreamed, wrote petitions and 'pleaders'—quite in the vein of Leo Tolstoy."

Lenin's tone is not, of course, generous to Tolstoy as thinker, as Mahatma. (He was enthusiastic about the novelist, but then we can all manage that.) And Mohit Sen's judgment and intelligence (like those of most Marxists I've read on Tolstoy and Gandhi) are confined by his vested interest in the subject. His argument has to end by showing that Lenin, as he says, "operated at an incomparably higher level of theoretical understanding" than either Mahatma, not to mention the level of action. But I believe that Tolstoy, and Gandhi have much to teach even Lenin about empire.

They were not always or simply antiimperialist. Both men responded strongly to the idea of national greatness, and the cultural greatness that comes in consequence; each man, early in his career, identified himself with the Russian and the British empires, respectively. As spokesman for the Russian warrior caste, Tolstoy wrote with enthusiasm about Russia's imperialist war in the Caucasus. And he admired the modern world system when he first met it. When he saw English and French armies in the Crimean War, he was much impressed by the average Western soldier: "He has good weapons and knows how to use them, he is young, he has ideas about politics and art and this gives him a feeling of dignity. On our side: senseless training, useless weapons, ill-treatment, delay everywhere, ignorance and shocking hygiene and food stifle the last spark of pride in a man." This might almost have been said by Peter the Great, beginning his work of modernizing Russia. But Peter was the man against whom the later Tolstoy pitted himself, in many ways.

The late Tolstoy, the Mahatma, saw the English and French example as one to be avoided at all costs. In his *Letter to a Hindu* (1908) (a pamphlet-letter in reply to a Hindu revolutionary who had written to him from exile) he urged India to resist the ideology of the English and to go back to Indian traditions. He spoke of "the deeply immoral forms of social order in which the English and other pseudo-moral Christian nations live today." He attacked Malthus, parliamentary democracy, and all modern and scientific thought. This was the message of the anti-imperialism that Gandhi took from him. It is not the English nation that rules India, he said, but modern civilization. And Gandhi translated Tolstoy's letter and had thousands of copies made.

This ambiguity, the alternation of the terms "imperialism" and "modern civilization," is of the greatest importance to understanding the Mahatmas. They ultimately decided that the two terms meant the same thing, but in their earlier years they thought, as most men did, that the two were almost antithetical.

A good description of modern civilization from the orthodox point of view is given by the German economist Georg Friedrich List in his *National System of Political Economy* of 1841:

> How miserable appears the ambition of those who attempted to establish universal domination upon the power of arms, in comparison with the great attempt of England to transform her whole territory into an immense manufacturing and commercial city, into an immense port, and to become to other nations what a vast city is to the country, the center of arts and knowledge, of an immense commerce, of opulence, of navigation, of naval and military power. . . .

Here we see the European mind celebrating its modern world system in the early nineteenth century. And over 100 years before, you can find Defoe praising the Dutch on just the same grounds, for making their country into one huge city far beyond the power of their countryside to feed, and to which other nations brought their raw materials to be manufactured. To their minds this was not imperialism, as List's description makes clear. This superseded empire. But this is the system against which Gandhi and Tolstoy rebelled in so many ways.

They also, of course, resisted empire in the ordinary sense, and by 1900 it was becoming clear that the modern world system *was* that, and that the differences between that and the old empire were superficial. We might demonstrate the growth of that awareness by the case of Gandhi's English disciple, C. F. Andrews, who came out from England to India as a missionary (but believing in the mission of the British Empire as well as that of Christianity) and was then converted by the Indian Mahatma. Andrews' father had given him, as a child, books like *Deeds that Won the*

Empire, and had told him tales of English heroism during the Indian Mutiny, and of soldier-leaders like Outram and the Lawrences. The boy learned that, though nominally an empire, what the English built was in fact a system of freedom. But out in India Andrews came to see that the English Empire was a system of white race domination. "I have watched, at close quarters, the determination of Englishmen to create a white dominion, from which coloured races shall be, as far as possible, excluded," he said in 1920. This could, he continued, lead to world disaster, for the British Empire is no exception to the general rule of history; it is an empire, and so it is doomed to perish. "Men who think deeply upon human problems and seek the guidance of history, with regard to the future, are turning away more and more from the barren 'civilizations' and 'Empires' of the past, however outwardly imposing." Our civilization is bound up with capitalism, and capitalism brings with it the slums of the poor, which disgrace and morally undermine those imposing imperial buildings that we erect in our pride. Gandhi is the enemy of the Englishmen's civilization in the same way as Moses was the enemy of the Egyptians', Jesus of the Romans', Mohammed of the Byzantines', Andrews said. This is the Mahatmas' view of history.

Gandhi had begun by believing in the British Empire, believing that it was an exception to the historical rule, or was not an empire in the invidious sense. Like many Indians, he attributed political significance to the private affection Queen Victoria showed for India—Victoria the great mother-figure—and he believed that England's future policies in the Empire would be those of the liberal reformers he read and corresponded with. In 1897 he composed the message for the Natal Indians to send to the Queen on her Jubilee: "Most generous sovereign and empress . . . we are proud to think that we are your subjects, the more so that we know that the peace we enjoy in India, and the confidence of security of life and prosperity which enables us to venture abroad, are due to that position. . . ." British liberals (including then Socialists and Radicals) believed then in the Empire as becoming a League of Nations, and Gandhi believed them. He accepted England's own account of itself. But by 1918 he saw the Empire as a form of the modern world system: "Ever since I read the history of the East India Company, my mind refuses to be loyal to the British Empire, and I have to make strenuous efforts to stem its tide of rebellion." And in 1921, "The British Empire today represents Satanism, and they who love God can afford to have no love for Satanism." He meant "the satanic character of the civilization that dominates Europe today."

It goes without saying that Gandhi was just as hostile to the imperialism of the Indian caste system, the Indian princes, and even of the other Indian classes' hoarded and flaunted jewelry. He often attacked the princes and millionaires "whose loud ornamentation, ugly-looking diamonds, rings, and studs, and still more loud and almost vulgar furniture offend the taste and present a terrible and sad contrast between them and the masses from whom they derive their wealth." And he said of the people, "But the bangled arms from wrist practically to elbow, the huge thick nose-rings with about a 3-inch diameter which could with difficulty be suspended from two holes, proved beyond endurance, and I gently remarked that this heavy ornamentation added nothing to the beauty of person, caused much discomfort, most often led to disease, and was, I could plainly see, a depository of dirt." Just because these are the signs of an old-fashioned imperialism, however, of an old world system, his concern about them is less far-reaching.

So much, then, for what Gandhi and Tolstoy stood for, and stand for. The history of the actual contact between the two Mahatmas is that Gandhi read Tolstoy's *The Kingdom of God Is Within You* in 1894, and was converted by it, and while in Natal also read (that we know of) Tolstoy's *What Then Must We Do?*, *The Gospels in Brief*, *The Four Gospels Harmonized*, "The Death of Ivan Ilyich," which moved him very much, and *Ivan the Fool*, which he translated into Gujerati. His disciple and secretary, Pyarelal, says that Tolstoy taught Gandhi three things: the importance of small changes in a nation's consciousness, the importance of a change of heart in one's opponent, and a sense of the subtleties of human psychology. These are all articles of faith essential to a spiritual politics, a Mahatma movement. He also says that, particularly in the 1920s, when Pyarelal first came to know him, Gandhi quoted Tolstoy's parables and metaphors and used key terms of his so frequently and casually that he seemed unconscious of borrowing them. And of course he had named his settlement in South Africa Tolstoy Farm.

In 1908, when Tolstoy was 80, Gandhi sent him a birthday greeting, and in 1909, while in London, he read Tolstoy's *Letter to a Hindu*. In the letter Tolstoy said that 200,000,000 Hindus could not have been enslaved by a commercial company had they not implicitly accepted its values as their own, and that they must resist the seductions of modernization and capitalization. "India will cease to be," he warned them, ". . . when she goes through the process of civilization," which he defined as "The reproduction on that sacred soil of gun factories." On October 1 of that year, Gandhi wrote to Tolstoy, asking for permission to copy and distribute his letter, and in November he wrote again, sending a copy of Joseph Doke's biography of himself. On April 10, 1910, he sent a copy of *Hind Swaraj*, his little book on Hindu self-rule, which expounded a very similar philosophy of history.

On April 20 Tolstoy wrote in his diary, "In the evening

read Gandhi about civilization; wonderful." And on April 21, "Read book about Gandhi. Very important. I should write to him." (He also said to friends that Gandhi's Hindu nationalism "spoiled everything," for Tolstoy was the more thorough anarchist, belonging as he did to an oppressor nation, not to one oppressed, like India.) In August Gandhi and his friend Kallenbach wrote to Tolstoy describing Tolstoy Farm. But at the end of that October Tolstoy began his final, fatal flight away from his family and his caste and his place in the world, in the course of which he died.

When his death was announced, *Indian Opinion*, Gandhi's paper in Natal, said, "He was to us more than one of the greatest men of his age. We have endeavoured, so far as possible, and so far as we understand it, to follow his teaching." And in 1928 Gandhi recommended Tolstoy's "progressive self-restraint" as still the one thing needful for the youth of India, now that Western literature, "full of the virus of self-indulgence," was flooding the country. For of course, as time passed, the modern world system waxed more vigorous and more manifold, and ever-new tentacles, including purely cultural ones, took hold of that older life that Tolstoy and Gandhi had tried to defend and restore.

If any men ever "fought the system"—giving that phrase its largest possible scope of meaning—they were Gandhi and Tolstoy; we cannot be surprised that they were defeated by it, that their lives ended tragically. Tolstoy was excommunicated by the Russian Orthodox Church for his criticism of its perversion of Christianity, and was insulted and threatened by many other groups, from the Marxist revolutionaries to the peasants of Yasnaya Polyana. But his crucial defeat was within his family. His wife made it impossible (she threatened and attempted suicide) for him to leave Yasnaya Polyana, though living there meant living in flagrant contradiction of his principles. Moreover, she insisted on monitoring what he wrote, and interfering in his relations with his disciples. She insisted on possessing him. Finally, on October 28, 1910, he awoke in the night to see her rifling his desk for his diaries. Before dawn he had gone, leaving her a letter but no clue to his destination. He died on the way to a new life in the railway station at Astopovo, still besieged by his wife and family, who had hired a special train to follow him, and by reporters and cameras from all over Russia and indeed Europe. His wife had always said his religion was vanity, a play for the world's admiration, and she proved it by making his deathbed a public spectacle.

Gandhi's death was a political, not a familial, tragedy. India got her independence in 1946, but was divided into two states, and also disgraced by Hindu-Muslim mutual massacres. Gandhi struggled with great success, but also with a great failure, to prevent these tragedies. Morover, his followers in the Congress party, now the rulers of India, were directing her development away from his beliefs. Pyarelal describes him as being, in 1947, the saddest man one could picture. On September 26 he said, "There was a time when India listened to me. Today I am a back number. I have been told I have no place in the new order, where we want machines, navy, air force, and what not. I can never be a party to that." On October 2, when he was offered birthday congratulations, he said, "Where do congratulations come in? It will be more appropriate to say condolences. There is nothing but anguish in my heart."

At the end of 1947 he fasted again, and again successfully, for peace between Hindus and Muslims, but a band of Hindu nationalists chanted "Let Gandhi die" beneath the windows of his room. Already on November 1 Nathuram Godse, a director of the Hindu nationalist paper of Poona, *Hindu Rashtra*, had called for his death. Godse and his co-director, Narayan Apte, were disciples of Vir Savarkar, the leader of fanatic Hindu nationalism. Gandhi had been clashing with Savarkar for forty years. *Hind Swaraj* is written as a dialogue between Gandhi and the Hindu fanatics with whom he had been talking in London, of whom the most extreme was Savarkar. In 1910 Savarkar was arrested for directing the Curzon Wyllie assassination in London. Deported to India and jailed, he was released in 1918, and organized the killing of the governor of the Punjab and an attempt on the life of the governor of Bombay. While Gandhi was leading his movement of nonviolent resistance to popular success, Savarkar had preached to a few devotees a great new Hindu empire, to be based on the nationalist morale of Hindutva.

When Godse and Apte heard of the success of Gandhi's fast (which resulted, among other things, in India's paying Pakistan a large sum that had been in dispute between the two countries), they decided to murder him. They flew first to Bombay, to get Savarkar's blessing, and then to Delhi, where Godse shot the Mahatma as he arrived to conduct his evening prayer meeting.

II

TALK ONE

My Visit to India

I MUST BEGIN with a somewhat simpleminded narrative of my visit to India, or at least a narrative framework for my impressions. I went to India at the beginning of November 1975, and when I landed at Delhi I saw everywhere huge posters bearing messages from the prime minister, like "The only magic to abolish poverty is hard work." These were the visitor's first signs of the state of emergency that Mrs. Gandhi had proclaimed. I of course expected to disapprove that state, and in fact the people I was to meet—painters, writers, critics, teachers, the liberal intelligentsia—were bitterly resentful of Mrs. Gandhi. Their hero was J. P. Narayan, the Gandhian Socialist, whom the prime minister had put in prison.

But another of those slogans read, "This is an era of discipline," which is a quotation from the *Mahabharata*, an epic that has in Indian culture a status something like what the Bible had in Western culture a hundred years ago. And this quotation had been sent to Mrs. Gandhi, written down as a slogan, a justification of her action, by Vinoba Bhave, who is the other great Gandhian figure in India today. He is not a political leader, as Narayan is. He is a spiritual leader, indeed a saint; he wrote this phrase down for Mrs. Gandhi after she went to consult him, because he had taken a vow of silence for a year.

J. P. Narayan is a saint himself, by comparison with most political leaders in the West. He is devoted to nonviolence; he fasts and meditates as part of his decision making; he is extraordinarily self-sacrificing. But Vinoba is, as it were, a professional saint; he is professionally interested in religion, and runs a convent where various spiritual disciplines are studied as well as practiced, and his life is extraordinarily austere. At the same time, his activities since 1948, when Gandhi was assassinated, have been political in the largest sense. He has led a Bhoodan movement, which collects land for the poor from the rich; a peace army; a movement for new education, in which manual labor takes the place of books; and one of his schemes, in the 1960s, was to found a stateless state for 100,000 to 1,000,000 people in the middle of India, which would pay taxes to Delhi but would accept no police, administrative, legal, or medical interference or services.

That is politics of an anarchist kind, in the Kropotkin sense of anarchism, and that is the style of J. P.'s politics, too. The two men have been close allies during most of the years since Gandhi's death. Thus Vinoba's gift to Mrs. Gandhi, that slogan justifying the state of emergency, has multiple resonances useful to the prime minister. It sanctifies the imprisonment of J. P. It means that the government cannot have attacked Gandhism as such, since it has the endorsement of the other great Gandhian of the age.

The point I want to make is not that J. P. or Vinoba are right, but that Indian politics is still much influenced by

Gandhism and Gandhians. I should admit that nearly all the Indians I met strenuously denied this, but it seems so to me. And that in Gandhism there is still an extraordinary interplay of politics and spirituality.

The car from which I saw the posters was enough to remind me of the non-Gandhian sides of India. It belonged to an Indian businessman who had boarded my plane at Teheran, fresh from business triumphs there, and in ten minutes was plotting my routes and hotels and insisting I stay with him at Vijayawad. He was a restless seatmate, constantly recrossing his legs, chewing or chomping on dry seeds, twitching his gaze around for something or someone to organize. He was, I reflected later, probably younger than I, but I'm sure that idea would have come as a shock to him—as it did to me. Being a man of the world, he must be older than any shy scholar. These things are not so much a matter of chronology as of caste—and nationality. He had been dealing recently in England (and France and Germany) and he condoled with me on the indiscipline of our working class. He thanked God his own workers were easier to handle. His firm was thriving, expanding; he had friends at the ministerial level in Delhi, whom he would put at my disposal.

In fact, in the matters in which he offered to direct me, he was quite inefficient. Not only did he know nothing about Gandhians but, having forced on me this ride in his car from the airport to my hotel (he himself flew on immediately to Vijayawada), he then kept me waiting forty-five minutes while he conferred with one of his subordinates who came to meet him. I and the chauffeur—he so much the subordinate as to be almost invisible and quite inaudible—just hung about; when I got my ride the car left me at a building that I discovered, after some confusion, to be a hostel for members of the Indian Parliament. So there was plenty to remind me of the overweening bustle of industrialism in modern India, as I contemplated those poster mottos. India was on the way *up*, as up was defined by my businessman friend, whose point of view was said to be shared by Mrs. Gandhi. Any quotations from the *Mahabharata* would have to yield meanings of service to that upward thrust.

So much for ideas I can attach retrospectively to the drive from the airport to Delhi. Arrived there, I went to the Gandhi Samadhi, where he is buried, and then to the Gandhi Museum, to look at the photographs and the relics, and at the film of Gandhi. However unscholarly that may sound, it was what I'd come for. Like most study trips, this was a sad waste of time and money as far as study goes. For that purpose one does better always to stay at home and cultivate one's reference librarian. It is what one sees that counts. And what I saw of Gandhi could be summed up under two heads, one his modernity, and the other his spirituality.

Under modernity I'm afraid I'm subsuming two separate concepts: his contemporaneity of style and his authenticity. I can't quite disentangle them, and anyway I mean them both. When one sees Gandhi in pictures with either his intellectual sponsors, like Rabindranath Tagore or Romain Rolland, or his political enemies, like Churchill or Jinnah, what strikes one is how modern he looks. The other men look stiff, posing, inflated, overdressed, beside him. He looks more natural, more self-defining, less affected by external criteria. He does not play to the camera, but the camera plays to him, because he does not freeze himself into the stately postures of protocol. He ignores the protocol of state occasions, and so the camera finds him out as the only natural person on the scene, time and time again. His style as a speaker and as a thinker, was antirhetorical; that is one way he is so unlike both his enemies and his friends and—incidentally—also his disciple, Martin Luther King. Gandhi was the reverse of the stately and rhetorical, even as a physical personality, and that, too, seems somehow especially modern. Sarojini Naidu, the poet, called him Mickey Mouse, and many people commented on his likeness to Charlie Chaplin; it was a likeness that signified his and our repudiation of the traditional trappings of power and privilege—a repudiation general to twentieth-century sensibility. Perhaps I can make my point more convincing by saying that if we had a picture of Gandhi standing with Hitler, I would not expect to find Gandhi looking clearly the more modern—or at least only in a more limited and special way. He would be more modern by virtue of his loincloth and suntan—by virtue of his character as living emblem of the ecological movement. But he would have no other edge over Hitler in twentieth centuryness.

Or compare him with other pre-1914 "idealists"—those thin-faced, upward-looking, bearded dreamers of the Edward Carpenter type in England (I can't recall if Carpenter himself had that face, but most such people did) and the corresponding types in France and Germany. They were all Christlike, icons of suffering, in the sense that means something weak and sentimental. You may remember D. H. Lawrence's strenuous efforts *not* to look like that, his dismay when Mexican peasants whispered "Cristo" behind him in the street, his delight when people said that he looked like a fox, a self-completing, self-delighting animal. Well, Gandhi *was* Christlike, but he didn't have that look.

What is missing from those faces, it seems to me, is aggression; the rewards of facing one's aggressiveness, the fruits of marrying that aggressiveness to purpose and belief. Gandhi's nature was much larger and firmer than theirs because it was full of aggression. He directed that force primarly against his own appetites, against his body, and to some degree against aggression itself. But it was always to be felt in him, and as a quite unashamed presence. Aggression, was the friend and ally of his will, which by its service swelled to a strength like a laser beam and carried other men out of themselves and beyond their limits.

Or compare the typical face of the Indian holy man: the refulgent eye, the regular ringlets, the smooth broad brow and radiant smile, of, say, Yogananda; the fulfilled man, advertising manhood. Gandhi doesn't have that look, either. He looks much more like us, it seems to me. He stands in a dry, clear, unmitigated light, to be known as we know ourselves, in the bathroom mirror, with the window open. He stands bathed in the spotlight that negates all spotlighting and merely reveals. And to us, that is a modern look.

His twentieth-century *look* naturally corresponds to something in his mind—something akin to *our* twentieth-century radicalized sensibilities. We can contrast him, again in this, with Tagore, and the point is all the sharper because Tagore seemed, and in some ways was, much more in tune with the advanced thought of his day. After the Bihar earthquake of January 1934, Gandhi issued a statement:

> A man like me cannot but believe that this earthquake is a divine chastisement sent by God for our sins. . . . For me there is a vital connection between the Bihar calamity and the untouchability campaign. The Bihar calamity is a sudden and accidental reminder of what we are and what God is; but untouchability is a calamity handed down to us from century to century. It is a curse brought upon ourselves by our own neglect of a portion of Hindu humanity.

Gandhi does not, you note, say anything to outrage the scientific attitude. In a statement a week later he defined the connection he drew between the two as a guess: "Guessing has its definite place in a man's life. It is an ennobling thing for me to guess that the Bihar calamity is due to the sin of untouchability . . . [but] I do not regard this chastisement as an exclusive punishment for the sin of untouchability." Nevertheless, in a country like India, where the scientific attitude was still struggling to establish itself, to connect the two in however qualified a way was to lend support to religion and superstition, and Tagore protested publicly against this unscientific view, too readily accepted by their countrymen. "As for us," he said, "we feel perfectly secure in the faith that our sins and errors, however enormous, have not enough force to drag down the structure of creation in ruins." There you have the crucial issue of faith. Is the structure of creation secure against humanity's sins? Gandhi answered a few days later, "I have the faith that our own sins have more force to ruin that structure than any mere physical phenomena. There is an indissoluble marriage between matter and spirit." He was not thinking, in that answer, of the ruin of the earth's ecology that modern scientists have expounded, but their work would not have been in any sense alien to him. I would suggest that it is Tagore, taking the modernist position, who sounds old-fashioned to us.

In a number of ways, then, Gandhi is close to us. But in other ways, ultimately more important, he is very remote. These are what I have summed up as his spirituality. Gandhi believed in an opposition between the body and the soul—the body understood as the corpus of a man's appetites and drives, and the emotions derived from them; the soul being those faculties named by the modern consciousness as the mind and the will, and the aspirations to transcendence and salvation. Gandhi believed that man could save his soul only if he fought out that war to the bitter end, destroyed his body in that sense, broke it down to become merely the physical machine of the soul, which deserves only that attention that makes it run efficiently. Thus food should be taken the way medicine is. You must care about what you eat, but you must not care for it. And sexuality is a brute appetite, and though it can of course be modified by affection and comradeship, any eroticism must be deceiving and dangerous.

In his autobiography Gandhi says, "By means of the body we practise a thousand things we would do better to avoid, cunning, self-indulgence, deceit, stealing, adultery, etc." And we hear the note of disgust in what follows: "If engrossed in pleasure, gorging itself the whole day with all variety of putrefying food, exuding evil odors, with limbs employed in thieving, the tongue uttering unworthy words, and taking in unwholesome things, the ears hearing, the eyes seeing and the nose smelling what they ought not to, the body is worse than hell." Many of us would recognize that tone by associating it with the fiercest medieval moralism, or with early Christian fathers like Tertullian. And even among medievalizing Christians, at least among literary and humanist types, no one has, I think, endorsed *this* sort of thing. And that is not merely out of liberal geniality and hedonism. Our intenser efforts at truth and goodness also have aimed away from this ideal. Gandhi said, "How can one who is attempting to realize Truth worship sensual passion? We know of no one who has realized Truth by leading a sensual life." He said that in 1930, and there must have been some among those who heard or read him who thought of D. H. Lawrence as having made just such an attempt.

In nearly every essay about Gandhi by a Westerner, a dissent is registered on this matter, and the best that his admirers can do is to treat his asceticism as an idiosyncrasy. For, as the journalist Arthur Moore said in the essays presented to Gandhi on his seventieth birthday, "Mr. Gandhi's attitude to sex is more completely opposed to modern psychology and medicine than one could have imagined it possible for any man to be." Not being himself a disciple, Mr. Moore puts the point robustly, not to say complacently.

He talks of Gandhi's ideals being "so far removed from the mass of humanity," as if that removed them equally far from serious consideration.

Gandhi believed that in the faculties of mind and will, in ideas and ideals, lay man's salvation as an individual and as a species .The story of his life as husband and father is, as you would expect from that, marked by bitter struggle and suffering, for others as well as for himself, though ultimately successful, as measured by the only criteria I can regard as realistic. And his triumphs as a national and international leader are all based on that ideology.

This set of beliefs is of course one of the oldest in the world. It plays a leading part in the history of most great churches. The Bible and the Upanishads both present spirituality as triumphing over competing religious beliefs that survive in only muted and mutilated forms in their records. In India the ancient materialism, which was also a sexual metaphysic, was called *Lokayata*. Originally it presented the cosmos as a macrocosm of the individual body, and as generated by male-female union. Later it was developed into a materialist system called Sankhya, which survived in opposition to a Vedantist idealism and was associated with obscure and obscene rituals, which have come down into modern India as Tantrism. Clearly, these cults are similar to those cults of Baal that we read of in the Bible as the enemy of Jehovah and Israel's calling—of Judaic monotheism and moralism. The imaginative life of our time has sought renewal in such cults, as one can see in cases like D. H. Lawrence and Otto Gross. Makhali Gosala was a prophet-martyr of the Lokayata, whom one might compare with Otto Gross across the distance of many centuries and lands.

Gandhism is as hostile to those cults as was Vedantic Brahminism, and also to the scientistic and antierotic materialism of the West. When J. P. Narayan came back to

Gandhi and to Vinoba in the 1950s, he announced his change as a conversion from materialism to spirituality. In 1952, in *Freedom First*, he wrote, "For many years I have worshipped at the shrine of the goddess—Dialectical Materialism—which seemed to me intellectually more satisfying then any other philosophy. But . . . it has become patent to me that materialism of any kind robs men of the means to become truly human . . . the task of social reconstruction cannot succeed under the inspiration of a materialistic philosophy."

But in the West in modern times it is those other beliefs that have been revived and have inspired our thinkers: forms of polytheism, eroticism, materialism, and so on. The only place we are likely to meet with spirituality, outside the established churches—and it is far to seek even there, except in traditional formulas—is in Gandhi and his great master, Tolstoy. (There are, of course, various "spiritual" movements, revolving around Maharishi figures, but I leave them out of account, as likely to be, judging by what little I know of them, effective merely psychologically, and merely effective—not impressive morally or intellectually.)

What bound Gandhi and Tolstoy together is merely caricatured by talk of influence or shared opinions, of ideas passed on from one to another. As far as I can see, they shared an identity. They strove, with equal passion, to embody the same idea—the idea of spirituality. Their circumstances differed, and I would include among circumstances congenital features of their personalities; and their success in embodying the idea varied, for one must call Gandhi simply more successful than Tolstoy. But they were the same in the idea they embodied and in the histories of their respective struggles to embody it. The story of Tolstoy as husband and father, for instance, is quite like Gandhi's, except that Gandhi won his battle. But that sweet-tempered gaiety and humorousness and charm of Gandhi's, that childlike simplicity which seems un-Tolstoyan, which seems Franciscan, which has drawn so many modern people to him by its promise of a stressless freedom—that innocence, make no mistake about it, arises directly from his conquest of his body. That gaiety is the zest of triumph, and what he is triumphing over is what the modern world calls love. It is the glee of escape—escaping from the human condition as we understand that (not, of course, as he understands that). There is an uncrossable gulf between Gandhi and many of his ostensible followers (in, for instance, ecological communes), people in rebellion against the modern world, people who live in service of love and growth.

So much for my reflections in or on the Gandhi Museum in Delhi. From there I went to Paunar, to Vinoba Bhave's ashram. This is a group of women who support themselves economically and agriculturally, by manual labor, while studying the various religious disciplines of India. This is a more radical innovation than it might seem, for there have been no convents in India, and only individual women have played any part at all in religious history. Gandhi and Vinoba have been feminists, and there is in fact a sizable feminist movement in India now. Vinoba says, in *Women's Power* (1975) that women should take over the direction of society. It would be very interesting to read the account of some American feminist's encounter with that movement, which is very different from our own. For instance, far from seeing salvation in the freeing of female sexuality, one of the prime aims of the Indian movement is to encourage women to say no to their husband's sexual initiatives—and not, you understand, in order to develop bolder initiatives of their own.

Thus in 1938 Gandhi said, "The Modern girl loves to be Juliet to half a dozen Romeos. She loves adventure . . . dresses to attract attention. She improves upon nature by painting herself and looking extraordinary. The nonviolent way is not for such girls." On the other hand he says that women have been deceived into becoming the weaker sex, and he promoted the participation of women in political life, both at the level of national leadership and at the level of picketing and marching. And in 1936 he told a conference of writers in Gujerat that women were exasperated at the sickly sentimentality of their depiction in literature: ". . . the vulgar way in which you dwell on their physical form. Does all their beauty and all their strength lie in their physical form, in their capacity to please the lustful eye of men?" And in 1944, "I have repeated times without number that nonviolence is the inherent quality of women. For ages men have had training in violence. In order to become nonviolent they have to cultivate the qualities of women. Ever since I have taken to nonviolence, I have become more and more of a woman." And some of the women among Gandhi's admirers—who do not strike me as at all silly—have commented on Gandhi's literal womanliness and motherliness as elements in his attraction for them.

Vinoba is not womanly or motherly, but he is Gandhi's closest disciple and truest adherent, who has followed up Gandhi's work on a wide variety of fronts. He is more an intellectual than Gandhi was. Vinoba is a mathematician, and some of his most brilliant imagery comes from mathematics—and though he has some political charisma, and a gift for devising symbolic action, still politically he is Gandhi's follower and imitator. The source of his energy, too, is spirituality. He is considerably more ascetic than Gandhi, in fact, more antierotic.

In his *Remarks on the Gita*, which is yet one of his most poetic and affirmative books, he says, "Night and day, the sewers of your body keep flowing, and even in spite of your indefatigable scavenging, it never gives up its uncleanness; is this body *you*? It is unclean; it is you who wash it." Unlike his master, Vinabo never married; he has had no such range of friendships; he has lived for many years now on nothing but curds flavored with honey and whatnot; and he is a good deal concerned with the danger to Indian morals of drunkenness, pornography, and so on. But to say that he is more ascetic than Gandhi is to use the term loosely, to apply it to the circumstances of his personality. If we turn to the inmost action of both men, their spirituality, we see that no one could be more ascetic than Gandhi. In the strict sense of asceticism—meaning spiritual growth by means of carnal discipline—Gandhi and Vinoba are identical, as Gandhi and Tolstoy were.

As for meeting Vinoba, I approached the encounter rather anxiously, because there are no rules for how to behave with saints, much less with world-saviors. This was to be the intensest epitome of all the encounters the journey would bring. The fact that this saint was by natural endowment irritable and cantankerous and uninterested in human intercourse—that, on the whole, attracted me to him (I would have been more at a loss at the prospect of meeting pure amiability), but still it meant I had to be on guard. "I have been by nature a sort of wild animal," he says in *Vinoba on Gandhi*. "It was Bapu who put down the flames of anger and lust that raged in me. His benedictions rained continuously on me." But Bapu had been gone twenty-seven years, and no one had taken his place.

There Vinoba lay, anyway, more or less in the open air, and more or less unguarded, on a verandah of the ashram, lifting up the pieces of his morning's mail to within an inch or two of his eyes, and dropping them expressionlessly. The image he composed was—apart from the grim impassivity—remarkably gay, like a piece of Pop Art. Though a Stephen Dedalus type when young, age has turned Vinoba into a Peter Pan; lying on his cot so limp and lank, emerging at the torso from a brown blanket that wrinkled away to far beyond where his feet could be. With his bright green earflapped snowcap, like Disney's Goofy, he was a garden goblin out of the *Just So Stories,* or out of Kenneth Graham or Arthur Ransom. His straggly beard, ageless eyes, and glossy skin give him just that look of merry malice. I had introduced myself in writing—partly because of his deafness and his vow of silence—and I now handed this to him. He read my communication—necessarily rather soulful and *ängstlich* —holding it up very close, to read it word by word. (I had asked him, among other things, to be the witness to my vow to abstain from alcohol, which I meant to be the first of a series of such Gandhian vows). He nodded, then beckoned for my pen and inscribed his reply: "No hurry, no worry," in Devanagari script, signed (as he always signs things) He Rama, Hail Lord. His secretary read out this message with appreciative laughter—Vinoba gazing at me, to see how I took it—and the audience, or rather the darshan, was over.

Later, I saw him standing up and moving about, and he looked much younger. His whole body is supple and glossy skinned. But lying down his movements were very slow and weary looking, or exhausted, though it might well not be physical exhaustion. But clearly very contrary elements blend in his personality, as they did in Gandhi's.

The ashram member who showed me round afterward assured me that all decisions there were taken democratically, and that Vinoba always refused to tell them what they should do. But I remained skeptical of that freedom, because everything else she said suggested that Vinoba wielded enormous prestige and power. I suspect that the democratic procedures are a pious fraud, as are, in another sense, those intimations of comedy and self-mockery in his appearance. In such an atmosphere, jokes really count for very little; if what you care about is jokes, you should go somewhere else. To put the same thing another way, the jokes are made to count for too much; talking about such places, people overemphasize the gaiety and make it the equivalent for all worldly humanist culture, whereas in fact it has nothing like the freedom and forcefulness—the wickedness, as we say—of the latter. One can get very tired of reading about how gay everyone was around Gandhi, and how boldly, unconstrainedly, people treated him and Vinoba. Gandhi's jokes are mostly rather simpleminded, and one can't take too many of them at a stretch. They depend for their effect on your knowledge that the great man was unbending with you.

That doesn't mean that the innocence and gaiety were just fraud, in either case. Within certain limits one *does* feel free and easy with such men, because of this "unimpressiveness"; one is glad of it. And the limits are unresented by those who *know*, once and for all, that these *are* great men and great saints. I found what Vinoba offered me wholly appropriate and edifying; not the fortune-cookie motto itself, but the bright glance of gaiety that went with it, which I read as an invitation to join him in enjoying the contrast between my painstaking address and his two-word reply, paralleling the contrast between my immensely long journey and this thirty-second interview. If I couldn't see that that contrast was all that was to be expected—all that was possible—then it was time I found out. Of course, if I'd fallen at his feet, as Mira Behn fell at Gandhi's when she arrived after her long journey, that would have been a different challenge, and he would have met it differently. Perhaps he would have raised me, as Gandhi raised Mira, saying, "You shall be my daughter." But Vinoba being himself, and I being myself, what passed between us was wholly right.

From Paunar I went to Mysore, where I have a friend who teaches in the English department of the university. There I relaxed from the tension of the extraordinary. I entered a world that would be familiar to us all, and particularly to those who have any familiarity with F. R.

Leavis' ideas. Just about everyone there in the English department is a Leavisite, and Leavis' essays and ideas are current in their translation into Kannada. (Kannada is their language.) But their world is familiar to a Leavisite even more in the sense that its main features—their main problems and opportunities in life—order themselves according to the moral scheme we learn from Leavis. For instance, they see a crucial difference and opposition between Indian writers in English and those who use the native languages; they are themselves novelists, culture-critics, filmmakers, in Kannada. They see Delhi and its cosmopolitan culture as a threat to, an enemy to, the best values of Indian cultural life. They are eager to translate into fictional terms the life of the Indian villages they grew up in, a life that has never been put into fiction. They want to evaluate and celebrate the strengths and weaknesses of that organic community life, which is still penetrated by religious and moral tradition to a degree scarcely imaginable here in the West. For them the challenge of Gandhi is very strong, but takes a form approximately like the form it has for us—though perhaps it also takes other, specifically Indian, forms—since they are engaged in cultural enterprises familiar to us.

Perhaps I should mention one more thing I saw in Mysore, and that is the Maharajah's palace' (built during Gandhi's time in South Africa). This is an incredibly gaudy and profuse and extravagant building, which yields nothing to Hollywood's versions of such places. I mean that more seriously than might appear. *Exactly* the same imagination dreamed up that palace as dreamed up *The Thief of Baghdad*. The marble hall, with its forest of shiny columns, the golden throne, the jewel-and-ivory-studded doors, the fierce and fretted swords and scimitars, the whole criminal and vulgar and foolish multiplication of mere money, are not especially Eastern or Western. It means the same thing all the world over, whether as the backdrop to a popular movie or as the dwelling of a great monarch. The Maharajahs of Mysore seem to have been, in the twentieth century, among the most intelligent and liberal, and certainly popular, of Indian princes. My friend remembers long ago joining student protests against the Maharajah, during his triumphal processions through the public streets —but doing so both in fear of popular reprisals and in knowledge that this was not the real enemy. The drab modern imperialism of the British was the enemy, not this foolish glitter, though this, too, must be denounced.

The palace made me reflect how cardinal a feature of Gandhi's movement was its good taste; the buildings of the ashram, the khadi cloth spun and woven there, the gentle manners and clear reasoning of the ashramites, all are, in no accidental way, the reverse of the Maharajah's. They are equally the reverse of the patched and crazy and dirty dwellings of the poor, and of the proto-Western modernities and luxuries of the middle class. Gandhism was a movement in taste as well as in politics and religion.

From Mysore I went south to Kodaikanal, a hill station where I stayed with Dr. Keithahn, an American missionary who has been in India since 1924, and who worked with Gandhi, and with his movement since Gandhi died. He was, among other things, one of the founders of Gandhigram, a big complex of educational institutions near Kodaikanal, where all kinds of training is given to people who want to renew the life of the villages—social workers, craftsmen, teachers for village schools. Dr. Keithahn feels that Gandhigram has fallen away from the radicalism of its beginnings, and in its Silver Jubilee publication his is the one voice raised in reproof instead of congratulation. He grew up in the world of Thorstein Veblen, and has a touch of the same daunting grimness.

For this reason he lives in some isolation, out of favor with the official patronage that supports Gandhigram, in-

humanists represent. (The anthropologists took their place—the ethos of *Tristes Tropiques* replaced that of *Mahatma Gandhi*—and that's an unGandhian ethos.) Modern high culture turned away from them and their protégé, Gandhi, at just the moment when he was about to perform a life that might have, should have, meant something enormous to men of thought and feeling. It was left to the journalists, to Louis Fischer, John Gunther, Edgar Snow, William Shirer, to discover and present Gandhi to us. The men of letters ignored him. Not in India, of course, where men of letters form a sizable group within the movement, attached to it by their educational and cultural interests. But that Indian culture, notably its literary consciousness, was premodernist.

From Kodaikanal I went north to Benares, where I visited the Institute for Gandhian Studies, founded by J. P. Narayan. The most interesting work they do there is in intermediate technology. (They also do a lot of social science, most of it pretty heart sinking.) They are in close touch with E. F. Schumacher, the author of *Small Is Beautiful*, and with American equivalents like the New Alchemists Farm and the Quaker Organization for a New Life. Gandhi is the great founder of this movement—his spinning wheel itself is a major piece of intermediate or small technology—and many of his lieutenants, notably J. C. Kumarappa, have written brilliantly on the subject. This movement, and the larger ecological movement to which it belongs, is the major survival of Gandhism alive on the world scene—together with various nonviolent resistance movements.

Benares, though one of the great holy cities of Hinduism, belongs more to Kipling's India than to Gandhi's. At least to a visitor's eye, its exravagant picturesqueness fits into the former Gestalt—Kipling's or the hippies'—the two are strikingly similar. The difference is just that Kim has now

left the Secret Service, to smoke pot all day. Being in
Benares, one is inevitably led to the Ganges and shown the
houseboats where the hippies live, as well as the temples
and their elaborate erotic sculptures. And it is of course the
polytheistic, idolatrous, and erotic layer of Indian religious
culture the hippies are attracted to. There is much about
Indian religious culture the hippies are attracted to. There
is much about Indian culture as a whole—its gentleness, its
colorfulness, the poverty and despair themselves—that
makes it possible for people there to lead a strikingly relaxed
life, what you might call a polymorphous perverse life. From
the point of view of Gandhism this is the lowest layer of
Indian religion. It is the opposite of Gandhi in spirituality,
politics, cultural taste. From this point of view, that hippie-
cum-temple eroticism is the slums of religion, away from
which Gandhi led the people, up the mountains of faith.

Back in Delhi, from which I was to fly home, I was again
submerged in political gossip. Everyone was full of rumours
of police brutality, corruption in high places, breaches in
the freedom of the press, and so on. J. P. had been released,
sick, and I was taken to see him, though at his hospital-room
door we were told that he could not give interviews. My
friends, all devoted to him, were torn between suspicions
that he had been poisoned and shame at their own prone-
ness to such suspicions. Reginald Reynolds compares the
wits and rebels of modern New Delhi with those of Joyce's
Dublin, for their self-fulfilling blackness of mood. He quotes
as typical an epigram passed around by journalists, about
someone "so crooked if he swallowed a nail it would come
out a corkscrew"; and he says that these men, even journalists, turn out not to know, and not to care, about any
ameliorative enterprise that is succeeding.

Indeed, several people told me, when they heard I was
working on Gandhi, that his name was never mentioned in
India now. That, I need hardly argue, is a gross exaggera-

tion. Even translated to mean that India has betrayed its Gandhian heritage, it is a foolish oversimplification. Indian politics, because of men like J. P. and Vinoba, who are big political figures, is different from politics elsewhere. Of course it is true, and of course it is tragic, that the Indian state is not organized according to Gandhian principles, nor are major policy decisions taken according to those principles. But Gandhism is in the air, as a potentiality one can feel. What that remark meant, I decided, was a reluctance to emerge from the bittersweet pleasures of recrimination into the keener, sharper air that Gandhi represents. They would rather chew the communal cud of outrage against Indira than enter the presence—answer the challenge—of Gandhi.

The real tragedy of India from a Gandhian point of view is not the current restrictions on political freedom, but the blind energy with which the country is plunging in pursuit of Westernism, in contradiction of all Gandhi's teaching. That plunge is indeed Indira's responsibility, but the men so indignant against her were not really resistant to it, even at the level of intention. From a Gandhian point of view they were in complicity with her, for all their indignation.*

I left Delhi Airport at 4:30 in the morning, a time when the runway lights were particularly clear and vivid, and the power of the plane particularly exciting; one heard all of modern life in the thunderous explosion of power inside the plane taking off, and in the muted thunder of another giant creeping along in line behind us. As we rose, the lights of Delhi, and even more the lights of New York when we came down there, were the epitome of modern beauty: the soft light of streetlamps, especially on suburban streets, the

---

* It is clear by now—clearer than it was to me at the time of my visit— that the state of emergency is a political tragedy for India. Several of the people I came to know in Delhi have been put in jail and worse. But still, from a Gandhian point of view, the larger tragedy is Westernization.

moving lights of long columns of traffic, crossing and swooping over each other, the piled, floor above floor, lights of tall office and apartment buildings, the winking and flashing and colored lights of advertising signs.

But as we took off I was reading a book by Vinoba, in which he describes Diwali, the festival at which everyone sets out lights at dusk, arranged in patterns; nowadays people also explode fireworks, as they did in Delhi when I arrived, for that was Diwali time. Vinoba says:

Diwali is the first clear, moonless night after the four months of the rainy season are ended. The Goddess of Night is revealed in the full wealth of her divinity. The empire of the moon is gone, and in its place the free stars, great and small, shine together in all their constellations in a splendid harmony of beauty.

I spent my childhood in Konkan, in a village among the hills. I remember how every year, as the season came round, we prepared to kindle the Diwali lamps. We used to go into the forest and collect the soft round fruits of Koranti, cut them in halves, and scrape out the soft pulp. What beautiful little lamp-saucers they made! We put a little sand into each and arranged the wicks in them, and then filled them with our pure swadeshi Konkan coconut oil. Ordinary cotton does not grow in Konkan, so we used tree-cotton for the wicks. Having got our lamps ready, we arranged them in patterns, squares, and triangles and circles. That was our Diwali.

There, of course, you have the crucial contrast of world history, in those two sets of lights. I am in no position to confront you with that contrast and pose you such problems. I bring merely this question. What accommodation, if any, may be made by a humanist deeply attracted to Gandhism with the fact that Gandhi wants no serious teaching of literature? In the subsequent talks I will elucidate and expound and even answer that question.

III

Post-Mahatma Politics

AT THIS POINT I think it might be advisable to say something about India after Gandhi. Like Tolstoy, Gandhi is overshadowed by the imputation, however inexplicit, of having been disproved by subsequent events—disproved as a political thesis, that is. And in some ways the most important aspect of the Mahatmas' work (promise and challenge) must be the political. Since the disaster facing us is political in its mechanism, though it will be or would be total in its destructiveness, we all grasp greedily at that promise. But we grasp it sullenly also, because if we came to believe it, we would have to act.

Seen from this political aspect, the Mahatmas differ, Tolstoy's teaching being much more radically anarchist than Gandhi's, more thoroughly opposed to all state power and state organization. For that reason, his is a less practical option—though we may yet have to abandon practicality as a criterion, and certainly if there are to be any postholocaust politics, Tolstoy will be a teacher to listen to. But for the moment, Gandhi must be the one to study, with that enormous achievement of Indian independence to his credit.

I don't intend to describe all that, however. There are many analyses in print of the movement he led, of which I will recommend Penderel Moon's and Geoffrey Ashe's to begin on, and Joan Bondurant's and Pyarelal's to continue with. But I would like to say something about the development of that movement since Gandhi's death, because the subsequent history of the Congress party and of free India, however vaguely known that history is, hangs like a chilling disappointment, a dumb cynicism, over all hopes born of that inspiration. It should at least be made clear that if the Gandhian movement failed, it must be in part because most of its prominent leaders never believed in Gandhi's principles.

It is easy to trace the steps by which India has departed from the Gandhian way. (Russia as a whole never began to follow Tolstoy's way, and any hope it might try was smashed, soon after his death, by the Bolshevik revolution.) It is essentially the story of Jawarhalal Nehru. At the end of his life, after independence was won, Gandhi sent Nehru a kind of political testament, in the form of a letter. In it he described the organization the new nonviolent India must have. "People will have to live in villages, not towns, in huts, not in palaces. Scores of people will never be able to live at peace with each other in towns and palaces. . . . We can realize the truth of nonviolence only in the simplicity of village life and this simplicity can best be found in the charkha [the spinning wheel]." Not, of course, that Gandhi confidently expected truth and simplicity to triumph. He knew the attractions of the modern world system. "It may be that India too will go that way, and like the proverbial moth burn itself eventually in the flame around which it dances more and more fiercely. But it is my bounden duty up to my last breath to try to protect India and through India the entire world from such a doom. . . ." (As this implies, Gandhi saw India as a world leader among the nations—a leader of the third world primarily, but not exclusively.)

He reminded Nehru that his fundamental beliefs had been written down, forty years before, in *Hindu Swaraj*, and that he had often endorsed them since. However, Nehru replied that he hadn't looked at that book for years, but that it had always struck him as being completely unrealistic. As for the rest, he said, there was no question of people living in palaces, but he didn't see why a lot more should not live in decent houses and be able to have a cultured life. (Of course a word like "cultured," clearly implying modern Western culture, by itself announces how completely he is on the other side, and against Gandhi.) And yet Nehru ended his letter by saying that the world seems bent on committing suicide, a course that is an inevitable growth from an evil seed in civilization itself, but what can we do?

This exchange, seen from a Gandhian point of view, throws a bad light on Nehru; he turns away from the Gandhian hope, retreats to a more comfortable and more commonplace despair. The exchange is undeniably typical of their relations over a quarter of a century, and yet that relationship was profoundly important to both of them, and a credit to both of them. For one thing, even these letters were frank and good humored on both sides, which could not have been easy, considering what they said. More important, that frankness also was typical; they had always been open with each other about their differences. Nehru had never pretended to agree with Gandhi about fundamental issues. He had always said that he found incomprehensible Gandhi's religiousness, his asceticism, his sexual views, and his disgust with modern civilization—everything that made him a Mahatma. "Sometimes his language was almost incomprehensible to an average modern," he says in his autobiography, which was published in Gandhi's lifetime. "Often we discussed his fads and peculiarities among ourselves, and said, half humorously, that when Swaraj came these fads must not be encouraged." So what Nehru said and did after 1946 was no contradiction of what he'd said before. He had liked Gandhi—more than liked, had loved and revered him—but with his heart, not his mind; though, indeed, since his liking was so acceptable to Gandhi, he must in fact have understood him, too. But he held himself apart, and could only lead India away from Gandhian ideals.

This conflict can be explained, must be explained, in terms of cultural as well as individual phychology. Nehru's father, Motilal, belonged to an Islamized-Hindu circle of families, a type that has traditionally found its models of civilized behavior in Muslim rather than in Hindu culture. And Jawaharlal clearly found Hindu religion and village life very alien. He was in every way an aristocrat, and felt his political responsibilities to the masses remotely—though powerfully. "The people produced, in the mass, a feeling of overwhelming pity, and a sense of ever-impending tragedy, though individually dull."

Moreover, Motilal Nehru was Anglicized as well as Islamized, and so was doubly of a ruling class. A self-made success as a lawyer, while Jawaharlal was a child he drove to the courthouse in Allahabad behind a pair of fine horses, sporting fierce moustaches and a Savile Row suit, with his servants wearing livery. He owned a motorcar by 1904, and bought each newest gadget as it appeared, dispensed wines and anecdotes in the evening, played tennis, traveled, and shot. A masterful, indeed kingly man, he broke the rules of Hindu religion, and was ready to break the rules of the British Raj if he found them unjust.

Jawaharlal describes his father in terms like "kingly" and "imperial," and "a Roman emperor's bust." He tells of an incident in 1924 when Gandhi saw an early photograph of Motilal before he wore moustaches; Gandhi started when he saw how hard the mouth appeared thus undisguised, and drily said that now he saw what he had to contend with. But in fact Motilal followed his son into a political alliance with Gandhi, and gave up his Anglicized life style—burned his Savile Row suits as foreign cloth, and so on. It was an extraordinary submission for such a man to make to his son, and to a prophet who must have been in many ways deeply uncongenial. Gandhi said that Motilal's love for India was his greatest quality, and that it derived from his love for Jawaharlal.

What is of most importance in this for understanding India today (partly because Indira Gandhi is a Nehru) is the extraordinary position Jawaharlal thus occupied, as the cynosure of all eyes, all his life. The male heir is always a little prince in an Indian family, a little idol adored and protected, and Jawaharlal was an unusually gifted child. He was given private tutors and read the books given to upper-class English boys of his time—and all the princes of the world—the books Vladimir Nabokov was reading also; first of all *Alice in Wonderland, Kim, The Prisoner of Zenda,* and then Dickens, Scott, Wells. He went to Harrow in 1907, was a star pupil there, and then on to Cambridge. He returned to India, already a nationalist, in 1912.

Around 1920 he began receiving marks of extraordinary affection and esteem from Gandhi, and from then on had in a sense two fathers competing for his love, who were two of the most remarkable men in India. The trio was perceptively nicknamed the Father, Son, and Holy Ghost. And the praise everyone lavished on Jawaharlal was in terms of his sensitivity, his fineness of feeling, his quality of mind. In 1927, replying to Motilal, who wanted his son made president of Congress, Gandhi said, "He is too high-souled to stand the anarchy and hooliganism that seem to be growing in Congress, and it would be cruel to expect him to evolve order all of a sudden out of chaos." In 1929, when

Gandhi did put Jawaharlal up for president, Sarojini Naidu wrote him, "You are so sensitive and so fastidious in your spiritual response and reaction, and you will suffer a hundred fold more poignantly than men and women of less fine fibre, and less vivid perception and apprehension, in dealing with the ugliness of weakness, falsehood, backsliding and betrayal. . . ."

Nehru was always seen as a prince, often as a brooding Hamlet. It is thus that Hallam Tennyson describes him, even late in his life, when prime minister of Free India: as a prisoner of fate, proud, brooding, and divided. Less kindly —by Indians—he has been seen as an Ashwini Kumara, a man determined to remain a young man all his life, a *Sonnenkind* (they have a parallel myth).* The most remarkable expression of that character of his is the article he published anonymously in 1937, written about himself as a politician, in which he describes himself in highly romantic, though critical, terms: his pale, hard face; this man that nobody knows; beware his Caesarism. But narcissist that he was, Nehru did recognize Gandhi for what *he* was, despite his protests of incomprehension, and that may have been unusually meritorious in him. Nehru was above all a connoisseur, one who recognized and assigned the comparative quality of things; Gandhi was a phenomenon that eluded connoisseurship, that defeated—or at least challenged—comparative judgments of quality.

Nehru rose to the challenge personally, but not politically or religiously. He often referred to Gandhi as a "magician," and in general treated him as politically "out of sight" or "out of this world." He ignored him intellectually, relied on him emotionally. After the assassination Nehru paid him a number of moving tributes, and in one of them said,

* The Ashwini Kumaras were twin sons of the sun and the sky, figures of eternal youth and beauty like Castor and Pollux, who drove a golden chariot drawn by horses or birds.

"Bapuji, here are flowers. Today, at least, I can offer them to your bones and ashes. Where will I offer them tomorrow, and to whom?" In fact, he offered them to no one; he took no other guru; but he was in some sense lost without one.

What he had to offer India himself can best be described as a kind of Fabianism. Fabian socialist ideas were those he had been most attracted to in England, and he kept up personal contacts with men of that persuasion. He says in his autobiography that the French and the Russian revolutions took the place for him that nature held for the Romantic poets, as the supreme manifestations of power, to thrill the mind. Like the Fabians, he was a technocrat in his sympathies and attracted to Russia as the great exemplar of technocratic socialism. Like them he closed his eyes to most of what was going on in Russia. He paid a glowing tribute to Stalin when the latter died. He sought advice from the Fabian scientist, P. M. S. Blackett, on the Indian defense system, and launched a series of five-year plans with the help of the Indian Statistical Institute. Shriman Narayan, who worked on the Planning Commission, says in his *Memoirs* that "Planning was some kind of an exhilarating experience for Panditji, and he was always prepared to push other matters into the background." Pyarelal, in the 1968 volume of Gandhi's biography, said that the Indian government, "after the long repression and frustration of British rule, developed early a weakness for State planning— which has an irresistible fascination for the town bred intellectual." Pyarelal remained loyal to his master's teaching, and critical of Nehru's government. In his essay on Gandhi's political techniques he said, "Only when the factors which affect the elementary well-being of the common man are compressed within the ken of his mental horizon will he be able to govern himself and realize true democracy." To present politics thus is Vinoba's aim, too, and it marks the Gandhians off from the Nehruites.

Gandhi's judgment on Fabianism may be indicated by his letter to Julian Huxley, in May 1947, replying to Huxley's request for comments on UNESCO's World Charter of Human Rights. Gandhi said that *all* rights derived from duties well performed; duties came first, rights only followed, and only conditionally; he said the same to H. G. Wells, about the latter's Five Points of international law for all individuals.

Gandhi's political philosophy was generally much more tough-minded than the Fabians' scientific humanism, which took the fulfillment of every individual's potential as the aim of life. (This is one of several points at which he can remind us of Kipling.) Vinoba expressed the same anti-hedonism in an essay published in 1951:

Our age has produced tons and tons of happiness, but it has, under its weight, crushed the mass of humanity all the world over. Bags of sugar are carried by the bullocks on their backs to make their way into the body of the epicure; and the astonishing outcome is that the epicure gets a bad liver and bullock a broken back. This is the miracle wrought by sugar, an article which is sweet beyond dispute. . . . And the problem of problems with which we are confronted today is how best we can free ourselves from its meshes [the meshes of the problem of how to share out happiness]. All the cogitations, agitations, and trepidations of the world are directed to this end.

That is why, like Gandhi, Vinoba has been cynical about the United Nations, scornful of the five-year plans, and indignant about American military aid.

It is understandable that Indian intellectuals have found Vinoba and Gandhi very bitter pills to swallow. Their effective sympathies have lain with Nehru in their attitudes to both Gandhism and India as a whole. We may take as an example D. F. Karaka, who says in *Out of Dust* (a tribute to Gandhi) of 1940, "The years at Oxford sometimes made it difficult for me to approach India in the

Indian way. Even now a simple approach does not come natural to me, and I find I have a sneaking regard for that which is subtle and sophisticated as opposed to things which I find in India, which are often simple and obvious. There are many others like me who have this mental make-up." Indeed, in recent months V. S. Naipaul has been publishing articles on India in the *New York Review of Books*, and Ved Mehta in the *New Yorker*, on Gandhi, that exemplify in more elegant form Karaka's "mental make-up" nearly forty years later. Though they can admire or respect this or that aspect of Gandhi, they are deeply and bitterly hostile to his basic self, his Mahatma self.

N. C. Chaudhuri's *Autobiography of an Unknown Indian* is perhaps the most interesting account and expression of the Indian intellectual's plight, written in a splendid prose that can at times be compared with Nabokov's. Like Nabokov, Chaudhuri has loved complexity, and the separation off of intellectual realms, with a passion like that with which Gandhi loved simplicity. (He can remind us of the Russian exile in many ways, as in his claim to have understood life not by means of love but by that of estrangement; to know the Indian environment all the better for his detachment from it—to see the country as from an airplane.) "L'Inde, c'est moi," he says, and that elegant affectation gives the tone of his whole book. He dedicates it "To the memory of the British Empire in India which conferred subjecthood on us but withheld citizenship; to which yet every one of us threw out the challenge Civis Britannicus Sum because all that was good and living within us was made, shaped, and quickened by the same British rule."

The splendor of empire, including the extra meaning I have given it here, the intellectual style of imperialism, is very dear to Chaudhuri. He belonged by ancestry, he says, to the Indian Renaissance, of which Tagore was one of the stars, and which began to break up 1916–1918. He himself early decided to become a scholar, in the style of Sylvestre Bonnard. He loved to study periods of imperial decline, to brood over events like the destruction of Athens' walls to the Piraeus after Sparta beat her. And in his own India he scented around him the decay of civilization again. Unable to watch the individuals he loved die, he says, he has instead watched the death of empires.

He blames Gandhi for the breakup of that Indian Renaissance, saying that Gandhi ended the employment of political knowledge and tradition in the nationalist movement. He simplified that movement, being "profoundly uneducated in the intellectual sense." Chaudhuri himself felt some revolutionary zeal in his youth, but transmuted that into a scholarly interest in military history. He could never think of collective action, he says, except as the calm and resolute action of formed bodies; he was profoundly mortified by the simian gesticulations and chatter of the wild and ragged mobs of the Indian freedom movement. He fell in love with the British regiments on parade, and found something dreamy and poetic in the young British soldiers who came out in the 1914 War. (In this and other ways he reminds one of Santayana.) He admires Churchill a lot, and thinks that had *he* been made viceroy, he might have saved India.

Though not enthusiastic about Nehru, Chaudhuri clearly feels some affinity with him; he is at ease with him as a ruler of India, as he would never have been with Gandhi. And in this Chaudhuri is no doubt representative of most educated Indians, who are committed to the modern world system, even though they know their part in it will be to be miserable. They formed the intellectual backbone of Nehru's constituency, and they would never have been Gandhians, with or without Nehru's leadership, because their minds belonged to the modern world system. Gandhism was a very difficult creed for an intellectual to accept.

But there were some true Gandhians left, and even some conversions to Gandhi, in Nehru's India. The most remarkable case was that of J. P. Narayan. He began his political life as a Gandhian, but during his university education abroad he changed allegiances and adopted a Western kind of radicalism. When he returned from America in 1929, at the age of twenty-seven, he was a Marxist, and he made an alliance of friendship with Nehru, addressing him as Bhai, elder brother. Nehru put him in charge of the Labor Research Department of the Congress party. They were the leaders of the secularist, socialist revolutionaries within the party. And a Marxist J. P. remained until 1952, when he broke with that creed after a twenty-one-day purification fast, and reapprenticed himself to Gandhi. He was then the leader of the Prabha Socialist party. In 1953 Nehru invited him to ally his party with Congress and to join the Cabinet himself also, but said that the Four-Year Minimum Program for National Reconstruction that J. P. was putting forward could not be done in the time, so J. P. remained in opposition.

In 1954 he vowed to devote the rest of his life to Vinoba's Bhooden campaign—in an act of self-giving, Jivandan, performed at Bodh Gaya, a sacred spot in Indian religious history. He wrote Nehru a letter about his decision: "My dear Bhai, I meet you after long periods, and get the impression that you are out of touch with us. You think we are doctrinaire about nationalization. You say you are not a 'formal' socialist. I have been rediscovering Gandhiji; one of the most vital thinkers of the modern age. I find his dynamic and incessant quest today only in Vinoba. You rate too highly the chits that foreigners have given your government." It was not doctrinaire socialism, as Nehru thought, but the teachings of the Mahatma that made J. P. dissatisfied with Nehru's India.

In the same year he said, "It is easy to see that the official machinery in India, the big business, the army, and the allied agencies and forces, serve only to strengthen the 'military power' above. Presently they seem to be gaining ascendancy, which bodes very ill for our country." He was referring to such facts as that only two years after India adopted her free Constitution in January 1950, she also adopted the Indo-American Technical Cooperation Agreement, which gave all U.S. personnel diplomatic privileges, and the U.S. government final say on all matters involved in that technical cooperation. Foreign capital entrenched itself more firmly than ever in India, and Indian businessmen entered into alliance with it.

Other Gandhians agreed with J. P. about these matters. Pyarelal, in the 1956 volume of Gandhi's biography, listed those of the Mahatma's forebodings about India's future that were coming true: the Indo-Pakistan arms race; power-bloc exploitation of the tensions between the two countries; going back on prohibition and the salt tax; taking revenue from gambling; interprovince feuds; the failure of Hindi to replace English; above all, the militarism. Another Gandhian, K. N. Katju, wrote in 1950, when governor of West Bengal, "Even in India . . . we have felt compelled to depart from the teaching of the master and place reliance on the strength of arms . . . ," including indiscriminate bombing. "When I read of or myself indulge in exhortations to the youth of the country for military training, I sadly reflect how rapidly we are turning towards . . ." every kind of armament, including the atom bomb. What was happening was clear enough; what could be done about it was not so clear, for the effective leadership in the party was anti-Gandhian, even though key offices of the state belonged to true Gandhians.

In some ways the purest representative of Gandhism in Nehru's India was Rajendra Prasad, the first president of the country. He was much more completely Indian than

Nehru or J.P.—much less touched by Western influence. He was a large, mild, slow man, a vegetarian and a khadi wearer, one who never drank or smoked, was devoted to the cow, and always bathed in holy rivers. As a politician he was conciliatory and rational. No orator, he convinced by expounding his ideas clearly and calmly. "Of such goodness of temper," his biographer says, "many people take advantage, for they consider him too weak to hit back."

His own style in talking about Gandhi will indicate how strikingly traditionalist his mind was. Gandhi, he said, was a modern version of Ganga, the Ganges. Ganga represented, and represents, the three attributes of the All-powerful. With her music she is mother, the Creator. With her silt she is plenty, the Protector. With her floods, she is the Destroyer. Gandhi was the modern Ganga. He, as she, derived from heavenly heights, and you had to go to him for all you needed in life; how much you took from him depended on the size of the cup or the lota (vase) you brought with you. The tragedy of modern India, from a Gandhian point of view, is that such a man, even though president of the country, wielded little power.

Prasad, his biographer tells us, gradually became very unhappy that Congress was coming to rely so much on the glamour surrounding one man—Nehru. As a result of that reliance, the party became a happy hunting-ground for seekers of posts, concessions, and favors. It turned away decisively from Prasad and the tradition of Gandhi. Nehru, says the same book (written while both men were alive), is in love with brilliant personalities more than anything else, whereas Prasad is in love with Gandhi's idea. Nehru's imagination "weaves dreams, governed by his egotism, wherein he sees himself as the centre of things, and people as created for him to fulfill his dreams. . . . His dreams count for everything, and he lets nothing come in their way. He has also the poetic faculty of imparting his enthusiasm to others and can sway mind and emotions like a magician."

He certainly did so more effectively than Prasad. Gandhi himself had had personal glamour, but Gandhi was dead. And Nehru's was magic of a kind more familiar than Gandhi's. Nehru was a brilliant, charming, and sophisticated man, in a style familiar to, and shaped by, European culture. The light that shone through him was the light of Europe, and it was toward that light, with all that it implied, that India turned. But it is not exclusively India's tragedy of which Nehru is the protagonist. He represents us, too, in his power to respond to much in Gandhi, and his impotence to respond to more, in his imaginative loyalty to the person and his political betrayal of the prophet. If the very facts of life in post-Gandhian India seemed anti-Gandhi, that was because of the criteria of reality, the measures of possibility, that Nehru accepted. The facts of our life look the same way, for the same reason.

IV

Empire and Culture

HERE I shall say less about Gandhi, though he will come in from time to time. Instead I want to speculate generally about the relations between empire and culture—that is, *our* relation, those of us who are men of culture by profession, to *our* imperialist civilization. Do we, just by being men of culture in this way, give power to that civilization, whatever our off-duty politics? First I must define empire and its general relation to art.

By empire I mean not only a country possessing colonies, but any state in which dominance and glory and power are politically manifest, because one racial or class or caste group is triumphant over others within or outside the country's borders. This definition obviously covers every state, though some more than others; its use is not to distinguish one from another as much as to bring out the character of empire they all share. It seems to me that the monuments of high culture—that is, any notable achievements in the arts or sciences or speculation—usually arise in significant relation to empire, and thus have a political character. By significant relation I mean that the former tends to support and promote the latter, or else tends to resist and oppose it, but always the culture is characterized by its relation to empire.

It is of course possible to take a contrary view. For instance, this of Rosa Luxemburg's, written in 1915: "The triumph of imperialism leads to the decay of culture— temporary decay during any modern war, or complete decay, if the era of world wars that has begun were to last and go on to its final conclusion. Now, therefore, we stand . . . before this culture, as in ancient Rome—devastation, depopulation, degeneration, a huge cemetery; or the victory of socialism. . . ." She disallows any possibility of a supportive relation between the two. That seems to me to imply too moralistic and exclusive a theory of culture. Half the great cultural achievements of the past, from the *Iliad* to Renaissance architecture, seem to me alive with the spirit of empire. (See Henry James' fine treatment of this idea in *Princess Casamassima*.) And in modern art, though the message is typically antiimperialist by intention, I find an imperialist impulse within the formal principle, as I shall show.

High culture may support the imperial power of its society, or it may resist that power. My own loyalty and enthusiasm goes to the second alternative, to those works of art that signify (and by that means elicit and reward) cultural resistance. But art includes more than them, and the other works are of equally high quality. From many points of view, to divide art into such semipolitical alternatives is at best irrelevant, though I won't admit it is ever illegitimate or infeasible. If, to take a geometrical metaphor, we represent the supportive tendency by a horizontal line directed to the right—running from culture to empire—

then the resistant tendency would be a horizontal line running to the left. Of course, any vertical line can be shown to incline somewhat to either the right or the left, toward either support or resistance; the only exception is the absolute 90° vertical, which would represent a pure aestheticism, one that disavowed every political bearing. And if we took Nabokov and Stevens as representing that direction in literature, then of course we would find that when their work is scrutinized by an eye concerned for political tendency, even they can be found at some point to incline to some degree from the vertical. Essentially they are in resistance, and that is the rule for all modern artists, as I shall try to show. But first, more definition of what I mean by empire.

On this subject I follow Wallerstein's *Modern World System*, whose argument is that during the sixteenth century the countries of Northwestern Europe established a hegemony over a number of others that was the equivalent of traditional empire, and in many ways more complete and efficient. Only they did so not by the traditional means of a unified tax-gathering bureaucracy, but by the varied and competitive means of modern capitalism and scientific technology. Far from being a unified empire, these countries even warred against each other; but this was in competition for the privilege of exploiting the lands outside their world system—either undeveloped countries like those of Africa and America, or foreign empires like China and India. And they held in subservience what Wallerstein calls the periphery of their system, the countries of Eastern Europe, and the semiperiphery, those of Southern Europe. Outside the world system a slave economy developed, most obviously in the undeveloped countries—for instance, the mines of South America and the sugar mills of the Caribbean; on the periphery there arose a serf economy—for instance, on the large agricultural domains of Poland and Hungary. These economies developed at just about the same time as something like the opposite was happening at the center of the system—the yeoman and artisans were emerging from feudal domination. Correspondingly, in the realm of politics, the core countries developed a strong state authority at the same time as the periphery countries grew politically feeble or chaotic. This happened during the sixteenth and seventeenth centuries.

One of the advantages of Wallerstein's theory of history is that it explains the otherwise paradoxical politics of freedom, equality, and fraternity, which went with the expansion of this empire as an ideological accompaniment. The merchants of the core states were the harbingers of freedom in foreign empires, in the slave economy of the undeveloped countries, and even on the periphery and semi-periphery. Another advantage is the way it brings into relief the enforced contribution of the exploited countries to the Industrial Revolution in the core states, notably the financing of that Industrial Revolution in England by gold looted from India, and then the destruction of the Indian textile industry to provide a market for the Lancashire industry thus constructed. This was the way exploitation worked in the modern world, flying the flag of individual enterprise rather than of imperial glory. The Emperor of India up to 1857 was a Moghul prince, although the power was in the hands of an English commercial company. Thus the energizing myth of modern empire is to be found in the novels of Defoe even more clearly than in those of Kipling.

As for culture, the particular stress I want to put on it is that given by Northrop Frye and Nabokov. Frye describes our universities as being our society's engagement with pure value, and our study of the arts and sciences as being society's gage of idealism. Culture is then our symbolic social contract, a declaration that we believe in and care for values other than those we can realize in our political and economic lives. And from Nabokov I'll take a few lines of the poem in *Pale Fire*:

> But who can teach the thoughts we should roll-call
> When morning finds us marching to the wall
> Under the stage direction of some goon
> Political, some uniformed baboon?
> We'll think of matters only known to us—
> Empires of rhyme, Indies of calculus.*

Both men, you see, declare an opposition between private culture and public, practical, politics, but find a political function for culture just in its privateness.

I chose these ideas because they bring out the resistance of culture to empire even among aesthetes. It seems to me that culture has resisted empire, in one way or another, to an increasing degree throughout the history of the modern world system. The men of culture have grown increasingly hostile to the men who wield power. Perhaps they always are, in all times and places. But I would think it a safer generalization to say that there has always been a rivalry between the two types. The men of culture have always attempted to build structures of thought and feeling, in some sense equivalent to the political, economic, and military structures of the men of empire. They have always been in love with power themselves, and whenever material or military power has flamed up, their imaginations have flamed up correspondingly, their ambition has blossomed more brilliantly. They have built, to use Nabokov's phrase, "Empires of rhyme, Indies of calculus," or scientific theories or theological summaries. But under the modern world system they have built in opposition to the men of power. Rivalry, of course, persists within resistance, as Nabokov's phrase suggests; we can plainly see writers like Mailer and Hemingway who rival the men of empire of their times. The difference is that pure rivalry does not preclude, as

* From Vladimir Nabokov, *Pale Fire* (New York: G. P. Putman's Sons, 1962). Copyright © 1962 by G. P. Putman's Sons. Reproduced with permission.

resistance surely does, some approval of and enthusiasm for empire. This allows for early works of culture like epic poems, which have a different relation to politics from the literature of modern times; the *Iliad* and the *Aeneid* were surely sung in support of empire. And it is difficult to see Shakespeare as writing in resistance to Elizabethan empire.

But as the modern world system developed its enormous and unprecedented powers to master the earth and all its materials; to annihilate time and space and nature itself at the behest of its ruling class; to multiply appetites and melt down cultural bonds fantastically; as this happened, it seems that the forces of culture became predominantly resistant at the level of intention. As I have said, there are plenty of partial exceptions, but when we encounter a really notable exception like Kipling, who cooperates imaginatively with the forces of empire, with the system, most of us feel ourselves, or show ourselves, at a loss. Of course, there is a profounder sympathy between the works of culture and those of empire in all ages, a familial connection, but the intention of resistance is none the less sincere.

When we speak of empire we must of course think primarily of the modern world system—must think of England as the imperial power and India as the native country, whoever bore the title of emperor. But it is important to note that these modern empires have thought of themselves as being antiimperialist. In the wars that ended at Waterloo, in Scott's time, England saw itself as an island people and a nation of shopkeepers, fighting an emperor crowned by a pope and embodying military glory. And in Defoe's time, the England that fought Louis XIV saw itself the same way. Marlborough and Wellington, heroes to Defoe and Scott, were generals who resisted empire. Even in Kipling's time, England's enemy was the kaiser, who embodied military glory; its general, Kitchener, was a figure of sobriety; its favorite hero, Lawrence of Arabia, was one man fighting the Turkish empire and inciting Arab tribesmen to reclaim their freedom. We still saw ourselves as being on the side of freedom for oppressed peoples. That England itself owned an empire, and held other people in subjection, was a profoundly uncomfortable fact to swallow, even after all that Kipling could do to gild the pill for us. Ideologically, we still belonged to the modern world system. We still wanted an art that named itself and us as antiimperial.

That kind of art, the kind that coexisted with our political and moral ideas in most unequivocal and happy correspondence, I am going to characterize by Defoe's adventure tales. Though they name themselves antiimperial (I will explain how later), in such tales the resistance to the modern world system is minimal—though it grows greater in authors later than Defoe—and the support is maximal; this is why, by certain modern criteria of "culture," such tales are unacceptable as part of literary culture. Opposite kinds of art, which often seem to have special claims to represent "culture," are in opposition to the modern world system even when those books' ideas are assertively unpolitical and amoral. An example from our own time would be the work of Nabokov.

But let me take an example, which corresponds to an old-style imperialism rather than to the modern world system, from the literature of India before British domination. *Shilappadikaram*, the Ankle Bracelet, is an erotic idyll written in Tamil toward the end of the third epoch of Tamil greatness, which lasted from A.D. 200 to 300. A merchant's son marries; both bride and groom are described to be exquisitely beautiful, and they live in the most exquisite luxury and happiness. Then he is seduced by a courtesan who is even more beautiful, and whose skills in singing and dancing are praised in great detail. The merchant having wasted his own and his wife's wealth on this courtesan, the married pair flee together in poverty. He sells her jewels to buy them food, and the last one is the ankle bracelet; because it is so valuable and he so poor, he is arrested as a thief and executed. Whereupon his wife, still in love with him, in her grief brings ruin down on the great city of Madurai.

This story obviously has some of the elements of *Daphnis and Chloe*, some of *Arcadia*, some of *Salome*. This is the art of a great empire, in which art and eroticism make a world unto themselves, defying the moral, religious, and political claims of "real life." It does not support the political and moral ideas of empire. The men of action who believe in those ideas will always find such art decadent. One may even say that such art, though obviously nonpolitical, always expresses some resistance to the imperial idea. But such resistance is only oblique and languid.

The modern world system, however, has evoked modes of cultural resistance that are clearly as energetic morally as the ideas they oppose. I am going to describe three of those modes, and I suggest that the conflict among them is the crucial conflict for those of us who are resisters, the choice among them our crucial choice. The last of the three is Gandhi's; the second we can call Marx's; and though the first is conglomerate, I can identify it briefly, because it has been fully described and analyzed. I mean the tradition of British culture criticism, which developed at the end of the nineteenth century but began with Burke and Cobbett, and continued to Leavis and Orwell. This is the tradition Raymond Williams presented to us in *Culture and Society*, and it is, by contrast with the other two modes, liberal rather than radical. It is also more a matter of art and thought; the resistances led by Gandhi and Marx are more a matter of politics and religion, and so direct themselves against rather different features of the modern world system.

As Williams himself brings out, there are some ambivalences within his writers' work, seen from the point of view of empire in the old-fashioned sense. Carlyle and Ruskin, central figures in this tradition, were on occasion trumpeters for the British Empire. But seen from the point of view of industrialism and the modern world system, they were all heroes of resistance. And they organized the hosts of art round them. By Carlyle's influence on more purely "creative" writers like Dickens and Tennyson, and by Ruskin's and Morris' influence on the visual artists, they spread the resistance style in art far and wide. *Middlemarch* and *War and Peace* may be taken as the supreme achievements in the novel of this liberal and humanist mode of resistance.

This was a very conscientious kind of art and culture, and many of us are conscious of owing a great deal to it. In a sense we owe it our self-respect as men of letters, because it gave us a quasi-political function as members of a resistance movement. Certainly it has been my roots and my home-base all my conscious life. But it ran into its own special problems, and nowadays is, I think, no longer viable. For the sake of freshness I want to illustrate these problems from the history of nineteenth-century Boston, rather than from that of England.

Let me note first that the founders of the Boston Athenaeum, who were in effect the founders of Boston Brahmin culture, were perfectly explicit about their motives and purposes. They proposed to build up a cultural establishment in Boston that should be a counterforce to the political establishment in Washington. Boston culture was in resistance from the beginning, but it was a loyal opposition, loyal to America, liberal, moderate.

Second, and paradoxically, what went wrong in the second half of the nineteenth century was that they succeeded too well. By building culture up so monumentally, by institutionalizing it, they created a counterempire that the liveliest radicalism of the time, even the liveliest art, found inimical, within which the radical artists refused to dwell. The history of Harvard is a good example. Under President Eliot and President Lowell Harvard grew big in number of students, number of courses, number of books and buildings. But the size was not merely a matter of numbers but of weight—the weight of learning deployed by professors in research and graduate courses; the weight and grandeur of the architecture; and the correspondingly weighty styles of personality. The vocabulary of kingliness, and legend, and hero and epic, used about professors and students in the memoirs of the time, shows that Harvard had become a shadow empire, a would-be empire, a mock empire, in funny-mirror relation to the great institutions of Washington. It became a place in which radicals, and not just political radicals, were ill at ease. One could not honorably teach Blake there—not to mention Rimbaud.

Finally I'll cite a couple of symbolic points of architectural history relating to the Boston Public Library. The main donation to make such a library possible came from Joshua Bates, who, as a poor boy, had to read books in a Boston bookstore. He volunteered the money from London after by chance reading George Ticknor's eloquent proposal. This was in 1852, and both men were inspired by the purest liberal idealism—the belief that if everyone had access to books he would naturally prefer the better to the worse, and so Boston would become a kind of slaveless Athens. Both men were fervent democrats as well as humanists. Nevertheless, Bates stipulated—it was his only stipulation—that the library's reading room should be not inferior in furnishings to the drawing rooms of the rich. "The architecture should be such that a student on entering it will be impressed and elevated, and feel a pride that such a place is free to him . . . niches for marble statues . . . the best works of the celebrated masters." If you will imagine what Thoreau would have said about marble statues and the works of the cele-

TALK TWO: *Empire and Culture*

brated masters, you will see that a fatal step has been taken toward associating the moral uplift of reading—the man alone with his book—with the class privileges of luxury and grandeur. Culture is being institutionalized, and that is not just a matter of regulations, but of imperialism—culture under the sign of empire.

In 1871, when the building was erected, the reading room was described as being "Fifty-two feet high clear, with three stories of alcoves on the sides." There were twenty-two massive pillars, with marble bases, supporting a richly orna-mented ceiling "whose elevation to an American is startling. . . . Few sounds break the silence, except the tap of the cancelling stamp at the desk, a football in the corri-dors, the rustle of book leaves. The noise of the street out-side sinks to a muffled hum, and one catches, through the windows, the sight of the verdure of the beautiful Common. There is no more civilizing place in the country." One sees there how inseparable the idea of civilization has become from the idea of a privileged and sumptuous seclusion.

And when the McKim building replaced the old Boston Public Library it was described by the Library Committee in 1894 as being "in the majestic and beautiful style of Italy in the great period of revival of learning and art. . . . The august and venerable prelate in the Vatican could hardly find a courtyard so noble for the solace of his meditative promenades." If you will recall the lurid and sinister asso-ciations of the Roman Catholic Church and Renaissance art in the earlier Boston, you will see what a marked change had come over the idea of culture during the century. Even a public library, surely the freest, the most anonymous, the most democratic of all cultural institutions, had become a kind of shadow-palace, a kind of mock-cathedral.

The threat of some similar institutionalization hung over all the tentatives of this first, liberal-humanist, mode of resistance. Just because it was a loyal opposition to the civilization of its times, and an honored presence within that civilization, it tended to lose its vigor of resistance, its component of radical intransigence. It could not make good its declarations of independence, of denial, of recalcitrance. Even the best of its books, like *Middlemarch* and *War and Peace*, involuntarily reinforced the self-respect of that civilization as much as the libraries and the universities. That is, of course, the charge that the radicals of the 1960s brought against us university liberals.

Let me turn now to the second kind of cultural resistance to the modern world system, one that employed a much more intransigent strategy and extremist tactics. I'm thinking of that mode of speculation and ideology developed at the German universities during the nineteenth century. I mean the work of Hegel, Marx, Schopenhauer, Nietzsche, taken as cultural artifacts and quasi-political forces, not as philosophical systems. It is the intellectual complexity, the scholarly weight, the moral and religious ambition, the character of that kind of speculation that I want to focus on. There is surely something imperially proud about that character, a pride new in the life of the mind, which went far beyond liberal humanism. How much happened during that movement, and why it gave birth to modernist culture, is measured by the distance between eighteenth-century British classical scholars like Bentley and Porson, and Nietzsche—whose classical scholarship issued, not in a weight of learning about a narrow field, but in a revolutionary ideology that applies to every branch of conduct.

The modern spirit has had other sources besides this, but these German universities are surely one source. Lionel Trilling has written well about this subject, particularly about Hegel in *Sincerity and Authenticity*. It seems clear that the historical causes of its development include the striking social alienation of both professors and students, an alienation that struck Anglo-Saxon observers of the period.

Germany at the beginning of the nineteenth century was divided into over 350 states, and some were so small that their universities were the largest things in them, or at least their star professors were bigger figures than some of the Dukes. The twin practices of *Lernfreiheit* and *Lehrfreiheit* had meant that the professors had accumulated stores of knowledge, systems of thought, and a boldness of speculation, not to be found in universities elsewhere, while the students were peculiarly free from social and moral disciplines. The professors were autocrats, little kings, and the students were Bacchanalian and Bohemian. Through these special conditions, these chinks in the structure of cultural tradition in Europe, the new forces of the modern world system made themselves felt.

The men of culture had, after all, participated in the new powers acquired by the men of empire—powers of technology and rationalization—and were intoxicated by them, in their own way. They wanted to do something equally large. So they developed a style of speculation that was implicitly and essentially rebellious against social pieties even where—as quite often occurred—the philosopher dedicated his system to the support of social orthodoxy.

Hegel's philosophy in his lifetime was taken to support the Prussian state system, but the philosophic heritage of his work, in the development given it by, for instance, Karl Marx, was revolutionary. I argue that that was no accident, and that the deepest tendency of all that nineteenth-century speculation was in rebellion against social piety. (That tendency was what made me, with my liberal humanist loyalties, so long hostile to modernism in both speculation and art.)

Gandhi commented, after reading *Das Kapital* in jail, that Marx was a great scholar in a way that he himself could not challenge, but that nevertheless he thought he could have argued the book's essential historical analysis better, because Marx had a genius for making simple things sound complicated. I take it that this, as is so often true of Gandhi's naive and casual comments, deserves considerable expansion; that Gandhi is here commenting on Marx from the point of view I have just put forward, as spiritually overweening. Certainly he is criticizing Marx's mode of resistance to empire in a way that would apply equally well to many others in the modernist arts and sciences as well as in speculation. Gandhi and Marx stand together in finding inadequate the resistance offered by my liberal humanism, but they stand in mutual opposition when it comes to prescribing an alternative mode of resistance.

As far as the propositions of historical analysis go, the two men were largely in agreement. It is in the moral and religious surround and source of that analysis that they are so different—in Gandhi's spirituality and its opposition to Marx's materialism—a difference manifested in the spirit of Marx's polemic and its oppositeness to the spirit of Gandhi's. Seen from this point of view, Marx seems to me fairly to be associated with that mode of cultural resistance that we see all around us in modern literature and modern art in general; that angry, obscure and obscene, tormented and tormenting art that has, in the twentieth century, replaced the nineteenth-century consensus humanism of *Middlemarch* and *War and Peace*. What we have now in the way of literature is an elaborate curse upon all modern civilization chanted by a Hell's Kitchen full of witches, and I take that to be in effective alliance with the Marx-to-Nietzsche range of culture criticism. And I take both allies to belong to the second mode of resistance. As Susan Sontag says in "On Style": "The intricate stylistic convolutions of modern art, for example, are clearly a function of the unprecedented *technical* extension of the human will by technology, and the devastating commitment of human will to a novel form of social and psychological order, one based on incessant change."*

Finally, I come to the third mode of resistance—that exemplified by Gandhi. I am not referring primarily to the political movement he led against the British empire, but to his cultural theory. Historically speaking, this was liberal-humanist in origin; Gandhi derived it from nineteenth-century theorists of the first mode of resistance, though he gradually altered its character completely. The main document, *Hind Swaraj*, written in 1908, is in many ways a very nineteenth-century-English book, descended from Ruskin and Morris, and Gandhi's Indian disciples found it very hard to take until they had read Edward Carpenter and Ruskin. (Men of politics like Nehru and Gokhale never *did* swallow *Hind Swaraj*; but even total Gandhians like Pyarelal say they first needed to read certain English books in the same line before they could accept *Hind Swaraj*.) Nevertheless, Gandhi altered what he took from that liberal-humanist tradition by combining with it the Christian extremism he learned from Tolstoy, and by harnessing to that various forces in the Indian religious traditions. His mode of resistance to empire tends toward an anarchist social organization and a spiritual personal morality.

Gandhi's politics were in tendency counterstate politics, though as long as the state in India was British, his resistance could fly the flag of Indian nationalism, and gained huge support thereby. But the first item of his Constructive Program for a free India, as revised in 1941, was to create a communal structure throughout the country, which would be a structure of culture, not of politics. He wanted the Congress party to dissolve itself as a political force at the moment of victory, and reconstitute itself as a force within the state, directed in some sense against statehood. He had

* From Susan Sontag, "On Style," in *Against Interpretation* (New York: Farrar, Straus & Giroux, 1966).

achieved this against the British; in the big cities during the campaigns of noncooperation, there was a whole administrative structure run by Gandhi and the Congress, in counterpart to the British system. And it is something like that that Vinoba and J. P. have worked toward—with limited success —since his death. It is, to use John Middleton Murry's phrase of the 1930s, a network of alternative communities "in the interstices of the totalitarian order."

Bishop Fisher says Gandhi epitomized postwar idealism (for example, he admired Woodrow Wilson as a true democrat and a great statesman). And Gunnar Myrdal describes him as an overoptimistic liberal of the post-Victorian English variety. I think this description fails to take seriously the religious radicalism of Gandhi's national politics, and even in international matters—his recommendations to the Jews and Czechs of how to resist Hitler by mass suicide was radical if ever policy was. But Myrdal's classification is a useful way to show that Gandhi was indeed no radical as Marxists define radicalism, and theirs is the definition that has prevailed in the Western world. It was Romain Rolland's endeavor in 1931, during their brief encounter, to teach Gandhi the new radicalism of postwar Europe, according to which the good man's enemy was to be international finance, and his mode of opposition unrelenting hatred. 1918, Rolland said, had demonstrated the failure of idealists like Wilson, though equally of old-style realists like Clemenceau, both of whom now belonged to history. But Gandhi resisted Rolland's teaching, and the two radicalisms are indeed mutually incompatible.

The 1928 International declared Gandhism a petty bourgeois ideology, and in 1954 the Great Soviet Encyclopedia said Gandhi had betrayed the people of India and helped the imperialists. In Gandhi's lifetime members of the C.P.I. flaunted Western-style suits, made from foreign cloth; their scorn for nonviolence can be judged by this account by Hiren Mukerjee of a Gandhi-led strike: "That it was, the leader insisted, to be undeviatingly 'non-violent' action, did not worry the masses, who were aching for a fight. . . . Patriots who spurned death's fears raided the armoury in Chittagong; unattracted by non-violence, they organized a network of revolutionaries who put cowering fear in bureaucracy's heart." The C.P.I., like Western men of politics, try to brush aside nonviolence with breezy phrases about its sickly sentimentality.

On the other side, Vinoba says in *Gandhi and Marx* (1951): "Communism being obviously an ideology of attachment, I never considered it worthy of a philosophical examination. . . ." And "It is not an edifice at all, but a pretentious jumble. Their vision is all yellow with intellectual jaundice. They believe the ultimate reality is conflict." There has been no fruitful dialogue between the two radicalisms.

There have also been many comparisons and contrasts drawn between Gandhi and Lenin—partly because the two men were born only a year apart. One of the best is René Fülop-Miller's, in a book published in London in 1927. He pointed out that both men undertook the heroic experiment of putting into practice the long-cherished dreams of many mere idealists: "Their profound feeling of responsibility for the sufferings of all the disinherited . . . [was] animated by some spirit of indictment of European culture." Thus they were each upheld by the ecstatic faith that his particular country was called to redeem the rest of the world. Both had, he said, the fascination, and the disturbing and repelling arrogance, of a Gospel. But the difference is that Lenin believed in an unlimited, though temporary, use of violence.

Fülop-Miller quoted Lenin's letter of 1913 to Gorky, about his love for music like Beethoven's *Appassionata*: "But I cannot listen to music often, it affects my nerves. I want to say amiable stupidities, and stroke the heads of the people who create such beauty in a filthy hell. But today is not the time to stroke people's heads; today's hands descend to split skulls open, split them open ruthlessly. . . ." And of course Lenin attacked all religion. He wrote to Gorky also in 1913, "Just because every religious idea, every idea of any God, nay, all coquetting with such thoughts, is an unutterable baseness, it is gladly suffered, often welcomed even, by the democratic bourgeoisie." He described Tolstoyans as worn-out, hysterical, pitiable rags of men, with their "imbecile preaching about not resisting evil with force." And Lenin became—in this, too, a marked contrast with Gandhi—an expert at codes, disguises, invisible inks, weapons, and so on. Zinoviev said, "As soon as you met him, you could observe in Lenin a deep unquenchable hate, which as it were shook a clenched fist in the face of the bourgeoisie. Even his face was changed in the course of time by this secret fury." This difference is emblematic of all the differences between the second and the third modes of resistance.

Gandhi was adamant against communism because of its violence; for instance, in 1940 he said, "The socialistic conception of the West was born in an environment reeking with violence. . . . I hold that the coming to power of the proletariat through violence is bound to fail in the end. What is gained by violence is bound to be lost before superior violence." And similarly, Tolstoy had said in 1905 that the Socialists in Russia "want to see the sufferings of the people intensified, to change the happy agricultural life for the improved factory life we have devised for them. . . . The servants of the people are like the servants of God [the established Church]—dissolute in life, uninterested in Him they serve, full of anger, dictatorial." Like Gandhi, Tolstoy wanted a mode of resistance quite unlike that of Marxist revolutionaries.

And so far it is easy to go with them. At least, speaking for myself, I find myself completely on their side thus far. But now—that is to say, at some point in this line of thought—

a large problem looms for people like us. The cultural monuments that arise from this third mode of resistance are not works of art or science or speculation, but the spinning wheel, the salt march, the burning of foreign cloth, the ashram, the fast, and the pilgrimage. Of course Gandhi did write books, and there are Tolstoyan works of art, but I think the spinning wheel and the salt march are the true achievements of Mahatma-culture. Indeed, Gandhi often offered those as being in competition with works of art and speculation, including those works of which the other modes of resistance approve. Gandhi's mode is the most philistine of the three. (The first is deeply sympathetic to all serious art; it is primarily a movement within the world of art, or at least within the world of high culture. That is its weakness politically and religiously. The second can be represented politically by several kinds of radicalism, but even the kind often said to be the most philistine—state communism— has, I think, a family resemblance to artistic modernism; is similarly committed to the modern world system while it rages against it.)

Gandhi often opposed the music of the spinning wheel to literal music, and quarreled with Tagore over the importance the latter attributed to poetry and to freedom of speculation. And one striking feature of the Gandhian movement is the number of men of talent whom he diverted from promising literary careers to his service—from book writing to cotton spinning and note taking—notably his two most important secretaries, Mahadev Desai and Pyarelal.

Romain Rolland gives an interesting account, in his journal *Inde*, of how he played Beethoven for Gandhi and his disciples at Villeneuve. Mira Behn and Mahadev Desai and especially Pyarelal, he says, "sont profondément pénétrés du culte de Beethoven," but Desai and Pyarelal had never heard him played, except on a gramophone. Mira had been at work on a biography of Beethoven before (at

Rolland's prompting) she turned her attention to Gandhi. They were all enraptured by the recital, but Gandhi's only comment was—as Rolland reports it—"Ce doit être beau, puisque vous me le dîtes," with a little laugh. He was very responsive to hymns and folk music and simple songs like Tagore's, but the elaborate and formally monumental music of the West was unsympathetic to him. And the anecdote may remind us of a passage in Tolstoy's *Journals* of 1896: "I recalled our incessant music on four grand pianos at Yasnaya Polyana, and it became clear to me that all this—the romances, the poems, the music—was not art, something important and necessary to the people in general, but a self-indulgence of robbers, parasites . . ."

The world of art is, from Tolstoy's and Gandhi's point of view, a culture in complicity with empire, although against its own intentions, because such culture absorbs all that energy that might go into effective resistance. If men spent their days reading or writing novels—remember Joyce's claim that his readers should devote their lives to reading his books, or remember our own lives—then Gandhi's great crusade would fail. Modernism in the arts expresses, in its symbolic way, a profound and energetic resistance to modern civilization; at the level of intention it rejects empire, but only at the level of intention and symbolism. And by virtue of its complexity, daring, intellectual and moral power and beauty, it is an alternative to Gandhi's and Tolstoy's mode of resistance. That is why, and not out of vulgar philistinism, they called for an art that anyone can understand.

So liberal humanism has its well-known "liberal" weaknesses as a mode of cultural resistance; Marxism-modernism is no option for a man opposed to violence; and Gandhism is antiintellectual and antiaesthetic.

This is what gives rise to the cruel dilemma facing any humanist who admires Gandhi. Quite apart from the problem of finding some positive action, of asking himself if he does anything *for* the Gandhian cause, he has the problem of negative action, of fearing that what he does and loves to do works *against* that cause; he faces, it seems, a choice between intellectual and moral suicide. Or can some acceptable accommodation be found?

V

Spirituality in the West, and Sexuality

I WAS soon aware of a resistance among my audience to the idea of spirituality, and its component of asceticism. The Mahatmas' opposition to war, and to empire, are nowadays easy to applaud. But to have those two causes linked to asceticism feels profoundly wrong, for moral reasons as much as hedonistic. Ultimately, I'm afraid, the obstacle is irremovable; the choice for or against asceticism is an existential one; but I want to say something to illuminate, if not alleviate, the difficulty.

We are bound to think of Gandhi as being in conflict with Western life and its intellectual traditions. But in fact there is much we have always said we believed in, and some modes of our actual behavior, that are in alliance with him. One way to demonstrate that is to show how much Gandhi himself took from us.

Gandhi came to England at the end of the 1880s, and

lived in London as a student. His legal studies did not take up all his energies, and he involved himself in some movements of the time, particularly in matters of religion and social reformation. He joined the Theosophical Society and was very active in the Vegetarian Society. Thoreau was a cult figure for vegetarians, and Whitman for similar enthusiasts, and Gandhi read both of them—both, of course, declared a debt to Indian culture. Moreover, Edwin Arnold, who was in the West London Food Reform Society with Gandhi, was also the poet whose version of the Gita was the one Gandhi first read. Thus Eastern and Western influences were inextricable in this world of ideas.

The England Gandhi came to know was dominated, says Pyarelal, by figures like the Webbs, Shaw, and William Morris. The last had recently renounced his brightly patterned fabrics and wallpapers in favor of whitewashed walls and wooden chairs and tables. This was the taste Gandhi took back to India, and put into practice in his ashrams, which seem descended from the Morris cottages in which people of this intellectual type lived in England. Also important to him were Edward Carpenter, who wore Indian sandals made in Kashmir; and Henry Salt, the vegetarian and biographer of Thoreau; and some Labor politicians with a strong nonconformist morality, like Keir Hardie and John Burns. These were the days of socialist leagues, and Ramsay Macdonald's Fellowship of the New Life, which later developed into the Fabian Society. Along with Macdonald, later to be England's first Labour prime minister, we might mention Maurice Hyndman, and Havelock Ellis, another liberator of minds from the shackles of nineteenth-century Europe. In 1887 Edward Carpenter founded the Sheffield Socialist Group, to which Hyndman, Annie Besant, and Prince Kropotkin also belonged. Another emblematic date is 1880, the founding year of Hyndman's Democratic Federation, Gurney's Society for Physical Research, the Theosophical Society, a Vegetarian Society, and an Anti-Vivisection Society. In this current of the Western tradition, Gandhi and Gandhism are perfectly at home, because that current ran close, in experimental if random ways, to spiritual religion.

But to show the most important connections between Gandhi and Christianity, it is probably better to stop asking who or what Gandhi knew, and to begin looking for correspondences, for Christian political movements parallel to his. Take, for example, the Holy Experiment in Pennsylvania, 1682–1755, in which the Mennonites and the Quakers were involved. The former were anabaptists who dwelt apart from the world in agricultural communities and refused to serve as soldiers, police, magistrates, or even as jurors. They were nonresisters of evil, following the policy Tolstoy advocated. The Quakers were nonviolent resisters, as was Gandhi. They accepted a state structure, but of a severely limited kind. They abolished the death penalty, and designed prisons to be rehabilitative, not punitive; they refused to bear arms, tolerated all religions, and treated the Indians with scrupulous fairness.

After 1755 the Quakers found the Colonial Assembly too worldly, and withdrew from it; thereafter the hope of a Christian state in America was lost. Still, nineteenth-century America was not without its absolute resisters to state force, and in the last part of the century Eugene Debs, Tom Mooney, and others tried to organize a nonviolent resistance on the part of labor against big business. Out of this tradition came such American disciples of Gandhi as Richard Gregg.

The same indebtedness is to be found in Tolstoy, who drew heavily on the writings of English and American Quakers, especially when he was beginning his adventure of nonresistance and Christian pacifism. It does not seem that Russian Orthodox Christianity had much guidance to offer him, at least that we know of. Only the Old Believers, schismatics driven out of the state church, included among them sects who practiced radical anarchism and state resistance from whom he could learn. In his late years, also, he turned to Indian, Chinese, and Japanese religions, combining their teaching with the English-speaking Quaker and Baptist tradition, and the German Mennonites and Moravians. He affiliated himself with the cranks. In the 1890s he entered into a correspondence with the New England Universalist Adin Ballou, a pacifist and social idealist who had in the 1840s, as Tolstoy said, preceded him along the paths of radical nonresistance.

These look like the byroads and detours of history, and so of course they are. But by now it is surely clear that the main road we have followed has been a mistake. We can no longer afford to dismiss the figures we dimly discern down those misty turnings. They are probably the ones who were *not* lost. The success of Gandhi's movement showed that one of those dim figures, inherently implausible on the great stage of history, could play a hero's part. He has given an extra dimension to the others, the lost men of Western history, so that now we have no excuse for our blindness to them; if we continue to be dazzled by the bright lights it is because we deliberately stare into them.

The realm of art, though dominated by the same forces as history, always gave more space to the exceptions—to the heroes of resistance. The West has always had traditions of quietism in the arts. Within English literature, for instance, Wordsworth has stood for contemplative withdrawal, and "stood for" it not only to scholars seeking to categorize his poetry; he had a considerable effect on the sensibility and no doubt on the behavior of a large body of nineteenth-century readers. Aldous Huxley has described how the influence of Wordsworth made a walk in the hills into a religious exercise for the Huxley family; the whole Lake District became inhabited by this spirit. E. M. Forster, in *Passage to India*, says that even the typical Anglo-Indian, Ronnie Heslop, was sensitive and earnest in the Lake District. In music, one might take Bach as a figure corresponding to Wordsworth. Romain Rolland told an Indian inquirer that the Eastern tradition of spirituality found its equivalent in the West in the cult of music. In painting one can point not only to specifically religious works like the altar pieces before Raphael, but also to Cezanne and Van Gogh.

The activity of appreciating art, and the activity of study itself, can be a mode of contemplation. In nearly every college or university you will find some genuine contemplatives. And even the busier and more worldly academics make a contrast with men of action outside, which gives them the character, for others, and intermittently for themselves, of being withdrawn from life's grosser conflicts and competitions.

Tolstoy, being a great novelist as well as a Mahatma, created literary images and legends to nourish a spiritual-religious sensibility. He embodied those values also in stories, novellas, and novels, notably "The Death of Ivan Ilyich," *The Kreutzer Sonata*, and *Resurrection*, which I must discuss later. Even more remarkable is his work in the line of the religious legend, the folktale, the fairy story, and so on, various genres of more-or-less anonymous fiction, which the main thrust of post-Renaissance writing passed by. Within these tales the heroes and heroines can be very meek and mild, virginal, humble, simply good. But the novel as a genre, "serious fiction" as well as the adventure tale, has not allowed such types.

The major images the arts have offered us for cultic contemplation are images of action, adventure, activism. They also depict figures and feelings that should remind us of Gandhi and Tolstoy. We should find nothing mysterious or mystic or Eastern about the latter; our feeling that they are alien arises only because such figures have always appeared before us under the ban of weakness and defeat—because our civilization rejected them. The realm of art obeyed the laws promulgated in the realm of politics—in this matter even the sharpest cultural resistance made no difference—and our understanding of manners and motives has been profoundly distorted.

For instance, if we try to define the temperament of the quintessential Gandhian or Tolstoyan, we find it very recognizable in Western terms. By the quintessential Gandhian, I do not mean the politicians among his followers, like Nehru and Sardar Patel, or the litterateurs, like Kalelkar and Desai, or even the fierce religious spirits, like Vinoba. It seems to me that men like Rajendra Prasad, Nirmal Kumar Bose, and Krishnadas, gentle, humble, nervous men, of no "personality," self-deprecating, reasonable, devoted, are the men molded in Gandhi's image. (Among Tolstoyans one might cite Bulgakov, Tolstoy's last secretary, on the evidence of his diary.)

One finds a vivid expression of this temperament in Krishnadas' *Seven Months with Mahatma Gandhi*—in the diarist's headaches and recurrent alarms and despondencies, his fear of crowds and agitation, his conviction of the feebleness of his own powers, his shy unwillingness to put himself forward, even to approach Gandhi. Gandhi himself has something of this manner in his autobiography, and what it reports of his life, particularly early on, in his relations with leonine figures like Sir Pherozeshah Mehta, where he speaks as "little me" and "who was I to hope to disagree with this great man." But Gandhi made himself with time absolutely fearless and commanding, a bold, in some ways genial and dominating personality. Nevertheless, he knew what manner of men were his natural disciples. In announcing the Bardoli campaign in 1921, he said he had chosen Bardoli because its people were so mild: "It is time people realized that only mild and docile people should enlist them-selves on our side in this battle . . . [the people of Bardoli] are as mild as lambs. This last is their special qualification."

Another interesting case of the Gandhian temperament is Shriman Narayan, a pioneer of commercial education and state planning in India. After his studies he spent a year in England in 1935, and in those days thought of himself as a poet, in the tradition of Tagore. He went to see Lascelles Abercrombie, John Drinkwater, and Wilfred Gibson, older poets who remembered Tagore, but complained that he and they themselves were neglected by the young men of letters of the 1930s. Narayan also called on Stephen Spender, and with him met two other of these new poets. Them he found brusque and haughty, and began to realize that being a poet —in this new style—was not for him: "All the three poets had the same careless and 'highbrow' bearing, which began to get on my nerves. So I hastened to take my leave, and left the young poets to themselves." When he returned to India he entered the Gandhi movement and gave up poetry, which had been appropriated by the Kshattriyas. The spiri-tual temperament, the meek man, was driven even out of literature.

No doubt political leaders in the West sometimes have secretaries like Krishnadas or Shriman Narayan. But we have lost the way of seeing them as morally impressive; the loss can be traced in literature over the last 200 years. Their temperament is one that I have always named to myself "Fanny Price," after the heroine of Jane Austen's *Mansfield Park*. Krishnadas is always being surprised to be thought of, always hanging back, needing to be encouraged, always aware of his slowness and unworthiness, longing to be allowed to wash Gandhi's dishes—just like Fanny. He even has a poetic prose about Nature, like hers. And Fanny has had few admirers. Most readers have preferred the bad girl of the novel, Mary Crawford.

Of course, temperament is a dangerous guide to spirituality, because it could make us concentrate exclusively on personal relations. There is another side to spirituality, which is bold and dangerous; this is indeed the larger half of the phenomenon, for—although Gandhi and Tolstoy were warm friends to many people—personal relations do not weigh as heavy in the scales of spirituality as in other measures of value. This boldness stands out in, for instance, their vision of history. The Mahatmas see life in much more vivid and dramatic terms than other people do, including their academic followers. Peace researchers all over the world, studying, for instance, Gandhi's methods, betray his intentions because they ignore the spiritual man's vision. What looks like something extemporaneous and disorganized and unsystematic in Gandhi's way—like something *they* can regularize and even improve on—is in fact ineradicable. That is Gandhi's truth, the duty to be discovered existentially, in the depths of the self as it lives in and lives out each particular crisis. And for Gandhi and Tolstoy the world is always in crisis; the unspeakable has always been occurring; the end of the world has always been at hand, because man is appallingly wicked. That sense is something that cannot be taken into any system of knowledge or any spirit of humanism; an enormous distance stretches between culture, at its most imaginative, and spirituality. The first has a geometrical sense of history, the second a topological; the substance of human experience can be stretched, and can be compressed, can crumple up into nothing; it does so stretch and crumple of itself—it is not a substance; our schemes of understanding, our forms of knowledge, are all a construct, artificial roofing that hides from us the vast abyss above. That is the heroic and overweening side of spiritual men. But probably that is less disconcerting than the slight, meager, faded, faltering aspect they may present in personal relations.

To return to the previous instance, most modern readers have found Fanny Price very hard to take. The imaginative mode of the West has been hostile to this temperament, and in alliance with the dashing styles of adventure and empire. This is one of the ways in which the study of literature is *not* in the service of contemplation. Dickens was one of the great scorners of nonconformist meekness of Fanny's kind, and it is of his Uriah Heep that I think at times, when Gandhi or one of his disciples seems *too* humble. (The temperament was, in the nineteenth century, superficially acceptable in a girl, like Esther Summerson in *Bleak House,* but the deeper mood of even that book is in a different key—the Esthers are finally inauthentic figures.) But I think of Heep only to realize that Dickens, and English literature as a whole, is no sure guide in this matter. This irritable turning away from meekness toward "spirit," "mettle," "fire," is by and large a bad thing—a self-commitment to the equivalent of imperial adventure.

Of course, literature is largely a recording device, and to that degree not to be blamed for what it records. In a nation like nineteenth-century England, committed to imperialist adventure, the authentic voices were likely to speak of mettle and fire. We would have more cause to reproach literature if it had spoken assertively for spiritual values in that culture, where they had either no voice or a falsetto one. Such values can easily be travestied and falsified.

That can be seen in politics as well as in literature. The last English upwelling of nonconformist meekness into a political movement, in the Labour party around 1900, discredited itself badly when it came into office in India. The Labour government under Ramsay Macdonald was not ready to do anything for India when it came into power in 1930, despite its long tradition of indignation against the imperialism of its rivals. Much of the moral conviction of the party was found to have seeped away over the preceding generation, as they approached office. Now they had power, the leaders found that the general climate of opinion had so changed that they could not any longer believe in their ideals—in that part of them that derived from nonconformist Christianity.

One can follow the course of this change, this defeat for spiritual values in English politics, in *Off the Beaten Track*, the autobiography of an English Gandhian, Wilfred Wellock, a man typical of the idealists among the Labour party at that time. Born in 1879 in Nelson, Lancashire, he went to work in the mills at the age of ten but managed to go to continuation classes in the evenings. But he got his education largely in the Noncomformist Church. From 1892–1902, he says, the church was the hub of his life, with its Sunday school, glee club, orchestra, hand-bell ringers, drama, and Mutual Improvement Society. It was inevitable that such a man would become an idealistic Socialist. He rejected from his Christianity the idea of sin, and preached sermons instead against stock exchange gambling in cotton prices. In 1914, "To me the whole idea of wars and military service was revolting and unthinkable," so he became a Conscientious Objector. He brought out a magazine against war, and was sent to prison—taking a portrait of Tolstoy with him—but still in some sense triumphant. For him, spirituality and politics blended in much the same way as they did later for members of Gandhi's movement in India.

When he emerged in 1918 he found a new world, different in its blatant sexuality and hedonism and in the decline of public interest in serious things. It was, he says, after the war that young Englishmen stopped going to church, and that those church-centers of creative social and religious activity, to which he owed so much, gradually disappeared. Before 1914 he and his friends had been all *optimistic* idealists, inspired by a fine galaxy of poets, and had thought that their only enemies were remnants of feudalism. After 1918 his sense of the movement of history was quite different: "As I reached middle age I began to notice that the idealists were declining in number . . . some years later came the biggest shock of all when I discovered that I had been swerved into a backwash by . . . [materialism] . . . people like me were relegated to the back stage. . . . I lived in a social wilderness." Wellock himself remained loyal to Gandhi but could bring him few English recruits, and had to watch his former friends turn away from the cause. Spirituality had gone out of fashion.

The same thing happened in the career of Gandhi's chief English disciple, C. F. Andrews. In the years after the war Andrews compiled three books, published in England, summarizing and quoting Gandhi's ideas. He became Gandhi's impresario with the English intellectual public. But he was, being an earnest evangelical missionary, quite the wrong person for the job. English intellectuals after 1918 were instinctively disrespectful of figures like him. He was what they called a creeping Jesus. (I will quote Orwell's use of the term later.) In fact he was, in 1921 in Kenya, dragged from his railway compartment by white settlers angered by his spiritual politics, who pulled him by the beard, saying, "Jesus wept." Even a letter to the press from an Indian in Kenya in those days complained of Andrews as one of the "insidious, bowing, cringing, khaddar-wearing barefooted white saddhus." In intellectuals some of the same philistinism revived or reemerged, under the sanction of modernist toughness of mind. There is a letter of 1934 to Gandhi from G. D. Birla, his supporter: "I had a long talk with Arthur Moore yesterday at my house lasting for about two and a half hours. Mr. Muggeridge, the new man, came with him. [Moore was the editor of the most important English newspaper in India, and Muggeridge was Malcolm.] Somehow or other, I find that these men do not take to Andrews and such with great kindness. They have no opinion of their intelligence and unfortunately have a sort of prejudice which I had not discovered until now." And from then on Birla tried to get Gandhi to use other intermediaries in dealing with the English, since spirituality was out of fashion. (Muggeridge was not yet *our* Malcolm.)

And yet in 1910 Gandhi could have felt, as Tolstoy seems to have felt, that everyone was coming over to his side. Tolstoy habitually talked, in the last decade of his life, as if it were only in governments that a foolish obstinacy in the old ways persisted, and the young men everywhere were refusing military service, and returning to the land, and so on. In the period just before the war there was a lot of intellectual, and more-than-intellectual, activity, besides the movement Wellock represented, that seemed to promise a speedy end to the patriarchal state and its imperialist enterprises.

For instance, in 1910 Gandhi found an article by G. K. Chesterton in the *Illustrated London News*, which so delighted him that he translated it and printed it in his newspaper. Chesterton attacked Herbert Spencer and his idea of progress, and used the case of India to make his point:

Suppose an Indian said: "I wish India had always been free from white men and all their works. Everything has its own faults and we prefer our own. Had we our own institutions, there would have been dynastic wars; but I prefer dying in battle to dying in hospital. There would have been despotism; but I prefer one king whom I hardly ever see to a hundred kings who regulate my diet and children. There would have been religious differences dangerous to public peace. But I think religion more important than peace. Life is very short; a man must live somehow and die somewhere; the amount of bodily comfort a peasant gets under your way of living is not so much more than mine. If you do not like our way of living, we never asked you to do so. Go, and leave us with it."

In effect, Chesterton attacked the modern world system, in the name of spiritual values.

Thus the new Catholicism and many other streams of thought then converged with Gandhi's. In a letter of 1909 Gandhi had written that Europeans had, before this time, much in common with Indians. "It is impertinence to change the world by the means of speedy locomotives. Medicine is black magic, and hospitals are the Devil's instruments." Not the British people but modern civilization rules India. If East is to meet West, it will be either because the latter throws modern civilization overboard, or because the former adopts it, but that second meeting would be in the Hall of Death, like the meeting to come between England and Germany. India's salvation is to unlearn what she has learned this last fifty years: "There was true wisdom in the sages of old having so regulated society as to limit the material conditions of the people; the rude plough of perhaps 5000 years ago is the plough of the husbandman today. Therein lies salvation."

And if in all this Gandhi sounds like Chesterton, he also sounds quite a bit like D. H. Lawrence, and the three together make a powerful consensus. Thus when Gandhi says in *Hind Swaraj*, "If you believe that because Italians rule Italy the Italian nation is happy, you are groping in darkness," it would be easy to find an exact equivalent in Lawrence, as it would be when he says, "I am not aiming at destroying railways or hospitals, though I would certainly welcome their natural destruction." But of course there is a crucial difference from Lawrence in *this*: "Ideally I would rule out all machinery, even as I would reject this body, which is not helpful to salvation . . . but machinery like the body is inevitable." And that rejection of the body would have offended Chesterton, too. The consensus is broken up on this rock.

The rejection of violence offended one body of potential enthusiasts—the political rebels—after 1918; the rejection of art and thought, another—those who followed T. S.

Eliot. But it was most of all his hostility to the body that proved fatal to Gandhi's reception by later English intellectuals, whether or not they called themselves followers of Lawrence. Seriousness, at least among men of letters, attached itself to one form or other of eroticism, and so opposed itself to most forms of spirituality.

In 1936 at the All India Literary Conference at Nagpur, Gandhi said, "Today a plethora of highly objectionable erotic literature seems to be in evidence in every province. Indeed, there are some who declare that barring the erotic, there is no other *rasa* [passion] worth the name; and . . . those who insist on restraint in literature, are held up to ridicule as devoid of all *rasa*. . . . If you will not be annoyed, I would say that the erotic is the lowest of all the rasas, and when it partakes of the obscene it is wholly to be eschewed." There is no reason to suppose that Gandhi would have exempted even Lawrence from the general category of erotic writers; this has meant that English men of letters, even those as morally earnest as Leavis, have not been his allies.

And yet they could have been, even in this matter of sexuality. However strikingly their routes diverge from his, even from the heritage of nineteenth-century humanism, the explorers among them come back toward him. I am thinking of Susan Sontag, who says in "The Pornographic Imagination" (1967): "There is, demonstrably, something incorrectly designed and potentially disorienting in the human sexual capacity—at least in the capacities of man-in-civilization. Man, the sick animal, bears within him an appetite which can drive him mad." Her dissent from the sexual orthodoxies of liberal humanism is like that of Norman O. Brown, and leads her, like Brown, to a choice between accepting obscenity, pornography, abjection, and accepting the ideal of chastity: "Human sexuality is, quite apart from Christian repressions, a highly questionable phenomenon, and belongs, at least potentially, among the ex-

treme rather than the ordinary experiences of humanity. . . .
[It is] one of the demonic forces in human consciousness. . . . Even on the level of simple physical sensation and
mood, making love surely resembles having an epileptic fit
at least as much, if not more, than it does eating a meal or
conversing with someone." That is exactly what Tolstoy and
Gandhi said.

It is, therefore, no accident that Susan Sontag sees
modern art as "a spiritual project," and that her culture
heroes are "perverse spiritual athletes," like Artaud,
Wittgenstein, Beckett, who drive their art and their thought
toward "silence." Her path in exploring modern sensibility,
though aggressively modernist and so angled more sharply
away from the Mahatmas' path than the liberal humanism
of Leavis, Trilling, Rolland, nevertheless brings her to this
chasm, this sexual dilemma, one leap across which is
Gandhism. But of course she does not take that leap. She
accepts and affirms pornography, not chastity. The difficulty
for liberal humanists, the obstacle my audience felt, is still
there. The difference is that it is now confronted.

VI

TALK THREE

Politics and Aesthetics

HERE AGAIN I want to talk about culture and empire—only this time about specific parallels and connections between politics and aesthetics, primarily in the work of Gandhi and Tolstoy. But I want to begin by addressing the subject at its most general.

The two fields, politics and aesthetics, lie far apart in our minds, a separation that causes lots of us distress. Part of our attraction to Gandhi and Tolstoy is that these two thinkers save us from that separation. But they do so at an enormous price, intellectually, by an enormous simplification of both fields and their connections. They reject so much that we value as art, and demand such simple kinds of social function from anything they accept—demand them so strenuously it amounts to a subordination of art. For them, everything is moral, but nothing is purely moral. They reject our categories, the purely political, the purely aesthetic, the purely moral, which are necessary to that complexity of consciousness that we value as our integrity as intellectuals. Or so we think. For first of all I want to show how closely the two kinds of experience in fact intertwine in our minds, unacknowledged by us, committed as we are to keeping them apart.

There are various ways of combining aesthetic categories with politics. Within a novel, for instance, besides describing political events and issues as part of the subject matter, there is the way followed by Nabokov in his *Invitation to a Beheading* and *Bend Sinister*. The protagonists of those stories despise politics and are involved with them only marginally, though fatally. But they rise superior to their oppressors even as they are killed by them. They proudly transcend politics, and the novelist cooperates with their pride by transforming reality in their service. Dictators and their henchmen become ludicrous puppets who literally come apart, and the place of execution becomes a stage-set that literally falls apart before our eyes.

And this approach to politics is not confined to novels. Randolph Churchill taught his adherents, so one of them tells us, to treat the conventions and institutions of British political life as if they were papier-maché stage-properties; to walk right through them on occasion. Jawarhalal Nehru wrote to Gandhi from the tragic scenes of the Hindu-Muslim massacres of 1947 that all the participants on both sides were equally degraded and disgusting. One of Nehru's essays on Gandhi after his death is entitled "The Perfect Artist," and says that all Gandhi's manifold activities became progressively a symphony; and that even in his death there was a magnificence and a complete artistry. It is not many steps from such categories of response to Nabokov's political categories of ennui and phoniness.

However, that mode of applying aesthetics to politics is a rather special case. Nabokov, Nehru, and Churchill were all men of aristocratic birth and temperament, all to some degree aesthetes, and all liable to spasms of perversity, of antipolitical irresponsibility. A less extreme case is provided by what we might call personality politics. Besides the state-run cults of personality, as of Che in Cuba and Stalin in Russia, the politics of Napoleonic France and Bismarckian Germany were dominated by giant personalities, and it is appropriate to analyze and criticize such politics by the categories of domination and subordination, of gesture and rhetoric, of power and grace of personality. The language of theater criticism is appropriate to quite a lot of politics as we know it. Norman Mailer's essays show how far such language can take us even today, and even in understanding a party as well as its leaders.

The language of symbol and myth also is appropriate to much of politics, notably Gandhian politics. Gandhi was a lawyer and journalist, skillful with constitutions and debates, rules of procedure and ballots; he was also a brilliant coiner of slogans and organizer of compromise resolutions. But his politics worked above all by means of the spinning wheel, the march to the sea to make salt, the burning of foreign cloth, his fastings and his pilgrimages. He reshaped the arena of politics and introduced into it forces of imagination, conscience, inspiration, which by traditional standards did not belong there. His operations demand to be described by political terms modified in the direction of aesthetic terms.

Nevertheless, *all* these are somewhat special cases. One might say that they all derive from the presentation and dramatization of political issues, not from the inner and original stuff of politics—the distribution of wealth, power, and status among different groups and classes. What interests me most are some recent intimations that to these, too, other categories, including aesthetic categories, apply.

I spent a holiday last summer in a fishing village in Devonshire. It was a charming place, and its charm lay in the fact that though people went there for holidays, it still made its living by fishing. Nevertheless, the regular inhabitants also rejoiced in its charm, its holiday qualities. I found this disconcerting because I had always assumed that such self-awareness was self-consciousness, sophistication, a late refinement that begins corruption. But this was not a late refinement. So far as I could make out from historical accounts, Appledore had been complacently aware of its own charms for hundreds of years. It had *always* seen itself as blessedly unlike cities, as being in touch with the ocean and with Nature, as offering a healing balm to harried man, and so on. Nor had its integrity suffered any violence from this sophistication.

So Appledore's ordinary and serious perception of itself is aesthetic as well as political. And this is, I would guess, true of fishing villages everywhere—not all, but many—and not only in Europe and North America. Of course it goes without saying that people from outside, from the cities, have seen them that way.

But perhaps this is true only of such small social units, left behind or outside the main currents of politics and civilization. Do the inhabitants of big cities think of themselves in aesthetic terms? Well, of course they do. Dickens' London and Mailer's New York leap to mind as examples of great cities aesthetically alive to their inhabitants, not merely in terms of their buildings or the types seen on the streets, but in terms of their life—the work done there, the workings of the law, the distribution of power; all are known in terms of myth, theater, caricature. Nor were Dickens and Mailer working against the normal consciousness of their fellow citizens. Being who they were, they saw *more*, which meant that to some degree they shocked and startled their readers, but once over that shock their contemporary readers acknowledged the truth of that vision. The writers had only organized and energized the citizens' perceptions.

Both town and country see themselves as imaginative, so partly as aesthetic entities. Fernand Brandel says that the confrontation of town and country is the first and longest-lived of a type that shapes history. Looking at each other, such antagonists constitute a theater, with expectations of each other—with *plots*—foreseeing the course of any competition, conflict, or other interchange. Thus nineteenth-century England was full of such feelings as, "The town is spreading and spreading, soon the countryside will be completely killed, and men will live and die never having seen green fields or sunlight."

And do not the social classes also between them constitute another theater? The bourgeoisie vs. the proletariat, the aristocracy vs. the middle class, the rich vs. the poor, all these pairs of terms start up expectations in our heads. We know facts about each other; we have principles about politics; but just as much we have scenarios. We have ideas and feelings about how anyone from one of those groups will behave toward a representative from another. And of course the same is even more obvious in international confrontations. Brandel says that civilizations play out a drama, one against another, like the class drama. An Englishman in India meets and carries a set of expectations to every encounter. We can of course choose among those expectations, and even evade all of them, but that is still evasion; they are still there, as the parameters of our behavior.

So deep in our sense of how political forces work lie various aesthetic categories, which are only artificially exorcised by "purely political" or "political science" studies. But I think the connection, or the identity, is even more challenging than that. To go back to those theaters that I was talking about, among the actors in them, some are more consciously and obviously histrionic than others. In the nineteenth century France seemed a histrionic nation to most Englishmen and Americans. And in most centuries the aristocracy has seemed a histrionic social class to the others. Goethe's *Wilhelm Meister* is the story of a middle-class boy with aspirations to both art and aristocracy. He transcends his social limitations by becoming first an actor and then an aristocrat. And he finds the two adventures follow and develop the one from the other, because aristocrats manifest themselves in their bodies, as actors do and as merchants do not. Aristocrats are on stage all the time, in the noblest sense of the phrase. It is their fate to manifest to society as a whole its general ideas—the ideas shared by all classes to some degree—grace, dignity, culture, power, magnificence, innocence, experience. This explains the itch to ennoble themselves we see among so many writers, including Goethe himself, Shakespeare, Defoe, and so on. It is not merely snobbery, or snobbery is not merely mean. And the same applies to people who are not writers. Snobbery is in many ways an inadequate word.

What is true of aristocrats is of course truer of kings. Perhaps it is less obvious that it is also true of all luxury living and luxury travel. In Delhi I stayed at the Imperial Hotel—to study antiimperialism—and in Madurai I stayed at the Pandyan Hotel, which was even more sumptuous. At first I thought it a sardonic incongruity that the name of ancient kings should be given to a modern hotel. But on reflection I decided that the Pandyans' palace must have been very like the hotel in magnificence of decor, in exaggeration of comfort, in quantities of servants, and in the eager servility of smiles and bows. I was living like a king. And may we not say that well-to-do people in the West all live in palaces when they travel? I don't mean only that we live on the sweat of others' brows, though that, too, is true. But what is at the root of all luxury? Surely it is fantasy—the indulgence of dreams. In luxury hotels we are buoyed up; we float away from the earth's gravity; we forget our limitations. Everything is designed to flatter our senses, our vanity, our pride, to make us feel more important than other people, than we know we are, than . . . any other term you can think of. It is a more-than feeling. We see ourselves enhanced in rose-colored mirrors.

But this applies best to luxury travel, which always carries with it the sense of impermanence and of contrast with a reality back home. If we are to talk of the palace-feeling—the banquet-feeling—as a permanent feature of our culture, we must trace the roots of fantasy further back. Of course the sense of contrast remains as contributory. We feel our homes as palaces, or *not* palaces, when we contrast them with our rivals' homes, or our own past homes, or other homes in general. Our minds, or at least our thoughts, are built of contrasts, and one cannot hope to exorcise them completely. But the root of fantasy, I would suggest, is the thrill of transcending not rivals but the body itself. That, the power to control the body and its environment, to make the senses register only pleasure, to make them dilate in expectation and flush in gratification, that is the essence of fantasy and luxury. That constitutes the luxury of the modern home, even when it is an apartment in a huge block, and exactly like hundreds of others.

Perhaps that becomes clearer if we think of the opposite extreme, Gandhi's ashram, where a new inmate's first duties were regularly to clean out the lavatories every day. This was realism, as opposed to fantasy. It was designed to prevent people from feeling like kings. In luxurious, fantasy living, every unpleasant object and duty is disposed of or minimized, every form of pleasure is amplified and varied. This exhilaration of fantasy can be felt without any sense of contrast with other people, or in a family whose ideology is wholly democratic. That exhilaration is what is expressed, for instance, by those American fathers who call their daughters Princess. Without feeling themselves in the least undemocratic, they are exhilarated by fantasy. The meals in many American homes are banquets—a procession of delicacies assembled from enormous distances—and feel like banquets even while the eaters feel themselves entirely average.

Kings, in other words, *were* men who lived lives of fantasy. So were aristocrats. And phrases like "to live like a king" and "to live like a lord" are fantastic not just by the accident that the speakers are not kings themselves, but in essence. Even for a king it is fantastic to live like a king. The whole structure of upper-class life is a dream. And the middle class of the West is the upper class of the world, and a realized dream, of course, which means that practical consequences followed from fantasy wishes. But it is still a self-indulgent illusion, a self-dramatization, in spite of a deeper reality —Gandhi's reality.

This, is, of course, the point of the legend of Gautama. He was brought up to be a king, and so was shielded from the sight of all disease, decay, and death. And once he caught sight of these aspects of life they made nonsense of the pursuit of pleasure for him. He gave up the life of a king because he saw that it was unreal—men are *not* kings. (As Tolstoy said about his family, "the conditions of superabundance in which we lived prevented us from understanding life.") So Gautama became the Buddha, by practicing and preaching the truths he had glimpsed through the walls society had erected around him—the same truths Gandhi and Tolstoy teach us.

And economically speaking, luxury has been of crucial importance in the development of capitalism and the modern world system, as Werner Sombart and Marcel Mauss have argued. It was after all the market for pepper and spices that drove trade in the later Middle Ages, the market for sugar in the sixteenth and seventeenth centuries that drove trade then, and the market for coffee, tea, and chocolate later—not to mention gold and silver, or alcohol and tobacco. These were what traders went far to seek, and customers paid extravagantly to buy, not the staples of nutrition. As Gaston Bachelard says, "the attainment of the superfluous causes greater spiritual excitement than the attainment of the necessities. Man is a creature of desire, not a creature of need." And Braudel says that though luxury changes its material forms with every age, the social drama that revolves around luxury abides forever: "The privileged and the onlookers—the masses who watch them —must of course agree to a certain amount of connivance. Luxury does not only represent rarity and vanity, but also social success, fascination, the dream that one day becomes reality for the poor. . . ." It is such dreams that hold a civilization together, Braudel says.

I recall Gandhi's complaints against the luxury of the Congress conference of 1938: "We have all become princes [a phrase that has a more precise reference for an Indian] . . . here there are petrol and oil engines and water pipes and stoves and electricity . . . toothpaste and toothbrush and scented hair-oil." To a Westerner these are likely to seem pitiful items for any list of princely luxuries, but they were clearly first steps toward the palace, even if we call this a palace for everyman.

Thus in a sense—in Gandhi's sense, but also in Norman O. Brown's sense—all civilized history has been a dream. And thus politics is intricately intertwined at its root with aesthetics, psychology, spirituality, despite the distance we set between these studies at the university and elsewhere. Our political ideas are aesthetic—are aspirations to Beauty and Pleasure—as much as our aesthetic judgments are political.

So our argument has brought us back to Gandhi and Tolstoy, who maintain in their world view an organic wholeness that unites aesthetics and politics, and all those other things. Their thought about both subjects runs parallel and close to ours for a time, and then suddenly jumps to the other edge of possibility.

Because of course all that intertwining of categories I described, so vivid for us, would be pointless ingenuity to the Mahatmas, who abolished the categories a priori. My point, my effect, depends on your having a vivid sense of how separate those ideas are. I am not saying the same thing as the Mahatmas; though my argument converges with theirs, it stops short at the meeting place and does not enter their country.

To give you a distant and aerial view of that country, let me remind you from what very English department sources Gandhi began. His three great book inspirations were Ruskin, Tolstoy, and Thoreau: *Unto This Last, The Kingdom of God Is Within You,* and *Civil Disobedience,* texts with which we are, some of us, professionally familiar, for which we are in some sense professionally responsible. *Hind Swaraj* is a criticism of industrialism and modern civilization generally, which might almost, as I have said, have been written by D. H. Lawrence. Using that book and its year of publication, 1909, as a base-point, it is easy to measure the divergence of the paths followed by the Lawrentians in England and the Gandhians in India.

The Gandhians took the path of politics, not that of aesthetics, and though they used symbolism, it was political symbolism. Gandhi's principal mechanism for achieving Indian independence was the spinning wheel, with which he identified all his ideas. By reintroducing the wheel—a part of the Indian past, driven out of use by the British textile factories—and by spreading its use, he hoped to make India independent of foreign cloth, and to make each peasant family independent of the periodicity of Indian agriculture. Primarily, therefore, the wheel was practical technology. But it was also, and just as importantly and by the same token, a symbol. Gandhi and his followers were to be *seen* sitting and spinning, and the yarn they spun was to be seen and handled; when woven it made white and brown khadi cloth, which they wore. To spin and wear it was the mark of the Congress party. Other people also bought it and wore it as "the livery of freedom," as Nehru called it. (Homespun cloth was of course one of the products of the Morris movement in England, but it never achieved anything like the political or economic significance that Gandhi gave it in India; that is representative of many of the differences between the two movements.) But as symbol the wheel was more than political and economic in its reference. It had spiritual, aesthetic, and historical dimensions; spiritually, Gandhi said the work of spinning composed his soul to peace like a prayer—it even restored his bodily health; aesthetically, he found its music beautiful—which meant, since Gandhi was always realistic, that he found it very ugly when the wheel was not working right; historically, he said that the spinning of the wheel was in the reverse direction to the turning of the world during the last three hundred years of history—that each man, as he spun, was setting the globe spinning back in the reverse direction toward health and peace.

These ideas, as you hear them from me, are little more than conceits. If you had heard them from Gandhi, they would all be magnificent symbols. The difference would have been that they would have come in the context of his incomparable manifold of activity and charged with his phenomenal forcefulness of will, but most of all they would have been different because Gandhi's reality is all one. It is not divided up among political and aesthetic and economic. All his symbols are resonant in all those dimensions. They are not similes or allegories because they do not reach across the gap that separates one of our categories from another. All reality is one, and it is all symbolic.

Since *we*, however, live in a category-ridden world, I shall take my major example of Gandhi's power of symbolism from what we call the world of literature. On his seventy-seventh birthday in 1946 an Englishwoman sent him congratulations and quoted the Blake stanza:

> I give you the end of a golden string
> Only wind it into a ball,
> It will lead you in at Heaven's gate
> Built in Jerusalem's wall.

"You also have put this thread in our hands," she said. Gandhi replied, "Have you ever noticed that my ball is an unending ball of cotton thread instead of Blake's 'golden string'? Blake's was the imagination of a poet, mine can become now and here the gateway to heaven if the billions of the earth will but spin the beautiful white ball of the slender and unbreakable thread." Could anyone else have met a poet like Blake on his own ground and, as it were, disarmed him—taken over his metaphor and improved upon it? Surely no other politician!

Gandhi, then, brought into the realm of politics—into all of practical life—the pleasures of the aesthetic resonance, the pleasures of symbolism, and fantasy, and form. He was a poet without benefit of verse, a poet of life. If we lived under his regime, we would need no separate realm of art in which to find our meanings. But what did he have to say about that separate realm that we have constructed for ourselves?

You may have noticed that Gandhi by implication assigned Blake, as poet, an orientation toward the future, while he, Gandhi, lived in the present. This is an idea that recurs in his remarks about art. In his controversy with Tagore, which was explicitly a controversy between the poet and the politician, Gandhi saluted Tagore as India's sentinel, whose ideas range forward toward the ideal and the future. The poet does not see, Gandhi said, the one thing needful, or the immediate present in all its circumstance.

This will not seem an immediately convincing idea of art, at least to those of us who grew up on the New Critics, who saw the poet as particularly intimate with the world's body in all its richness, while men of ideas and men of action dealt with schemes and skeletons. But Northrop Frye may save us from dismissing Gandhi's idea out of hand. Frye speaks of art as being often "utopian," using that word to cover all vivid and intense descriptions of intense and vivid things. Thus a description of a flower can be utopian, much more that of two people in love, in the sense that the description gives us a taste of perfection and draws us on to demand more of life. I think that is the idea Gandhi has in mind.

He is certainly very much to the point in his main reproach to and rebuttal of Tagore. Tagore had complained—this was in the early 1920s—that the Gandhian movement was narrowing the freedom of Indian patriots, above all their freedom of mind and imagination. India had long been an impoverished country, and what it needed was to expand its imagination, to rejoice in varieties of splendor, and to reconcile them. The symbol of the spinning wheel was crowding out other symbols, and it was in itself a symbol of negation, of poverty, of asceticism. Gandhi replied that the life of the mind proceeds by negation as much as by affirmation. And if you know Tagore's work, you will agree that that is the perfect reply. Tagore was a Goethean yea-sayer, whose weakness was that he lived completely among the beautitudes, all benignity and radiance at every cost to precision and complexity.

When Gandhi was founding his ashram at Sabarmati, after his return to India from South Africa, his path and Tagore's were diverging from what had seemed a close correspondence. In origin both were religious but heretical, both were nationalist but nonviolent, both were deeply influenced by the West and Christianity. Tagore had been preaching villagism, *swadeshi*, national education, and an end to caste and creed divisions, long before Gandhi. But in the years when the latter became more and more austere and ascetic, Tagore's accent was, as Sibnarayan Ray says, increasingly on "the dynamic aspects of reality—on life's élan and ever-changing forms, its movement and fluidity, its inexhaustible youth and energy, its urge for freedom and adventure." That is a report on his motives from a point of view flatteringly close to his own, though true enough in its own terms, but at any rate he turned away from Gandhi. In 1921 he wrote to Andrews, "I refuse to waste my manhood in lighting fires of anger and spreading it from house to house . . . it would be an insult to humanity if I use the sacred energy of my moral indignation for the purpose of spreading a blind passion all over my country. It would be like using the fire from the altar . . . for the purpose of incendiarism." He decided that Gandhi's movement was directed against reason itself. When Gandhi asked him to endorse the use of the spinning wheel, he said that in India life was already leveled down into death, and that a cult of the wheel would increase that effect.

In 1920 he had praised Gandhi as the Indian Tolstoy; indeed, as Tolstoy's superior, since Gandhi was natural, simple, modest, and pure, while in Tolstoy pride fought against pride, anger against anger, and everything was violent. But Tagore already then regretted that Gandhi's moral fervor was poured into the frail vessel of politics, and he found "noncooperation" all too negative. He felt, he said, a horror at all that says no, and preferred the Brahman ideal of purifying life's joys to the Buddhist ideal of negating them. (Gandhi replied that human effort is made up of negatives, too, and India had forgotten how to say no.)

On March 5, 1921, Tagore wrote of his inner resistance to the national excitement; the voice within him said, "Your place is on 'the seashore of worlds,' with children; there is your peace and I am with you there. . . ." And he continued, "But while I play, the whole creation is amused, for are not flowers and leaves never-ending experiments in metre? Is not my God an eternal waster of time? . . . But where am I among the crowd, pushed from behind, pressed from all sides? And what is this noise about me? If it is a song, then my own sitar can catch the tune. . . . But if it is a shout, then my voice is wrecked, and I am lost in bewilderment." There is enough truth in all this to be poignant, but of course it is hard to find it impressive.

Gandhi replied that the poet seemed to be satisfied with beautiful words and song, when India was a house on fire where the people were dying of hunger: "To a people famishing and idle, the only acceptable form in which God can dare appear is as work and the promise of food as wages." This was of course unanswerable in a public debate like that. But it is worth noting that Gandhi had many other things to say and said them first. He used his heavy guns sparingly and, as it were, reluctantly.

Generally, however, what Gandhi said about art as art is not very interesting in itself. No doubt he never gave more than one-half of 1 percent of his attention to the subject. His genius lay in his wholeness, in seeing things' togetherness, not their separateness. In any case, much of the discussion he engages in is vitiated from the start by the assumption—made by his opponents as much as by himself —that art is in the service of beauty, and that, through beauty, it inspires men. This theory led Gandhi, naturally enough, to retort to aesthetes that he found all the beauty he needed in Nature, and that much of modern art seemed to him far from inspiring. (He took Oscar Wilde to be a representative of modern art.) The truth, of course, is that great art as we know it—I mean modern and modernist art —has very little to do with beauty, or with inspiration, in that major meaning of the term that relates to serving mankind.

It makes more sense, I think, to see all the arts and sciences as transpositions into an ideal mode of just the same energies as practical men put into the pursuit of wealth and power, construction and destruction. They may serve beauty or ugliness; truth, or power, or pride; or whatever the artist or thinker wishes—that the national culture offers him. The arts and sciences participate in the national energies of their times. At different epochs of national development, the mode of reflection will differ, too; at one time it may enhance, at another degrade, now celebrate, now caricature. And during the last 300 years, the epoch of Western imperialism, the men of culture have of course participated in the feverish energy of that economy, that technology, that militarism, and that politics. Their art has reacted against that but participated in it, has been sublime rather than beautiful, to use Lionel Trilling's terms. So Western *culture* has been imperialist, too, even in its resistance to Western civilization; imperialist by virtue of its inordinate centrifugal powers and energies.

This was of course what Gandhi said about Western technology, economy, politics, militarism; but he did not know, I think, quite how it manifested itself in the arts and sciences and speculation. These he fairly simply disapproved. But the important fiction and poetry written during his lifetime, the important music and painting, were as formidable constructions of wit and will as his own work, and demand from those who would appreciate them quantities of devotion and patience comparable to those expunged by Gandhi's followers.*

* Think of *Ulysses, The Magic Mountain, The Four Quartets, A La Recherche du Temps Perdu*, and so on. And think of the work we put into understanding them.

As Susan Sontag says in "The Pornographic Imagination," art in the last century has "been invested with an unprecedented stature—the nearest thing to a sacramental human activity acknowledged by a secular society." And in "The Aesthetics of Silence" she says, "As an abstract and fragmented replica of the positive nihilism expounded by the radical religious myths, the serious art of our time has moved increasingly toward the most excruciating inflections of consciousness." This is quite a different idea of art from even *Middlemarch* and *War and Peace*. "Positive nihilism" is what Gandhi and Tolstoy teach, and some modern art is indeed related to that teaching—but related as "an abstract and fragmented replica."

Gandhi had some sense of that. Even expending only one-half of 1 percent of his attention he saw more than most people. But his response was only anger. He thought what he called specialization in the arts, and what he called hair splitting in their appreciation, was a perverse turning away from the most real, art's desertion of its social duty. "I want art for the millions," he said, as Tolstoy had said in *What Is Art?*

This is, as I have said, a philistine position, however intelligent, however noble. Gandhi and Tolstoy refuse to listen to the modern artist, refuse to give him a chance, because he demands too much latitude. We who ally ourselves with contemporary art *must* find something inadequate in Gandhi's and Tolstoy's aesthetics. After all, modern artists are not being personally perverse and willful in creating such complex works, or in insulting beauty and inspiration. The rules of the game have changed on them, and they can only obey. The arts and speculation are responding to the same situation as Gandhi's politics did when he had to give up his loyalty to the British Empire, and launch out as a rebel and a revolutionary; modern art is responding just as sincerely and with just as agonized an effort.

Nevertheless, art's protest against corruptive modern civilization is also a mode of operation *of* modern civilization. It is destructive, in its anger against our society, of the ancient bonds of social piety. It is not, for instance, on the side of health. The decay of traditional sexual morality, something that exercised Gandhi and Tolstoy a great deal, is something exploited and fostered by modern art. The kind of art they could approve was pious, in the service of society at least 90 percent, though of course it might savagely attack some particular abuse of power and privilege, even in the central authority of the state.

This kind of art is to our taste rather philistine. This is true even in the case of genius—the case of Tolstoy's late work. It lacks the freedom and vigor and boldness, as art, to which we are accustomed—a freedom that derives from the separation of art from the rest of life to be a whole kingdom in itself, where the whole range of human energies and ambitions act themselves out.

But on the borders of art, where it shades into politics, where the unity of these separated realms reemerges, the advantages are reversed. Within the area marked out by their aesthetic, Gandhi—and of course Tolstoy—move with perfect authority.

In his speech of 1916 at the opening of Benares Hindu University—the speech that made Vinoba his disciple—Gandhi demanded action, not words, and temple cleaning instead of the parade of jeweled princes he saw on the platform beside him: "I'm sure it is not the desire of the King-Emperor or Lord Hardinge that in order to show the truest loyalty to our King-Emperor, it is necessary for us to ransack our jewelry boxes and to appear bedecked from head to toe. I would undertake, at peril of my life, to bring to you a message from King George himself that he expects nothing of the kind." He was of course invoking their sense of the plainness and manliness of style of the English themselves—

they would never appear bedecked, or have jewel boxes to ransack. And in 1927 in *Young India* he attacked the treasures of the temples and the princes' palaces: "If you gave me a contract for furnishing all the rich palaces, I should give you the same thing for one-tenth of the money, and give you more comfort and fresh air, and secure a certificate from the best artists in India that I had furnished your houses in the most artistic manner possible."

We recognize in passages like this a hero of taste, not merely of politics. That is both what shows as his wholeness, and what is shown by that authenticity of style I spoke of before. So let me give a couple of more anecdotal examples.

You may have heard of his remark after meeting George V in 1931. The reporters had of course been much excited by his loincloth and shawl, and when he left Buckingham Palace they crowded round to ask him if he had not felt underdressed among all the elegance and the uniforms. "No," he replied, "his Majesty was wearing enough for both of us." If you have seen pictures of George V—who was, incidentally, a stickler for correct dress—you will know that that was the perfect comment.

Even Winston Churchill's style, though forceful enough in its way, suffers by contrast with Gandhi's. You may remember Churchill's indignant description of Gandhi as "formerly a Middle Temple lawyer, now posing as a fakir of a type well-known in the East, striding half-naked up the steps of the Viceroy's palace to confer with the representatives of the King-Emperor," a spectacle Churchill found "nauseating and humilitating." That whole passage, of course, owes a great deal to Kipling, in concept and phrasing.

Well, in 1944 Gandhi wrote to Churchill thus:

Dear Prime Minister, You are reported to have the desire to crush the "naked fakir," as you are said to have described me. I have been long trying to be a fakir and that naked—a more difficult task. I, therefore, regard the expression as a compliment, though unintended. I approach you, then, as such, and ask you to trust and use me for the sake of your people and mine, and through them those of the world.

Your sincere friend, M. K. Gandhi

He got no reply, but do we not hear in that contrast just what we see in the pictures of the two men—that Churchill's prose is overstuffed and attitudinizing, adorned with borrowed jewels and hired medals, while Gandhi's is deft, simple, natural, authentic? Gandhi had increased enormously the dimensions of the political arena, let imaginative sunlight onto the stage from so many angles that Churchill's theatrics seem preposterous.

Finally, I want to offer you an example of another area of sensibility in which Gandhi and Tolstoy seem strikingly authentic and modern—and like the literary sensibility of this century, though also strikingly unlike. This is the area of excrement—what Gandhi calls nightsoil, what modern literature calls shit. Finding an intermediary word is difficult, for excellent reasons, so I shall stick by the most neutral option, excrement.

Everyone has noticed that twentieth-century literature is a literature of shit. That is one of the most illuminating and comprehensive ways of describing it. Joyce is one of its inaugurators within English; for instance, Stephen's vision of hell in *Portrait*, and the first Bloom scene in *Ulysses*, not to mention Nighttown. D. H. Lawrence was too much of the nineteenth century to mention shit, or too little of that twentieth-century second mode of cultural resistance that has become dominant in the literature of our times. He is in this way an old-fashioned author. When, in *Lady Chatterly*, he uses the four-letter words for sexual functions, it is in order, he tells us, to redeem them for tender uses. It is worth noticing that Leavis, among others, objects to that novel, and just because, I think, that four-letter vocabulary belongs to the same lexical subset as shit. Those words, he feels, *cannot* be reclaimed for tenderness. They are after all expletives rather than nouns or verbs.

And since World War II, and above all in America, this is the literary mode that has become dominant. Norman Mailer discovered in the wartime army that shit is the soldier's word for soul, which is of course a paradox, since it is really a word for the opposite, a word to deny soul; in *Cannibals and Christians* he develops an elaborate philosophy of shit. There is plenty of it in Bellow and in Pynchon —one long sequence in *Gravity's Rainbow* narrates a character's adventures after being flushed down a lavatory. And in the world of speculation we have Norman O. Brown's brilliant chapter on filthy lucre in *Life Against Death*.

Another vivid case is Moravia's *The Red Book and the Great Wall* (which discusses the consumer society in those terms on pages thirteen to seventeen of the English translation). "Producer and consumer then represent one the forward extremity and the other the posterior of the same earth-worm.... The end of modern civilization is consumption, that is, excrement. One consumes all one can, and in the greatest variety: the consumer's ideal is consumption and he strives to live up to this ideal. But the final result is excrement. Consumer civilization is excremental." And Lévi-Strauss uses the same imagery.

I think it is clear enough what modern literature is up to here. Its rhetoric of shit is another of its many devices for protesting against the complacency of modern civilization, for disturbing its composure. It sometimes claims not to be cursing but merely speaking in the name of healthy realism, against a false modern refinement; but surely this does not ring true, either of its own motives or of human consciousness generally. In fact, the most primitive villagers in India are as emotional in their revulsion from excrement as we are. Norman O. Brown is surely in the right about this, as against

D. H. Lawrence. You may remember that Lawrence complains about Swift's poem with the climax, "But—Celia, Celia, Celia shits." Lawrence's comments are in the name of healthy normality—what else would Swift have the poor girl do? Swift is merely sick. But Brown says that Swift is pointing to something that is disturbing to the healthiest of us—the incompatibility of romantic love with the animal functions. At any rate, it is surely Brown's sense of the matter that is reflected in modern literature, where the shit is a missile most often.

To turn now to Gandhi and Tolstoy, both laid a primary stress on the fact of nightsoil, above all on the duty of each man and woman to dispose of his own, and not to employ servants for the purpose. Thus Tolstoy, in his "A Letter to Romain Rolland":

> The first sign of the sincerity of the men of our class, who profess Christian, philosophical, or humanitarian principles, is a striving to free themselves as much as possible from this [social] injustice.
>
> The simplest and handiest means for attaining this is manual labor, which begins by attending to one's own needs.
>
> I will never believe in the sincerity of the philosophical and moral principles of a man who makes his chambermaid carry out his vessel.

By "vessel" he means, of course, chamberpot.

And in Gandhi's case there were two extra dimensions to the subject: one, the need for the nightsoil to be used to fertilize infertile Indian earth; and two, the need to rescue the whole Indian subcaste of sweepers, who were employed exclusively in labor of that kind. There is a great deal of expertise about nightsoil in the Gandhi literature. And a great many exhortations: "A small spade is the means of salvation from a great nuisance. Leaving nightsoil, cleaning the nose, or spitting on the road is a sin against God as well as humanity." Mira Behn, his English disciple, who was in some sense in love with him, he forced to become an expert in the subject—and not by means of theory (when she lived in the village of Sindi, she had to clean the roads each morning of the villagers' droppings). Gandhi always looked after his own lavatory, and often claimed that it was as fresh and dainty as a drawing room. You are shown it today as one of his memorabilia.

The differences between this and modern literature are obvious enough. Though for Gandhi and Tolstoy nightsoil is clearly and proudly symbolic, it is not part of a rhetoric of disgust but of realism. Above all, it is not merely symbolic but also factual, an economic, agricultural, political fact, which it isn't really for modern writers. But the likeness is important, too. Both groups draw our attention to excrement because they are rebelling against the false, inflated, fantastic idealism of upper-class civilized culture—the culture, to take a literary case, of Tagore. (And in fact, when Gandhi visited Tagore's ashram and college in 1915, he got the students to dismiss the servants and start cleaning out the lavatories themselves. Tagore did not protest when he returned, but the experiment was very short lived.) Gandhi was rebelling against the privilege of Indian poets and teachers, lawyers and politicians—he started cleaning out the lavatories at the first Congress meeting he attended.

So in this area, too, teachers of modern literature should feel themselves very close to Gandhi and at ease with him in one way. He is of our times and our temper. But much more, as I need hardly emphasize again, they should feel themselves very distant from and uneasy with him. The Mahatmas reestablish the relevance of politics and aesthetics to each other, and to so much else, but at the cost of literature's independence and integrity.

VII

Tolstoy as Mahatma

O F THE TWO MAHATMAS, Gandhi is the more challenging politically, and more vivid because he is closer in time. But to men of letters like my audience, Tolstoy must be the more familiar and the more challenging intellectually, because we knew him, many of us, very intimately; we had known and loved that mind as well as any in the world; he is one of the patrons of that liberal humanism to which we had aspired in our best selves. To see him change so willfully, condemn all that he had been (and we would be) so totally, abolish that mind and self we loved, is an extremely upsetting experience. We see one of us become a Mahatma, and we see a great humanist and a great poet repudiate poetry and humanity. While I was actually giving the talks, I felt that this material was too painful to force on my audience, too clearly an attack on our own choices, but now that I am writing in book form, I can tell this part of the story, too.

After his conversion Tolstoy was led, step by step, to renounce and to denounce things that had been very dear to him before. Among these things were the imperial expansion of Russia, and even ordinary patriotism; art, including his own work as a novelist, and including music, of which he was passionately fond; and love, domestic as well as romantic, of which he had been the greatest celebrant. His writings were now filled with this renunciation and denunciation.

His essay, "Of Patriotism," of 1895, is a brilliantly satirical account of the visits exchanged between the French and Russian fleets in 1894, and other similar effusions and manipulations of "patriotic" feeling. In 1898 he condemned the American part in the Spanish-American War as imperialist, and contrasted such adventures with the sufferings of the Doukhobors, a Christian sect that was just then refusing military service to the Russian government. And in 1901, when he was asked to send a message to the American people, he wrote the following (published in the *North American Review* in April 1901):

> When I read your letter it seemed to me impossible that I could send any message to the American people. But thinking over at night, it came to me that, if I had to address the American people, I should like to thank them for their writers who flourished about the '50s. I would mention Garrison, Parker, Emerson, Ballou, and Thoreau, not as the greatest, but as those who, I think, specially influenced me. Other names are Channing, Whittier, Lowell, Walt Whitman—a bright constellation, such as is rarely to be found in the literature of the world.
>
> And I should like to ask the American people why they do not pay more attention to those voices (hardly to be replaced by those of financial and industrial millionaires, or successful generals and admirals), and continue the good work in which they made such hopeful progress.

He called for the renunciation of war, and of those adventures and ambitions that inevitably lead to war. He called for the dismantling of governments and armies and prisons, and half the apparatus of civilized life. And the things we normally cite as the justifying fruits of our civilization—the arts and the sciences—he had dismissed in advance. What would follow from such dismantling—and how to reconcile his demands with the major drives of our nature—Tolstoy did not explain. The claims of the ideal, he thought, never could be reconciled with, or harmonized with, the desires of unredeemed nature. He symbolized the conflict in the image of a river. The gospel of Jesus, that of the Buddha, and that of all the other great prophets of spirituality, is that we should swim for dear life to the opposite bank. But the river is in us as well as outside us, and the currents of our appetites and ambitions urge us faster and faster forward. We must exert our wills and minds desperately to force our way across, by unceasing, exhausting, unrewarded effort.

Turning from the theme of militarism to that of art, we find in his *Journals* for 1896 "The principal thing which I wanted to say about art is that it does not exist in the sense of some great manifestation of the human spirit." He is referring, of course, to Romantic and post-Romantic art, and even more to post-Romantic feelings about art. That is, the novels that the people around him appreciated (including the novels he himself had written), and even more the way they appreciated them, were both spiritually overweening in their claims, and radically false in themselves. True art, such as peasants appreciate, is quite a different thing, and also a humbler thing. He believed that culture, in the sense of the arts, sciences, and thought, had become for most men the ultimate value in life, and he was deeply convinced that that evaluation was wrong. In 1900, in *The Slavery of Our Times*, he wrote: "Nowadays men say 'Fiat cultura, pereat justitia,' instead of 'Fiat justitia, pereat mundus.'" And in *What Then Must We Do?*: "What good are these products of the arts and sciences? . . . Now we have pure science and art for art's sake, because culture has liberated itself from duty. . . . Artists and scientists aim at personal advantage as much as restaurateurs, jockeys,

modistes, and whores; all of them add a pleasure to life."
Tolstoy's writings on this subject, like *What Is Art?* and his
essay on Shakespeare, have aroused far more wrath than his
attack on war and patriotism. Thus I find a liberal critic
writing in 1971 of Tolstoy's "malevolent, deliberately stupid,
and bullying affectation of deafness."

But even his theory of art has not provoked as much anger
as his theory, and still more his practice, of love. This is not
so much a matter of his writings as of his life. We cannot
forgive him his part in ruining that family life he had celebrated for us in the great novels—the life of the Rostovs in
War and Peace, of the Levins in *Anna Karenina*. In 1882
in a quarrel with his wife he said that his fondest desire was
to run away from his family; for the twenty-eight years that
remained to him, that was what he yearned for. Sonya
Tolstoy wrote in her diary after that quarrel, "As long as I
live I shall remember the sincerity of that cry which broke
my heart. I yearn for death with all my strength, for I
cannot live without his love. . . . My love weighs me down,
but it only irritates him. He is filled with his Christian
ideals of self-perfection. I am jealous of him." As so often,
she displays a startling flash of insight in that last sentence.
But her story is a tragedy of the limitations of self-knowledge, and in the years that followed she acted not out of her
knowledge of her jealousy, but out of that jealousy itself,
resisting Tolstoy at every turn. And she carried most of the
children with her. Soon he wrote about his family, "What
seems to count for them is not the meaning of my words but
the fact that I have the deplorable habit of repeating them."
And their memoirs confirm this. Ilya Tolstoy writes, "We
all found him tiresome and uninteresting. . . . What hope
was there of reconciling 'life according to God' . . . with the
invariable duty of taking soup and cutlets at dinner, of
talking French and English, or preparing for the Gymnase
and the University, of learning one's part for theatricals?"

And he symbolizes the conflict as being between "life according to God" and "Anke Pie."

Anke Pie was a particularly good cake that Sonya and her sister Tanya baked for feast days in their families. It had been a feature of their own childhood (in the Behr's family life, depicted as the Rostovs' in *War and Peace*) and they brought the recipe, and the tradition, and many other such, with them when they married and had their own children. In the summers, Tanya (the Natasha of *War and Peace*) brought her family to Yasnaya Polyana, and she and Sonya (the Kitty of *Anna Karenina*) organized family life as a series of feasts with ceremonies that Tolstoy labeled as all versions of "Anke Pie." It was that which he now asked them to give up; that intensification and theatricalization of family life, that institutionalization of its self-worship, which he had celebrated in the novels; and that was what Sonya hated him for, since she was a priestess of that cult. And it is that that we have hated him for.

One of the major documents of his conversion is *What Then Must We Do?* of 1866. (It takes its title from the gospel according to St. Matthew.) In it Tolstoy describes his move to Moscow in 1881, and his horror at the poverty he saw there and at its contrast with his own home. The move was deeply depressing to him domestically also, because it was a sign that his children from now on needed (in their mother's estimation) to live in the city. Tolstoy had always been unhappy there, and had built his family life in the country most deliberately. It was there that his older children had passed their childhood, in a much simpler style and setting, but from now on the family would spend only summer holidays at Yasnaya Polyana. But *What Then Must We Do?* dealt with his domestic situation only glancingly.

Tolstoy tells us that he took part in the Moscow city census in 1881 and visited the homes of the poorest and most depraved. Horrified by what he saw, he devised a philanthropic scheme to accompany the census, and solicited his rich friends for contributions. But he found it impossible, in various ways, to help the poor by such means —he found that philanthropy corrupted giver and receiver: "Yes, before doing good I must myself stand outside evil. . . . But my whole life is nothing but evil." He describes his despair at finding his eighteen-year-old son in bed at 11 A.M., while a peasant built him a fire in the stove in his room. How could you teach a boy of his class and up-bringing the value of suffering? And yet "Only in suffering is the spiritual world born."

What he said, what he thought, what he wrote, of course made others besides his family and friends uneasy or angry. He felt the hostility of the whole world. In 1887, in his "Letter to N. N.," he wrote, "Help me! My heart bursts from despair, because we have all gone astray; and when I struggle with all my might and main, you, at every deviation of mine, instead of pitying yourself or me, push me into the swamp and shout in delight: 'See, he is in the swamp with us.' " People thought him pretentious and posing, as well as destructive and sadistic.

And one thing that made the situation so difficult for all concerned then is just what makes it so fascinating for us now, that Tolstoy had been of all writers the greatest cele-brant of the pleasures he was now condemning. He had even written fiction in celebration of imperialist adventure, as I have said. And his two major works, though they clearly belong to the first, liberal humanist, mode of cultural re-sistance, are not really radical in their criticism of Russian civilization. The good life *is* there to be lived by Kitty and Levin, though not by Anna and Vronsky; by Pierre and Natasha, though not by Napoleon. There is even a military hero in *War and Peace*—Kutuzov and the "natural" forces he embodies—"the unconscious, swarm-life of mankind" that uses kings as an instrument for its own ends, while in

Anna Karenina we are told that it is the Russian people's destiny to occupy new virgin lands continually. Above all, of course, we are shown the love between Kitty and Levin, and Dolly and her children, and bade worship it.

The late art is very unlike that. Perhaps the most famous story is "The Death of Ivan Ilyich" of 1886, which describes the death of a man made to seem ordinary, average, representative of our culture. His death is physically slow and agonizing, but Tolstoy lays even more stress on its moral and spiritual character, as the man finds the relationships he has built up and lived on all fail him, all reveal themselves to have been false. The only person who can help him in his last extremities is the servant, Gerasim, just because he is not part of Ivan Ilyich's life—because of his simplicity. (The simplicity Tolstoy recommends is not exactly a moral virtue, but an ontological primitiveness possible only in a personality that has not been "developed" according to the ideals of modern culture.)

Then "Master and Man," of 1895, describes how V. A. Brekhanov goes to buy a forest, taking with him Nikita, a reformed drunkard whom he exploits as a servant. Brekhanov's "business" zeal drives them both to their doom in a snowstorm. When their sled gets stuck, Brekhanov rides away on the horse, leaving Nikita to die. But he gets lost again, and the horse leads him back to the sled. Half-repentant, he lies on top of Nikita, who is dying, and dies himself, feeling happy. Nikita recovers, but died, the narrator says, "this year." "Whether he is better off, or worse off, there, in the place where he awoke after that real death, whether he was disappointed or found things there just as he expected, is what we shall all of us soon learn."

The Kreutzer Sonata of 1888 has epigraphs from St. Matthew, and tells of the disastrous marriage of Pozdnishev, and his murder of his wife. Having been immoral himself, he had sought out, at thirty, a girl pure and idealistic enough to deserve to be his wife. He found such a girl (as Tolstoy had) and they fell in love, though he sees now, after the murder, both the falsity of that romantic love in both of them, and the erotic and seductive training she had received, which was inseparable from her idealism: "You see our too abundant and exciting food, coupled with a perfectly idle existence, is nothing else than a systematic incitement to lust." The peasant escapes both lust and the illusion of love conjured up to cover it (idealism); he escapes them because he works and lives poorly. The sexual prerogatives of men have enslaved women, and they in turn have enslaved men. His wife's sexuality—much intensified when she ceased to bear children—in fact drives Pozdnishev to murder.

He had found soon after marriage that they had nothing to say to each other; when they quarreled he began to see a harsh cold hostility in her face, which was only displaced by the excitement of lust and the illusion that ornamented that. Finally she began to flirt with a violinist called Tukhachevsky, excited by his music and by all the things she associated with it—all parts of the illusion, the idealism, that covers sexual excitement. Music, Tolstoy says, does not elevate but excite; it falsifies one's mood, and should be played only in grave circumstances. Pozdnishev became jealous, and his jealousy became a passion, and disaster followed.

In a "Sequel" to the story Tolstoy explained (at the request of a disciple) what his story "meant": (1) that it is wrong to think sexual intercourse good, especially when precautions are taken against conception; (2) that infidelity, and romantic love, should be recognized as simply evil. And so on, through five such points. Married people should aim at a love like that of brother for sister. The human race does not need to be perpetuated.

One would have thought that meaning clear enough

without the sequel, but even with it, the introduction to the edition I read says that the story is much misunderstood; that foolish readers take the ravings of Pozdnishev, a self-confessed lunatic, for Tolstoy's own views; that really the whole thing is a study in Pozdnishev's morbidity.

What we see here is the blindness of the liberal humanist brought up against this particular phenomenon, an involuntary blink that ruins that steadiness of vision on which he of all men depends. Gandhi, of course, read the story literally, loved it, and recommended it widely. Sonya Tolstoy wrote a riposte, "Who Is to Blame?," as did their son, Leo Tolstoy, who blamed his father in his "Prelude of Chopin." But the story, or its diagnosis and prognosis, was corroborated by subsequent history, for in 1896 Sonya fell in love with a pianist, Taneyev.

Finally, his one novel of those late years, *Resurrection* (1899), which tells how Prince Nekhludov at eighteen seduced Katusha Maslova, and meets her much later as the prostitute she has become in consequence of that seduction. He had been an idealist, and innocently in love with her, until his training as a Guards officer taught him a different morality. The story begins when he serves as a juryman in a trial in which she is accused of having poisoned a client. Tolstoy gives a very realistic account of the law, and prisons, and guards, and all the apparatus of legal justice, seen as a caricature of true justice. Nekhludov is gradually drawn more and more into repentance for what he has done, and disgust at the life he presently leads, pampered by all the privileges of an unjust society. Having failed to secure Maslova's acquittal, he follows her to Siberia, and on the convict train meets many varieties of revolutionary, so described as to distinguish Tolstoyan from Marxist kinds of radicalism. He and Maslova do not become lovers again. The promise of the ending points toward a purely Christian union between them in charity.

Tolstoy's late art then presents a strenuous challenge to all of us, and there are many examples of how upset connoisseurs of literature have been by it. Let us take, for instance, Logan Speirs, in *Tolstoy and Chekhov* of 1971. He tells us that Tolstoy's late tales "are written out of the false wisdom of old age under the guise of lofty condescension." In *Resurrection*, he tells us, Tolstoy's bitterness at the imperfectibility of man overflows, so that there is not a single attractive personality in the book. And apropos of "Ivan Ilych," "It is too late in the day to try to convince people that they may sprout wings on their death-beds, and this is what Tolstoy suddenly does . . . his customary power has turned into something like bullying." He contrasts that story with Chekhov's "A Dreary Story," very much to Chekhov's advantage, though he ends, "The major contrast between the two stories is that Tolstoy's really is a work of despair. It has the smell of death in it." But this, we are to understand, is a fault in the story. Chekhov is always the hero of Speirs' comparisons—of his philosophy of literature: "Chekhov's realism involves the perception that one can make no judgments about life which are not liable to be cancelled out by fresh evidence. . . . He sees that nothing stands for long, and that the theories and presuppositions one brings to experience are never adequate to it." But these are metaphysical or religious *dogma*—the dogma of the liberal humanist.

This anger, as is obvious, directs itself against Tolstoy as a whole, as a man, not just against his late stories. And something similar is to be found in other books about Tolstoy. Another vivid example is Edward Crankshaw's 1974 book called *Tolstoy*. Crankshaw's tone about his subject is extraordinarily aggressive, considering the kind of book he is writing. He says that Tolstoy could never truly love those nearest to him, even when young, and he developed into an insufferable and sometimes revolting young man, full of "violence and devilish pride." His fanatically literal mind had not a breath of poetry in it, and he quarreled with Turgenev because he knew that Turgenev was his moral superior. He was such a materialist, behaviorist, determinist, that he "could not believe in the reality of other people." The clumsiness and congestion of his prose expresses his determination to allow words no life or poetry of their own but to direct the reader every inch of the way, and make him see only and exactly what Tolstoy saw. He was, Crankshaw agrees with Orwell, of bad character. As a human being, Tolstoy was a failure.

Why then should we concern ourselves with him? Because of his art, because of the novels he wrote before he tried to become a prophet: "His greatness lay elsewhere. Everyone knows about that. It blazes across a century of human suffering; a signal of hope, a fixed point of orientation, a monument to a man who refused to take any stock in what seems hope to most of us, a celebration of life by a man who turned his back on it."*

What is striking here is not only the anger, the ungenerosity of judgment, but the discomposure of the judicial stance. This is after all an extraordinary tone for a critic to take to a great author, an extraordinary tone for any man to take about any other, let alone about a great man whose work he admires. The liberal humanist, the man of culture, shows himself challenged in his own identity by Tolstoy—he shudders at the sudden breath of a phenomenon beyond the management of intelligence, beyond the scope of taste.

---

* From Edward Crankshaw, *Tolstoy: The Making of a Novelist* (New York: Viking Press, 1974).

VIII

Our Options as Men

of Letters

At THIS POINT I think it would be useful to draw the contrast between my situation as a man of letters in America, and the situation of the friend I was visiting in Mysore, Anantha Murthy. I had know him ten years before, in Birmingham, England, and then our two situations had seemed much the same. At least, I hadn't then thought to compare them in terms of sameness, but when I met him again I was forced to think in terms of difference. And analyzing those differences leads us back, by a different route, to Gandhi's challenge to us, as American men of letters.

First, however, a few words about the situation of the Indian man of letters, and the difference Gandhi brought to him. There will be two parts to these preliminaries, one relating more to the problems of India's writers, the other to her readers and critics.

A writer and college teacher of literature in India operates within a situation in some ways strikingly like that in England. Because England so long ruled India, imposed English as the national language, and English literature as India's literature, generations have grown up reciting Milton and Burke and T. S. Eliot, and thinking of certain events in English history as key steps in the world's development of democracy. They have even become involved in the politics of English literature, so that a word like "Bloomsbury" is a call to action stations for some Indian intellectuals just as for some Englishmen. But while the key poems, the critical slogans, the charts of debate are the same for them, the life experience is of course very different, and so the relation between the map and the land is different, too. To put it crudely, that relation must always be more difficult for an Indian, who must, I think, always feel some guilt at teaching English literature, some resentment at needing to acquire laboriously what Englishmen know without effort, some shame at being forever making mistakes—in matters so superficial and yet unignorable as pronunciation—that even the stupidest Englishman never commits.

Gandhi was concerned about the Indian inferiority complex—that was indeed as much as anything the center of his concerns—and he led a movement to replace English with Hindi as the national language. It is a significant problem for contemporary India that that movement did not succeed, and that English is still the central medium of communication. Writers in one of the native languages—though they may have an audience of 25 million—cannot be read by writers in the neighboring language, and must communicate with them via English. One of the friendly commissions I was given by the people I met was to find support in the United States for a program of translation, to translate the significant new fiction and verse of Kannada, Malayalam, Bengali, and so on, into English, so that these writers could read each other. Socially they know each other quite well, some of them, conversing in English, but they have never read each other's imaginative work.

Besides trying to abolish the dependence of Indian writers on English language and literature, Gandhi tried to remove the teaching of literature from English-style institutions. As a part of his noncooperation program of 1920, he called on Indians not to use government titles and medals, not to practice in or appeal to government courts of law, and not to go, or send their children, to government schools and colleges. Besides being a political tactic, this was in line with his general attack on Western forms of life, written out in *Hind Swaraj*. It was a historical strategy for India. A great many students and quite a few teachers left the government colleges, and new Indian institutions were formed, called *vidyapiths*, where *Indian* culture was taught —Indian languages and literatures, taught in an Indian style. Gandhi himself, without mounting any campaign against English intellectual things, filled his discourses with references to the Gita, the Ramayana, and the Mahabharata. These things taken together can be called Gandhi's policy toward the teaching of literature.

It has left the writers and critics of India with a severe problem, and a division of loyalties. On the one hand, they want to follow Gandhi into the native languages and literatures, and preserve that cultural integrity that is obviously necessary to their personal integrity as men of letters. But that way leads to past achievements, things already known, belonging to earlier phases of civilization, and scarcely renewable as twentieth-century enterprises. On the other hand, they hear of and read brilliant new experimental work done by Western writers (nearly always written in denunciation of Western civilization), modernist art that is infinitely more exciting but only achieved by means in defiance of Gandhi. To take a concrete example, I met some of the young writers in Kannada, the language of Mysore, among them Sriskrisna Alanahalli, a young novelist whose work is, I was told, both serious and popular, and shocking or daring in both subject and technique. He was eager to talk to me of John Updike, and it occurred to me that he himself was the John Updike of Kannada. At the same time, I also gathered from my friends that there was in some way a comical phrase. He is not, no one is, the John Updike of Kannada. Kannada does not *have* John Updikes. Which means, I'm afraid, that Kannada is not a literary culture to set beside English in equality. "Why should it be?," we quickly ask. But we would not say that so blithely if we were writers in Kannada, because they, you see, read the same books we do. For them, to work in a small culture is not only to work for a small audience, but within a small workshop—to make small works of art. They have an audience that attends closely to everything they do, and they have all the advantages and disadvantages of that situation. I shall say more of that later.

It is the disadvantages of that situation that the Indian-writers-in-English are avoiding. They have at least the hope of a worldwide audience and so can write in a worldwide way; one of them who has realized that hope, R. K. Narayan, also lives in Mysore. The writers in Kannada there seemed to have both respect and affection for Narayan, but also to regard his work as a symbol of the literary and moral weaknesses they set themselves against. And then beyond Narayan, in the direction of rootless internationalism, stand such figures as Ved Mehta and V. S. Naipaul, both of whom have been writing about India recently. The tone of both men's writing about Gandhi was extraordinarily flat and unresonant, and one could only guess at the complex of contradictory feelings that were strangling the voice. Of course,

Narayan's fictional treatment of the Mahatma is also very flat. The cramps of the Indian-writer-in-English are never more crippling than when he tackles that subject.

But I also want to describe, before I begin my main comparison, the position of the head of the English department at Mysore, because his career, too, illustrates the options and dilemmas of Indian readers and critics facing Gandhi. His name is C. D. Narasimhaiah, he was born in Mysore in 1919, and studied at the University of Cambridge, where he became a disciple of F. R. Leavis, like so many students from the Commonwealth. This means that he inherited an embattled position on many issues of English cultural politics, and when he came back to India in 1942 he founded a literary critical magazine like Leavis' *Scrutiny* (his was called *The Literary Criterion*) and conducted campaigns of literary and cultural warfare like Leavis'. He has been, in the eyes of many, a hero of the literary consciousness in India, relating literary to social issues, but finding the essentially literary cruces that express the social problem. But these campaigns were on English-literature topics at first. In recent years he has begun to turn his attention to Indian writers, and to preach independence of English masters, including Leavis. He has written a book about the novelist Raja Rao; he praises the poet and mystic Aurobindo very highly; and he has two books on Gandhi.

The first of these, *The Writer's Gandhi*, was published in 1967, and is a series of lectures given at Punjabi University. Narasimhaiah was, he tells us, never a Gandhian, even before Gandhi's disciples had made that term ridiculous. This was because he had always found Gandhi so distant and different from the rest of the world, setting such impossible standards. Narasimhaiah had never thought of emulating Gandhi's example; he had not even, till recently, studied his work. He had come to Gandhi through his enthusiasm for Nehru. Admiring Nehru as he did, he had come to admit that he must admire Gandhi, too, as Nehru's master.

I must not talk about Nehru here, for it would take me too far off my track, but I must say that for me this is an extraordinary choice, because Nehru is so infinitely less interesting a figure, so infinitely more limited, so all-too-comprehensible. I'm quite prepared to admire him as a head of state or head of party, but to admit him to any more personal relation, as personal hero, is incomprehensible to me.

Nevertheless, the second chapter in Narasimhaiah's book on Gandhi is really all about Nehru, examining his funeral oration on his master, and exalting it above all the other orations then delivered. Nehru was of course an amateur of letters, which offers Narasimhaiah a flattering role as a professional and tutor. He praises Nehru's oration on grounds of style, grounds that are in turn based on criteria of contemporaneity. As Narasimhaiah says, Gandhi himself broke the chains of those cumbrous Victorian periods that had enslaved Indian writers, and Nehru's prose is modern, and the better for it, as compared with Sarojini Naidu's. It is Mrs. Naidu's oration, and her poem on Gandhi, on which Narasimhaiah is hardest. Mrs. Naidu was a Gandhian politician but a Swinburnian or pre-Raphaelite stylist, and Narasimhaiah is performing the same scavenging work on Indian literature as Leavis and Eliot did for England in the 1920s. But though Gandhi's prose is modern, it is far from modernist, and most of the writers in the Gandhian movement—and elsewhere in India—were more old-fashioned than he; so the effect of this scavenging work is embarrassingly close to a sweeping away of the whole movement's literary work into the critical dustbin. The only Gandhian writer fit to be taken seriously is Nehru, who apprenticed himself to modern English masters, and so implicitly submitted himself to Narasimhaiah's criteria of judgment.

In other ways, too, Narasimhaiah maintains a stance that gives him, as literary critic, an overwhelming superiority to politicians. Thus, describing Gandhism, he invokes T. S. Eliot's *Idea of a Christian Society*, citing Eliot's recommendation that we should reascend to our origins in order to return, with greater spiritual knowledge, to our own situation. Narasimhaiah says, "These words could as well have been written by Gandhi, who does to Hinduism, India, and the world what a poet like Eliot has tried to do to Christianity, to Western civilization, and to Poetry, and therefore to the whole of mankind." He gives Gandhi dignity by translating him into the terms of poetry and criticism. And he says, "No man, no patriot in politics, did a fraction of what Yeats did to win respect for his country and its culture," and yet in "Easter 1916" Yeats did not hesitate to criticize Ireland. That statement may be acceptable in itself, but it belongs to a logic whose next step, though it is usually left implicit, would be "Thus the poet's achievement is more real than the politician's." We see the man of letters dealing with politics from a position of all too much strength.

Narasimhaiah's second book on Gandhi is a collection of essays he edited, entitled *Gandhi and the West*, published in 1969, whose strategy is quite different. Here he in some sense defends Gandhi from literary scrutiny. He objects to people assimilating him to Western intellectuals. He objects, for instance, to Payarelal saying that the vegetarianism and the handicrafts movements that Gandhi met in England influenced him. Narasimhaiah will allow only that the Englishmen's approximation and sophisticated articulation of these Indian practices "may have pleasantly surprised Gandhi"—but they and he were essentially Indian. He cites G. B. Shaw's way of condemning cow slaughter—"a typically [clever] Shavian remark"—as proof that these intellectuals could not have brought much conviction to their thinking. He contrasts Shaw's remark (something about cow slaughter being like sending one's mother to the poorhouse when she stops giving suck) with Gandhi's remark that the cow is a poem of pity. The two phrases seem to Narasimhaiah to represent styles as remote from each other as Heaven and Hell. What makes that difference so large a fact to him is a large shift of intellectual taste.

Shaw, like Wells and Chesterton and a whole world of pre-1914 intellectuals, is inaccessible to Narasimhaiah (as to Leavisites in general, and to Leavis himself). He cannot credit Shaw and his friends with any seriousness, though in fact they were much closer in their thinking to Gandhi than the intellectuals who came to power in England after 1918; see, for instance, how many Gandhian themes, like nonviolent action, Shaw treats in his plays. Shaw, Wells, Chesterton were great simplifiers and humanists, like Gandhi himself; since 1918 literature has been in the grip of complicators and separators, more serious but with a seriousness quite unlike most of the Mahatmas.

Thus Narasimhaiah makes Gandhi out a unique phenomenon, inexplicable in intellectual terms, and those who are said to be like him are really quite different. Even Tolstoy is essentially only a *writer*. This puts Narasimhaiah in the position of knowing more about Gandhi than any Westerner, more about literature than any Gandhian, and being the sole maintainer of standards of discrimination. This is another, all-too-predictable way to bring literary training to bear on the Gandhian challenge.

Narasimhaiah is nevertheless a strong personality, much respected even by his enemies. And there is something to respect. He is a bold and incisive spokesman, though for ideas I think to be hopelessly wrong. Moreover, I have a strong enough sense of the difficulties of his position; a clear enough understanding that my own position is not that different; and a doubtful enough grasp of the policies I am evolving to deal with it, to respect a bold spokesman for another party.

But now to Anantha Murthy. As I said, I came to know him in Birmingham, England, in 1965, and one thing that brought us together was what we both owed to F. R. Leavis, the literary and cultural critic. From Leavis we both took a complex of ideas that defined and structured the lives of men like us, men of letters; men concerned, professionally but more than professionally, with language, literature, and culture; writers, readers, critics of society and members of society. Another link was the admiration we both felt for Gandhi.

Since meeting Anantha again, ten years later, I have been struck by how much our lives have diverged. Anantha's experience seems to me even better structured by Leavis' ideas than it was before. He can understand what he does and what happens to him in terms of those ideas with great satisfaction, whereas to my life those ideas now seem irrelevant, outdated, unusable. That divergence is what I want to analyze here.

Perhaps I should first say a word or two about which ideas of Leavis' I mean. I'll take four main propositions. First, that within any literature there is a great tradition of significant works to be rigorously distinguished from the rest. The rest will include works of great ingenuity and talent and seriousness of purpose, and the task of discriminating the significant and maintaining critical standards is a full-time activity. (This idea clearly relates to the reader-and-critic function of the man of letters I mentioned before.)

Second, the significant works of a literature will all embody—though in no obvious or simpleminded way—the values created by men as they live in "organic communities." In such communities (and Leavis has in mind the best of rural life in preindustrial England) everyone made something and contributed that object and its cultural meaning to the common life—the idea at the root of Gandhian Nai Talim. These values can be detected, by the critical eye, in the literature of even postindustrial England, and to detect them is a crucial clue to the significant works. (This idea relates to the man of letters as member of society.)

Third, Leavis leads a battle against the modishness of taste that is likely to develop in the metropolitan centers of a culture. Literature is always likely to be appropriated as the property of a ruling class, as another mode of their luxury and their privilege. His main example of that in his own England was Bloomsbury, which he accused of frivolity, sophistication, and even perversity of taste. (This idea relates to the man of letters as critic of society.)

And finally he takes a mystical view of language (and literature) as a depository of "the people's" creative tradition. In a recent book, *The Living Principle*, he describes language as an "immemorial human creative collaborativity"; he reproaches both Wittgenstein and T. S. Eliot for their inadequate sense of that. Eliot could be a poet only by grace of the English language, created not by him but by the English people, and he would have been a better poet if he had worked with language in that spirit. (This idea relates to the man of letters as writer.)

You will see, by the way, a distinct political bias to these ideas, in the more general sense of "political." Leavis has always refused to acknowledge any connection between his criticism and any political party or ideology but it clearly belongs to a generally left-wing field.

Let me now turn to our two careers as men of letters. I will take Anantha first. As a writer he has written two novels, in Kannada, and about Mysore village life; novels that examine the weaknesses and the strengths of that life, against an implicit background of more modern modes of life. He is read by all other writers in Kannada, and gets letters or messages from all kinds of Kannada-speaking reader. He is a member of a cultural movement, even of a cultural family. He is bringing within the scope of the novel, and the sophisticated consciousness served by the novel form, material that has never been explored before—the life of his people, the life of their organic communities.

His publisher lives in a village, brings out only those books he wants to see in print, does not expect to make money by publishing. His first novel, *Samskara*, was made into a film, on the lowest of budgets; several of his friends participated in making the film, as actors, composers, or in other ways. The film is about a social issue of caste, and so encountered censorship trouble at first, but once accepted and successful, it opened the way for other such explorations of the unexplored. Thus in his situation even film, the popular art of our time, yields itself to serious cultural purposes.

Now for his life as reader and critic: He reads everything in Kannada that seems likely to be significant, as it comes out. He is the friend of most of the other writers, at least those belonging to his own, left-wing, movement. In his critical essays he leads them against those writers who write in English and who try to adapt the fashions of New York and London. As a representative of Kannada literature, he meets the representatives of Bengali, Hindi, Malayalam writing, and they make common cause against the cosmo-politan-metropolitan tendencies we might associate with Delhi—against the equivalents for him of Bloomsbury.

As teacher and citizen, within English literature he is able to teach the taste of Leavis himself—modified of course by his own dissents and innovations—and his students can work out the analogies between the English situation and the Mysore situation in which they and he live. And politically, his sympathies go to Jayaprakash Narayan, who represents in Indian politics and culture very much what Leavis—and Orwell—represent in English culture.

I'm sure you take my point—how completely Leavis' ideas support and interpret Anantha's life in India, justifying him and explaining his successes and failures, his pleasures and pains. (Gandhi's ideas, on the other hand, challenge and trouble him, but that trouble we can take for granted as being true of all men of letters.) In many ways those ideas suit Anantha's situation better than they did Leavis' own. As Leavis often said, the organic life of England's villages had disappeared, was only a memory, in his lifetime. His work has been to conjure up the ghost of that life, those values, preserved within literature. This may have something to do with Leavis' unkindness to the new writers of his own time—and with why he has not, like Anantha, written any novels himself. Mysore villages are still alive. It is not yet a forlorn hope to try to preserve what is valuable in them.

(Perhaps it might sharpen my point to say how different the position of the Indian writer is from that of the Indian painter. The latter is in a much less favorable situation, much more dependent on "metropolitan-cosmopolitan" taste. There is no barrier of language to shelter him from the imperious influence of Western fashions, and he must please the taste of very rich patrons. Literature like Anantha's has a middle-class audience, but painting is controlled by plutocrats whose standards are much influenced by the West.)

Now for my own situation. When I left Birmingham, it was not to go back home, in any sense, but to Boston—though I don't think that my situation would have been significantly better if I had stayed in England, even if I had taken a house in the village I grew up in.

When we met again, I, too, was writing a novel. But mine is science fiction, a futuristic fantasy, set in the Congo, a place I have never even visited. The book is based on an alternate version of our earth, which has had a radically different history from ours since the seventeenth century.

There are scenes after a nuclear holocaust; my hero is a cyborg, a partly mechanical man; and I employ a wild variety of characters and narrative voices.

My nonfiction books have concerned themselves with nineteenth-century Germans and twentieth-century Russians, psychiatry and sociology as much as literature, and the structuring ideas have been myths from speculative cultural anthropology. In other words, nothing that Leavis could approve. *My* publishers live in a skyscraper off Fifth Avenue. If a film were made from one of my books it would be in Hollywood, and I would have no control of it. My readers do not find that reading me makes them partners in a cultural enterprise.

As reader and critic I have to watch—to some degree enter—the hectic whirlpool of Western cultural ideas. I am a consumer, to use Susan Sontag's phrase, of our ceaseless flow of cultural goods; new ideas, new subject matters, present themselves all the time, ideas that have no social application, or only within the smallest of most privileged groups.

As teacher, my experience probably contrasts less sharply with Anantha's. But as a citizen, it is a lot harder for me to find any congenial political leader or cause. When I was presented with all the competing radicalisms of 1968–1972, I found none of them congenial, and I realized that the inner life of my cultural convictions was basically antisocial. I could not describe even theoretically the kind of political radicalism that I could subscribe to authentically. (In other words, this is another version of the contrast between two modes of cultural resistance that I discussed before. Anantha's and Leavis' is essentially a version of the first mode, though of course both are too much of the twentieth century not to have to deal with modernism and to some degree participate in it. But my mode is—unwittingly and unwillingly—modernist in its essential structure. The third,

Gandhian mode is not in direct sense a synthesis of the two, but it is of course an alternative, and does look to me now like a way to transcend the conflict.)

So much for our divergence, which makes for a pretty complete contrast. But so far I have described everything from a point of view implicitly Leavisite, and so Anantha appears as the saved soul, I as the damned. But I don't really believe it is so simple as that. That Leavisite point of view produces a cultural map that in fact needs to be revised.

In Leavis' scenario, the good men engage in a virtuous resistance to a cultural center corrupted by power. The marks of that corruption he sometimes calls "academic" or "club" values, and he often associates them with Oxford. Representative figures are Professor Walter Raleigh and, in a more modern style, Charles Williams and T. S. Eliot. Their attitude to literary-cultural issues is marked by relaxation, epicureanism, an enjoyment of class privileges. And that I don't acknowledge in my own case.

But of course Leavis also names a rootless modernism and experimentation as the marks of corruption. This he associates with Ezra Pound, and to some degree with T. S. Eliot, and he often nowadays names it "American." That I do acknowledge in my own case, but I don't admit that it is a mere modern variant on academic hedonism or class corruption. Modernism is not just the modern form of establishment art, but something radically new. In our day the palace of art—that Tennysonian phrase seems to me the best for Leavis' enemies—has been replaced by a skyscraper that is also an Electric Kool-Aid Acid Test. (Tom Wolfe's book with that title gives a good idea of what I mean.) I mean that it is an attack upon reality, since reality is established by consensus, and modernism attacks consensus. And this is not a modish perversity of a few artists. It is the inevitable result of a law of cultural development that is as important as those laws Leavis cites.

Western culture in the last 200 years has been developing powers of control—over matter and mind—quite unprecedented in their scope and moreover accelerating all the time. It was to be expected that the life of high culture—of the arts and sciences and speculation—would change, too. With so much wealth and power came leisure and pride, and an intoxicated exaltation of the intellect and imagination, so that the scope formerly assigned to philosophy and to poetry no longer satisfied. The human race has in a sense gone mad, and its high culture must go mad with it. That is, from the standpoint of previous ages, men now move in a drunken dream of unlimited powers, save that the dream is reality. We lead fantastic lives—more fantastic than earlier generations lived. Modern culture is imperialist in a sense never known before.

That, then, is where I find myself: at the imperial capital of that culture, to which Leavis' kind of virtuous resistance is inappropriate. New York City is not Oxford. The maelstrom of ideas and art there is not merely to be resisted or deplored. It is indeed one of the most wonderful achievements of human culture ever seen. My job must be to navigate the maelstrom, to yield to it enough to know it, and to discriminate between better and worse.

Clearly one cannot label these diverging fates, Anantha's and mine, as better and worse, or even lucky and unlucky. If one *could*, then his would be the lucky one. If I were an Indian, even one who'd been to the West, I think I should try to follow his pattern there. But if he were an Englishman, or an American, I think he would be forced to follow mine. What we have are just two more or less parallel paths through a jungle mapped out for both of us by Leavis in terms of cultural place, but by Gandhi in terms of right and wrong. The one gives us a north and south, the other an east and west, and we must make what we can of the map.

IX

The Problem of Sincerity

I SAID it was my job just to know modern culture. But in fact a job I can believe in has to have a more active and ambitious element than that, however grandiloquent it makes me sound. I have to aim at mastering and answering that culture, in a way comparable to Leavis'.

But it has to be a different way, which seems to me more radical. We live on the brink of disaster in a simpler and more terrible sense than any that Leavis could invoke, and our sensibilities are thereby radicalized. We must admit that all art is the product of energies freed from direct social service and social loyalty. But modern art is so in exaggerated degree, and it demands from us, I believe, some imaginative renunciation of the whole thing, even as we appreciate it. It is so closely related to the military and technological intoxication of Western culture that even when it protests against the latter, it is implicated with it; simply to participate in that art prevents one from working against that culture. At the same time, as Gandhi said about railways and factories, since they are here we may not destroy them, but must learn to use them and make them harmless.

It would have been better that they should never have come into existence, but since they did we must deal with them. Thus it is—while I'm being grandiloquent—a Gandhian philosophy of art I am working toward.

And what could a Gandhian philosophy of art mean? For this first preliminary sketch I must lay it out clearly even if crudely. It means to study art in terms of imperialism; to approach art as he approached politics, and analyze its phenomena according to its hidden principles of dominance, exploitation, exultation; and to understand the whole subject matter against the implicit contrast of other values—Gandhian values. It means to live with the death of the mind as he lived with the death of the body—the death of the mind meaning the renunciation of art—and thus to accept and reject art as he accepted and rejected politics; to nevertheless master art as he mastered politics; to become a master-critic, as he was a master-politician; to accept fully all the phenomena of art, in the sense of understanding them, making them harmless; and of course to combine such criticism with other kinds of Gandhian activity, that is, with more simply and straightforwardly Gandhian movements in politics and economics and religion.

At this point I am compelled (by the logic of my enterprise) to ask a question about myself, more naked than is usual in a book like this. But without asking it, I think I could not hope to keep the confidence of my readers, or not for long. It amounts to asking where I myself stand in relation to these imperatives and alternatives, and if "where I stand" and "the project of a Gandhian criticism" can be called sincere.

It was easy for me to show that, for instance, Tolstoy and his late writings cannot be dismissed as Speirs and Crankshaw dismiss him. They offended against their own liberal-humanist decorum as critics; indeed, we should be grateful to them for scorning to protect themselves against reproach on that score—for speaking out what they thought, despite decorum. They made it easy for me to show, by purely reasonable criteria, the limitations of their purely reasonable, liberal-humanist approaches to spiritual phenomena on this scale. But what then can carry one beyond those limitations? Merely more flexibility of imagination? That does not seem likely. Merely criticizing Crankshaw and Speirs of course gives one an illusion of passing through barriers, of expansion, of transcendence. But surely that must be an illusion. As long as one is merely writing an appreciative book about Tolstoy and Gandhi, surely the crucial barriers are still there.

To put it another way, by expounding Gandhi and Tolstoy so sympathetically, I am identifying myself with them, and sharing in their triumph over these critics who fail to measure up to their challenge. But have I the right to identify myself with them? Am I not more similar to those critics, in my general equipment, social place, and purpose, than to Tolstoy and Gandhi?

To put it yet another way, this book will seem in some degree insincere if I have to admit at the end that for me the subject has been just another subject in a series—that I shall be moving on to something else after this, looking for another good subject to write about. The only tone adequate to expounding Gandhi and Tolstoy is one that implies conviction, a resolution, a resting place. If I second their call for a change, I imply that I myself have heard and somehow or other responded to that call.

I have many reasons for doubting whether that is true of myself, innumerable unmentionable reasons. But I can mention, as one way to suggest all the rest, one evening I remember when I ate dinner in the garden restaurant of the Pandyan Hotel in Madurai. I ate alone, reading something by Vinoba, and, since this was after my meeting with Vinoba, I had nothing to drink. But I realized, as I prepared to leave, that I was on the verge of laughing aloud, all my stomach already convulsed in giggles—that I was in effect drunk. On what? Well, drunk on the exquisitely spicy food (rajas food, such as Gandhi warned his followers against) and on the flourishing deference, the hustle and bustle, of the many waiters; drunk on the music of a group, one of whose singers looked and dressed like the young Sinatra, and sang "Stop the World I Want to Get Off" in blurred English but metronomic rhythm, shaking his sex at us like a chime of bells in time to the tune; drunk on the other diners, the men all wearing khadi dhotis like Gandhians but obviously (how it was obvious I couldn't say) provincial tycoons, squat spiders of usury, giving their richly dressed spouses a Hollywood night out. (I'd watched those couples before, slowly parading the hotel's empty halls in classic provincial boredom.) I was drunk on all those things, but even more on the consciousness of myself at their center. That was what sharpened all those shapes into electric absurdity. Me reading Vinoba, thinking about Gandhi, being so serious, in the middle of so much gaudy nonsense.

That was classic Western laughter, the musical accompaniment to "Things-fall-apart" or "Joy-in-destruction." It was the laughter against which Bernanos warns men in particular, because it is the solvent of manhood. It was a laughter more profoundly subversive of Gandhism than any reasoned philistinism or worldly selfishness could ever be. It was the laughter of England after 1918, that fatal mortal sense of humor in which we educated each other.

What was I doing in the Pandyan Hotel? Was this trip anything more than an escape from those insoluble problems of domestic life, those failures that prolong themselves and compound themselves forever, making one guilty in advance of what one knows will be unpardonable? Wasn't the India I was visiting further from Gandhi than the America I lived in? Wasn't this hotel further from an ashram than my own home? In Madras, I remembered, waiting for the airport bus, I'd sought out the most splendid of the hotel lobbies to sit and read in, one where the porters wore high turbans and aiguillettes, and the desk clerks wore Rajput silk coats tailored for musical comedy, and the loungers included some flamboyant femmes-de-luxe—cocktails of femininity. I felt at home there.

But the point is not to reproach myself—here and now would hardly be the place for that—but to suggest the grounds my readers have to doubt whether simpleminded sincerity forms the substance of my interest in these matters. And if it must be a complex interest, what part does sincerity play in it? What am I prepared to *do* in service of my conviction, however that may be compounded? That is something they are bound, sooner or later, to ask.

Not that action as opposed to thought seems to me a necessary criterion of sincerity. Indeed, action as opposed to thought seems a decidedly dangerous criterion for an intellectual—one that positively invites insincerity. But the thought has to be serious, of a seriousness of which one guarantee would be a readiness for action. That action need not be sharply distinguished from thinking, but it should be distinguishable from writing.

The only sincere writing about such a subject is that which might be the very last writing you would ever do. This is a manifestation in purely intellectual terms of that constant concern with death that I have pointed to in Gandhi and Tolstoy. Could one believe in this new idea enough to give up writing for it—give up the pleasures and freedoms of thought? Would anything short of that show sincerity, or be adequate to the idea's demands?

Perhaps I can make my point by comparing what I am saying with another critic's response to the problem—a problem that he sees, I think, in almost exactly the same terms. In "Art and Fortune," Lionel Trilling says:

> Surely the great work of our time is the restoration and reconstitution of the will. I know that with some the opinion prevails that, apart from what very well *may* happen by way of Apocalypse, what *should* happen is that we advance farther and farther into the darkness, seeing to it that the will finally exhausts and expends itself to the end that we purge our minds of all the old ways of thought and feeling, giving up all hope of ever reconstituting the great former will of humanism, which, as they imply, has brought us to this pass. One must always listen when this opinion is offered in true passion. But for the vision and ideal of apocalyptic renovation one must either be a particular kind of moral genius with an attachment to life that goes beyond attachment to any particular form of life—D. H. Lawrence was such a genius—or a person deficient in attachment to life in any of its forms.

This has been the classic way in our time for humanists to formulate their position. We shall see later that both Leavis and Orwell attribute that deficiency in life-attachment to men of spirituality—to Gandhi and Tolstoy in Orwell's case, to T. S. Eliot in Leavis'. And both invoke Lawrence as the alternative, as the life of the spirit in its healthy form—which is of course an acceptable proposition only to those within the erotic movement. Trilling concludes about these two alternatives, moral-genius or life-rejection, "Most of us are neither one nor the other, and our notions of renovation and reconstitution are social and pragmatic and in the literal sense of the word conservative. To the restoration and reconstitution of the will thus understood the novelistic intelligence is most apt." And just because that seems to me so true, I am forced to ask whether *anything* I could say about novels, however I intended it, could do anything but renovate and reinforce that will, which is so deeply involved in all our disasters.

Trilling is worth citing because he was so clearly aware of that alliance between the arts and spirituality that imposes obligations on us. In "The Meaning of a Literary Idea" he speaks of "the strong contemporary wish to establish, in a world of unremitting action and effectiveness, the legitimacy of contemplation, which it is now no longer convenient to associate with the exercises of religion but which may be associated with the experiences of art." This is the idea of modern art that Susan Sontag has taken up, speaking of it as a spiritual project. She goes further than Trilling, and says in "The Aesthetics of Silence," "As some people know now, there are ways of thinking that we don't yet know about. Nothing could be more important or precious than that knowledge, however unborn. The sense of urgency, the spiritual restlessness it engenders, cannot be appeased, and continues to fuel the radical art of this century." And she speaks of the best art and thought of our time validating itself by transcending itself into silence, like the art and thought of Rimbaud and Wittgenstein. But the Gandhian mode of resistance, though it *is* silent in this sense, cannot conceive of itself as silence, and cannot commend itself to us as anything but a mode of action.

What then could Gandhian action be, for a man of letters? I find it rather striking that so little has been said so far along these lines. Almost the only program I find sketched out is Y. G. Krishnamurti's. He published two pamphlets just after the assassination, *Gandhism for Millions* and *Gandhism Will Survive*, that address themselves to creating a cultural program for Gandhians.

In the first he describes the world situation with some grimness: "To put it brutally, today cynicism is the only form of emotional greatness," but says that luckily there is a chance of the world staging a deathbed repentance and accepting Gandhi's new moral wares. Being an enemy to every shape of tyranny or brutalization, Gandhism is the only possible alternative to the threat inherent in the atomic bomb.

He appeals to Indian intellectuals to realize that Gandhism is the living armor of the world spirit. They should extend the axis of its utopia to the ends of the earth. The martyred heart of Gandhi holds its subtle enchantment. Gandhism is the magic link that binds the petals of a world culture into a radiant pattern.

In the second book he calls for a Gandhian Institute, with a radio station, orchestra, museums, and chains of magazines. He sketches a structure for the institute, names officers and activities, all on the largest scale. He would have decorative styles, toys, textiles, posters, banners, dance-drama, and theatre; a whole Morris-like battery of activities, directed to "deepen cosmic awareness."

Of course nothing came of this in 1949, and it is difficult now to imagine how it ever could have. And though I find his idea—frankly, it seems to me rather the idea *of* an idea—more attractive than the actual Institute of Gandhian Studies, with its aridly social-science approach, still I could not compose or propose anything comparable. My idea would have to be much smaller in scale, dimmer in color, grimmer in tone and intent.

But indeed, though I made my question about sincerity challenging and specific, I shall make my answer much more general and vague. The function of both question and answer is only to persuade the reader that I have faced the issue. What exactly must be done about it I think it would be foolish to say, especially in advance of trying. There are many ways in which whatever I wrote would read crassly or foolishly. But I can say what kinds of activity are in question.

All that it seems to me at all realistic to propose is some effort to change the consciousness of one country, England, in this one matter of imperialism. That seems to me realistic because there the old consciousness is already decayed, along with so many of the old institutions of England, and there is a search on all parts for a new idea. At the moment what we have is not so much an idea as, on the one side, shame, and on the other, anger. By speaking of two sides I point of course to the confrontation of the immigrants with the native-born English, a confrontation that inspires all our worst fears and best hopes. It is comparable with that sharpest confrontation of rich and poor in late nineteenth-century England, out of which came that fruitful movement of criticism—literary but more-than-literary criticism—to which Orwell and Leavis and Raymond Williams belonged. It seems to me that out of the present confrontation an equally fruitful intellectual growth could come, if we build a criticism that relates to the theme "the empire" as that earlier criticism related to the theme "the people." I have more to say about this in my sixth talk (chapter 12).

But to change a country's consciousness, if the project claims Gandhian auspices, must involve something more strenuous than speculation. To be as specific as possible, the secondary schools of England must be persuaded to teach the novel of adventure in the context of the history of British imperialism. Not, of course, with the idea of teaching the students to hate adventure, or to hate British history—any such loaded message would be, I think, self-defeating—but with the idea of bringing out both their attractive and their unattractive aspects, and achieving some balance or stasis between them. There should be enough stasis to allow individuals and groups to know the highly charged feelings that lie behind their and others' judgments, and to induce immigrants and native-born both to ask how they come to be where they are and, if possible, to understand each others' feelings about that.

Along with such teaching would go involvement with England's social problems—the problems of a multiracial society; these are not the problems of Gandhi's India, and yet they are sufficiently similar for his techniques to be a reasonable guide. Of course, a Gandhian criticism could not allow itself to be purely literary or purely intellectual. It must engage in social action to some degree, and education is the obvious primary mode of such action—it was the mode of Tolstoy and Gandhi themselves.

But no less manifold than the problems in England are the possibilities, for here before our eyes is the breakup of an empire, and of an imperial city. Surely here, if anywhere, the antiimperial idea can take root, the Gandhian idea. Surely here, if anywhere, the third world could find a center.

There are then three dimensions to the project: one intellectual and critical, one pedagogical and educational, one social and perhaps religious. All this would not be to save the world. The world, it seems, would not be saved by Gandhi, so we need not torment ourselves with such ideas. All we can aim at is to save our honor. The world, surely we all know, is doomed. Presumably in our lifetime its end will come. But to presume is presumptuous. All that I am concerned with here is sincerity.

X

TALK FIVE

Brahmins, in India

and America

THE TOPIC of this talk is a bit out of line with the argument so far, but I'm sure that deep down it is closely related. I've been impressed by the similarity between the social situation of the college teacher of humanities in America—us—and that of the Brahmins proper in Hindu culture. But the relation of similarity is of course a large loose category, and this similarity is not one of the least partial and peripheral. I use it mostly to introduce another idea, on which my stress will fall more firmly—the challenge Gandhi offers to all kinds of Brahmin. And that, of course, is only another way to name the main subject of all these talks—his and Tolstoy's challenge to us.

The idea of caste has some general advantages over the idea of class in speculation about cultural typology. Tolstoy, for instance, when he says that he was born into the warrior caste in Russia, says also that therefore the official teachings of the Christian church about sex—the official recommendation of chastity, for instance—never reached him. It was there, in Russian culture; obviously he had heard that recommendation a thousand times; and yet it was *not* there for him, so that he discovered it for himself, late in life, as a new idea. And the same was obviously true of the official church injunctions against violence, war, fighting, and so on.

Now the word "class" could not be substituted for the word "caste" in that idea. Tolstoy could not have said that the upper class in Russia did not regard Christianity as having anything to do with them. It is the image of the warrior, with its stress on men as opposed to women, and on fighting as opposed to drawing rents, that explains everything.

He was taught, he says in *My Religion*, that Christ's teaching was lofty but impracticable: "I was taught to judge and punish. Then I was taught to make war, that is to resist evil men with murder, and the military caste, of which I was a member, was called the Christ-loving military. . . ." And that was the spirit he carried into his early writing, which was reviewed by liberal critics as "reactionary" and "a downright refusal to acknowledge all that has been and still is going on in literature and life. . . ." And we have seen him acknowledge in that passage from an early draft of *War and Peace* that he could not write about peasants, merchants, and theology students, much as the contemporary public might desire that, because he was of the aristocracy.

In saying that, he was fighting off his identity as a man of letters—as one of the group that contained Turgenev, Nekrassov, and Chernyshevsky. He was naming himself a

Kshattriya. We can see American writers like Hemingway and Mailer attempt the same self-nomination. But in the long run Tolstoy had to acknowledge that all novelists, however great, are men of letters—are Brahmins. How much more are college teachers of the humanities. The same could be said of teachers of all subjects and at all levels, to some degree, but I think it is most true of college professors of cultural subjects. I think of them as Brahmins primarily because of their position of privilege without power, or rather than power; because of their work in expounding their society's sacred texts; and because of their position vis-à-vis the other major elements in American society—the men of executive and military power, the Kshattriyas; the men of commercial and industrial wealth, the Vaisyas; and the laborers or working class, the Sudras. And of course we have our outcastes, too. Do not typical representatives of these other groups look on college teachers rather as if they were Brahmins, protected and privileged by a system of ideas to which the men of other castes give only a notional assent?

But first I should say that I am using the term "caste" to refer to the four great *varnas* just named. They could be called not so much castes as groups of castes, or perhaps ideas of caste. Into these large loose categories the *jatis*, the subcastes, which have a much more specific and local character, much more factual and less theoretical, fit quite artificially. My idea of caste is theoretical, not factual, but there are good precedents for that usage. Swami Dayanand, the founder of the Arya Samaj, even held that no one could be born a Brahmin or a Kshattriya; that these were titles to be deserved and won by merit. Sociologists, describing the facts of caste life, give us a very different picture, but Dayanand's usage (which is first cousin to my own) corresponds to something in general Hindu thinking on the subject. Caste identity is there, in the Indian mind, as it is not in ours. But it is there, for most Indians, as a notion, a potentiality, rather than an actuality.

For instance, the warrior-ruler caste are said to be characterized, in individual psychology, by meat eating, fighting, alcohol drinking, splendor, and rough humor. Edward Thompson tells us of a Central Indian prince who said to him, "To me, as a Rajput, the doctrine of ahimsa [nonviolence] is inconceivable! It is Rajput's *duty* to kill and be warlike." Now obviously Indians know that not every individual, or every jati, belonging to the Kshattriya varna has all those traits strongly developed. Nevertheless, the statement is meaningful. Such is the character of the ideal Kshattriya, and the individual belonging to that varna defines himself in terms of those traits—as himself possessing or not possessing them. And in matters not crucial to his personal self-definition, he is likely to be carried along inertially into conformity. Something similar can be said of the Russian military-nobleman identity, as Tolstoy implies, and presumably of West Point families in America. I want to make a comparable definition of us as a caste.

The Brahmins have, at least in theory, a more definite cultural typology than any of the other varnas, and that is both a help and a hindrance to my comparison. The primary social function of real Brahmins is of course to be priests, which we are not—but not priests in the evangelical sense so much as in the pedagogical. At least since the Vedic Age, Brahmins seem to have been closer to rabbis than to, let us say, Wesley, or John Knox, or Teresa de Avila. Brahmins are the memorizers of the ancient texts, legendary as well as theological, the masters and guardians of the traditional rituals and the great temples. They are contemplative men, in the ideal sense mendicants, supported by the contributions from the rest of society, and socially privileged as being purer and closer to the common ideal than those others who support them.

Sometimes they administrated whole states, as prime ministers, usually under rulers of another caste; but originally they learned from each other, they memorized and so preserved, the thousand Vedic hymns. (These hymns were written down about 600 B.C., which reduced the need for memorization, but by then their language was already archaic and arcane, so they needed and still need study and interpretation by Brahmins.) They also study the Upanishads and Vedas, the Smriti, sacred law, and the Ayurveda, traditional medicine, plus such philosophy as is ancillary to such matters. They advise in spiritual, occult, and ritual matters, and are paid by gift. They take disciples, *chelas*, into their homes and teach them the methods of exegesis and disputation.

The picturesque details of what they teach and of their rituals of separation from the world are of course unlike any of ours. They don't have the long years of thesis writing, the oral defense, or Freshman English sections. They assume a sacred thread at the upanamaya ceremony and are thereupon born again, as a bird is born again when it emerges from its shell. Before eating (usually only vegetarian food) they sprinkle water round their plates in a clockwise direction, and lay something aside for the birds and for the poor. They must avoid all contact, even of their clothes, with children or dogs, or Untouchables, before eating. All the details are quite different, but the underlying reality is the same.

For the key characteristic of Brahmin castes, literal and metaphorical, is separation and withdrawal. They withdraw, in defined and limited ways, from the aggressive and competitive and violent activities of their societies. They are contemplative guardians of knowledge. In our society, then, college teachers are even more the Brahmins than are the churchmen—at least if we take the secular clergy to characterize the Christian churches, because they, at their best, are active rather than contemplative and think of themselves as engaged in every social problem. But of course in other ways churchmen are Brahmins, too.

Our Brahmins acquire their caste by examination and not by birth, which makes an enormous difference. Still, it is not a total difference. It is often possible to recognize the sons of academic families, even those who have chosen another life for themselves, as nevertheless Brahmin. Upon this recognition, for instance, depends the performance of Jack Nicholson in *Five Easy Pieces*. In India, too, some Brahmins are illiterate, many are cooks, and their privileges are often purely theoretical. And yet, in both countries, those privileges are always potentially there, even if they are actualized mostly in the resentment of the unprivileged. It is in India a sacred crime to kill a Brahmin, a holy Brahmin, which provokes much irony among men of the other castes. And headlines like "College Professor Slain" or "English Teacher Arrested" can have a similar ironic flavor for us.

The sacred texts expounded by modern American Brahmins are of rather a different character from the Vedas and the Upanishads. English department reading is likely to include "The White Negro" and *Soul on Ice*; if the major texts are *Moby Dick* and *The Scarlet Letter*, the commentaries are likely to include *Love and Death in the American Novel* and *Regeneration Through Violence*; that is to say, the texts are related to society and its pieties in quite a revolutionary way. The History department, though it may teach the Constitution, will almost certainly also teach *Capital*; and even the Theology department is quite likely to teach *Waiting for Godot*. Nevertheless, these *are* the sacred texts of our society. So explosively angry is this culture, so centrifugally dynamic, that the more violent and antisocial a manifesto is, the more eagerly it is claimed by the culture as its own voice, its meaning. Of course, it is true that such texts cannot be expounded in the same way as texts in support of orthodox piety. For one thing, many of our texts make the social role of teacher, of liberal intellectual, one of their main targets.

But we recognize in their attacks the same impulse of pride as led Tolstoy to claim that he was an aristocrat, a Kshattriya, and not a man of letters, a Brahmin. Many of our fiercest modern writers are Brahmins-against-Brahminism, or to use a more Christian expression, spoiled priests. Katherine Mansfield used to call Middleton Murry a monk in search of a monastery, and the same phrase may well have been used about *their* husbands—certainly the same complaint was made—by Sonya Tolstoy and Frieda Lawrence. And these were the two great celebrants of anti-Brahmin values, life-values. One need only glance at the faces of Kafka, Proust, Dostoevsky, Rolland, to see what priests or monks *they* would have made, in another culture. Our culture invites such men into literature, not religion, calls them artists, not saints; but they are just as clearly the spokesmen of the spirit to the rest of us.

The practitioners of modernist art call themselves sometimes Kshattriyas, sometimes saddhus, and the interpreters and teachers of their work do the same, by infection. But it is a hollow pretense, and their readers and students know that these are Brahmins, after all—sheep in wolves' clothing. This we see more clearly by adopting the caste metaphor.

Another advantage to the metaphor is that the Brahmins of India have always faced challenges from the holy men of their culture, the saddhus, the rishis, the Mahatmas, similar to what we face from Gandhi. As Nagendranath Gupta says, "There can be no doubt that the doctrines of the Buddha were bitterly resented by the Brahmins and the priests, and sometimes insulting remarks were addressed to him." The Buddha accepted no distinctions of caste, and if he had had his way the Brahmins would have lost their occupation. Most important, for our purposes, they, too, met that challenge from Gandhi. Gandhi clashed with the orthodoxy of Hinduism, embodied in the Brahmins, socially and spiritually and in other ways.

Nevertheless, Gandhi was, culturally speaking, conservative, even reactionary, in that he wanted to revive and purify traditional Hinduism. Many intellectuals, for instance, Tagore, quarreled with him over that. Gandhi said repeatedly that he considered himself a sanatani (orthodox) Hindu. In *Hind Swaraj* he described true civilization as being where men live in traditional huts in villages, doing traditional work, and governed by priests, not kings. But the orthodoxy he believed in, the past he wanted to return to, was an ideal one. The actuality had never been what he wanted—nor did he suppose it had—but it had set itself ideals by which he still held.

"Where is the real Brahmin today, content with a bare living, and giving all his time to study and teaching?" he asked in 1939. "Where is the Kshattriya, ready to lay down his life for the honor of his fellowmen, or of his country? Where is the Vaisya, glorifying in adding to the nation's wealth, and using his own wealth for the benefit of the poor?" Translated into our categories, this rhetoric has a Ruskinian ring, not to say Moral Rearmament, which must sound foolish and reactionary to ears trained in Marxism. But if we take a Gandhian attitude to the modern world system, we must be ready to be "reactionary." We must learn to dissociate reaction from oppression, and from illiberal and unexperimental thought.

Gandhi described his future by means of ideas that he named from India's past, and to this extent he accepted the caste structure. But he said he wished all twice-born Hindus to lay aside their privileges and consider themselves as Sudras: "There is only one varna today—all of us are Sudras, or, if you please, Harijans."* At the Faizpur Congress (1936) he had the sanitation arrangements run by Brahmins, led by an ex-professor. He said that if it could ever be proven to him that anything in the sacred texts justified untouchability, then he would forswear Hinduism. And in certain ways he did rebel against caste more and more as he grew older. Early in his career he disapproved of intercaste marriages, but by the end it was only marriages between a caste Hindu and an Untouchable that he would attend. There was then much in the caste system he valued, or transvalued; much that he tolerated, allowing politics more latitude than religion; and there was something that he could not tolerate. And this issue is doubly interesting to us because it related, in Gandhi's mind, to another of our key ideas, empire. Both the privileged position of the Brahmin caste, as guardians of Hindu culture, and the intolerable oppression of the outcastes were evidence to him of a native Indian imperialism. Empire was not exclusively a British phenomenon, nor were Indians only victims of empire. Caste is indeed probably racial in origin, and even includes a distinct element of color prejudice. The official term for the backward races was Kaliparaj, or dark people, and the opposite was Ujali-paraj, fair people. Hindu culture, Aryan or Sanskrit culture, is essentially something that has been imposed on subject peoples.

Gandhi was not the only Indian to see that. Tagore said in 1915, "In India, where the upper classes ruled over the lower, they forged their own chains. Europe is closely following Brahmin India, when she looks upon Asia and Africa as her legitimate fields for exploitation." It was not hard to see that truth. The hard thing was to see what to do about it—

* Harijan, meaning child of God, was his name for the outcasts.

how to acknowledge India's guilt but still protest her victimization.

Gandhi said, "We have driven the pariahs from our midst and have thereby become the pariahs of the British Empire. . . . We are all guilty of having oppressed our brothers. We make them crawl on their bellies before us, and rub their noses on the ground. With eyes red with rage we push them out of railway carriages. Has the English Government ever inflicted anything worse on us?" And his way of naming the problem was always as hard as Tagore's on the caste Indians, even though he opposed any secession of the Untouchables.

And Gandhi's disciples followed him in their tone about Brahminism. His Christian disciple, J. C. Kumarappa, has a striking passage on a Brahmin seat of Sanskrit study, which taught certain mantras to a certain Brahmin sect and allowed no Harijans to enter. These men, said Kumarappa, are not Brahmins, they are India's true untouchables: "Can there be anything more heart-rending than the pride and arrogance of these untouchable Brahmins of our land? Learning ancient lore is no more culture than vomiting is digesting. . . . Our so-called sacred threads bind us to death's heads and degradation. . . . The Brahmin has misappropriated his privileges as custodians of the race's purity and the nation's culture." This is just what Tolstoy said about people like us, modern men of letters. If Gandhi supported the caste system, his support was conditional upon changes from within.

But let me return to the theme of education, always the Brahmins' prime province, in India and in America. The idea of education that Gandhi devised, and that his followers, notably Vinoba Bhave, have developed, called itself antiliterary. The word "literary" is used by Gandhians as we might use "academic" or "mandarin"—because the traditional Sanskrit culture in the Brahmins' keeping was based on ancient texts that needed to be translated and expounded and interpreted. Gandhian education, which is called Nai Talim or New Education, is centered on practical corporal work, and though it includes literacy, that is taught for purely practical purposes. Gandhi said on one occasion, "People read and read until they almost lose their power of thinking. This is a class to which many of us belong." And when his secretary, Mahadev Desai, died, he wrote, "His dreams rose above scholarship or learning. . . . God had blessed him with high intellect and versatile tastes, but what his soul thirsted for was the devotional spirit. . . . A word to litterateurs. He delighted in spinning for hours."

Tolstoy, discussing his school at Yasnaya Polyana, says, "If you teach a boy to enter the world of art, he will no longer breathe with full lungs; and it will be painful and injurious to him to breathe the pure air, if by chance he happens to go into it." He describes teaching the peasant boy Fedka the way to choose the details to perfect a story, and seeing the artistic instinct in the boy awaken and develop. Tolstoy says he himself went pale with excitement, but felt he was committing a sacrilege—that he was a debauchee who corrupted children: "Only two or three times in my life had I ever experienced such a powerful emotion."

Kaka Kalelkar, another Brahmin among Gandhi's followers, tells of an American visitor asking Gandhi a number of leading questions, which climaxed in, "What causes you the most concern—what keeps you awake at night?" "Bapu paused a moment to think, then said, 'The hardness of heart of the educated.' " After hearing that, it was Kalelkar's turn not to sleep, because his job in life was education. He was in charge of the Gujerati Vidyapith, a Gandhian institution set up to replace the British-style universities, but it was still a place of education, and Kalelkar was shocked to face the fundamental distrust his master felt for the process.

Vinoba will not have even specifically religious instruction, because he believes that the valuable lessons of religion are learned only by means of association with good men. He would have students learn some passages of sacred text by heart, but as literature, for the benefit of their beauty, a benefit that he compares with refreshing effect of sleep. It is clear that he would have no analysis of these texts, no thinking about them or expounding of them. He trusts to their emotional power, and the fervent response of teacher or parent, to make them take a strong effect on the pupil. In other words, he advocates a non-Brahmin education, whether we think of Indian or American Brahmins.

This is what one should expect from Gandhi and Tolstoy. Their set of symbols is single, and so the life they shape, in the individual and in the community, is simple. To have a literary education and a literary class to supervise it is the mark of a society and a culture that have fallen apart into specialization; that have failed in simplicity and manhood; that are imperial. And Brahmins, because of the profits and privileges they derive from the system, seem especially attainted by it.

And if this is true of the Hindu Brahmin, it must be even more so of the modern American version. For our modern culture is so much more complex and strenuous, it demands so much more of its devotees—in emotional and moral endurance as well as intellectual—it is so much *more* specialized. Comparatively speaking, the Vedas and the Upanishads are so much more simply related to the pieties of Hindu life, however enigmatic in themselves, however open to ingenious interpretation, however richly embroidered with legend. To expound our sacred texts and their relation to the pieties of our life is much more dangerous and all-absorbing a task. What would Gandhi say to that?

What Gandhi said he wanted of Brahmins was that they should be *good* Brahmins—truly devoted to tradition, truly unworldly and mendicant in spirit, truly religious, and so on. But I doubt if we can rely on a good record as literature teachers to exempt us from his reproach. If we are to find any pride of self adequate to his challenge to us, we would do well to abandon the Brahmin analogy, and even our sense of Gandhi at this point, and revert to our own vocabulary.

As I said in the preceding talk (chapter 8), I cannot believe that Gandhi or even Tolstoy fully understood this modern culture we represent. Destructive though it is, it is also a great manifesto of spirituality in defiance of modern industrial and imperial civilization. It employs energies of mind and spirit comparable with their own, and calls for comparable efforts of participation by its adherents. At the level of intention it constitutes a rebellion against established evil as great as their own.

To speak of the level of intention is of course to admit the great difference at the level of effect. One cannot hope, if one persists in this profession, to change the way people live. A life spent teaching literature will always be one long wander in the forest of symbols, a meander in Illyria. But then was even Gandhi effective? If the answer must be either yes or no, then it must be yes. But he was also ineffective. At the end of his life, the two largest facts about India's situation were facts against which he had struggled all his life. The country was divided into two states, with Hindus and Moslems bitterly hostile to each other. And the Hindu state was embarking eagerly on a career of industrialization and militarism. Those facts were for Gandhi large and terrible, and he did regard himself as having failed.

I would never say that, but I would say that the lessons of history, even those of Gandhian history, are never clear enough to draw one who is a Brahmin by temperament into the sphere of other-caste effectiveness, the world of action. The only thing that can give so clear a lesson, can reliably promise that action is the right option, is faith in *oneself as*, say, a Kshattriya, a prior commitment, a prior temperamental contract. To jump into the stream of action without that faith is no more responsible than to wonder in the forest of symbols.

We must, then, find a way to deal with modern culture that will be a mode of action, will disinfect modern culture of its virulence. That will not be easy. Our literature is deeply compromised by its dependence on the establishment it intentionally attacks. Unlike Gandhi's movement, it does not start again from scratch, but accepts a parasitical dependence on established society, living off it and enjoying its favors. And therefore it hates itself, and its emotional climate is hot, hateful, hellish, as it clings desperately to life —the opposite of Gandhi's clear, bright affirmation against the background of death. And I think—though this is not a topic I can dwell on—that life-affirmation of the Mahatmas' kind *can* only be made against an acceptance of death of that kind, so that to follow them we should have to find some equivalent.

By the background of death I mean primarily the Mahatmas' readiness to die, a readiness Gandhi renewed at the level of intention every day, and demonstrated in action a hundred times, perhaps most notably on the occasions of assassination. There were two such occasions, the first in South Africa, when the blow was deflected, though Gandhi was still badly hurt. Both times he said He Ram as he collapsed.

On another occasion he sent this message to commemorate the martyrdom of a coworker:

My Ahimsa will also be perfect if I could die similarly peacefully with axe blows on my head. I have always been dreaming of such a death, and I wish to treasure this dream. How noble that death will be—a dagger attack at me from one side; an axe blow from another; a lathi wound administered from yet another direction, and kicks and abuses from all sides, and if in the midst of these I could rise to the occasion and remain nonviolent and peaceful and could ask others to act and behave likewise, and finally I could die with cheer on my face and a smile on my lips, then and then alone my Ahimsa will be perfect and true. I am hankering after such an opportunity.

This is of course a very shocking thing to hear said, and an even more shocking thing to say. There is not, to my mind, any way to discuss it. What we find individually as an equivalent for that must be a private or a religious matter. There is a public and intellectual equivalent—but it is no equivalent.

I spoke of a death of the mind as our equivalent for his death of the body; a renunciation of the pleasures of art, the habit of those pleasures, of appreciation and analysis, like his renunciation of the pleasures and habits of the body. This is symbolic renunciation—made once and for all and yet every day—and so in some sense unreal, and yet it must be sincere. That analogy, between the two renunciations, must be very partial, and even then it remains absurd. But that is just why Gandhi's example is so useful to us. It announces the leap of faith. It is anagogical, as we used to say when we were much concerned with the four levels of interpretation of a literary text. The anagogical was the top level, the farthest away from the literal, the leap of the mind up toward the supreme and the divine.

But let us turn from the consciousness of death, which is for the moment only peripheral, only strategic, to the central question of the vocation of Brahminism. The lessons of history, I have said, can give us only negative reasons for remaining what we are. But for me at least there is a positive reason—that I see great power, paradoxical as it may seem, in the idea of a Gandhian criticism of our culture.

This is of course what I was talking about in the previous talk. I justify the claim to the title "Gandhian" in three ways. First, a teacher could combine such work with orthodox Gandhian politics, and serve as a direction signal for younger people still more easily able to commit themselves totally to that option. But that is necessarily somewhat external to the inner life of criticism; it is Gandhian enough, but not very literary. Second, this criticism should involve as complete a commitment to and at the same time disengagement from the world of culture as Gandhi's commitment to and disengagement from that of power politics. Gandhi was a man of paradoxes, too, and one of the sharpest he mastered was that he, a man of spirituality, in search of salvation always, in search of God, spent his life among the competitions, rivalries, challenges, angers, conflicts, betrayals, publicity of politics. It would be no harder to be a Gandhian critic of culture than to be a Gandhian leader in politics. This second point is internal enough in its reference to the critic's self-consciousness, but not very specific about his practical activity. So, finally, I would take inspiration from Gandhi's example in that, having engaged in the difficult and doubtful game of politics, he went on to master it—to deal successfully with the British Empire, with the Communist party of India, with the Hindu nationalists, and so on. One cannot claim, alas, that he won every battle, but one can claim that any comparable level of success would be quite enough to aim at. And that is surely easy enough to translate into terms of literary critical activity; there are new books, authors, careers, to know; new relations of literature to society to theorize; new points of view to attain, from which even the familiar achievements will look quite different; new alliances to forge between literary and political or economic forces. And what all this means in the concrete terms of an empire-centered theory of literary history I shall be describing later.

XI

The Mahatmas' Feeling

for the Arts and

Sciences

TOLSTOY'S AND GANDHI'S judgment on Brahmins and on culture was indeed harsh, but no harsher than that of other, more familiar commentators, deeply involved themselves with Western culture as its critics, its artists, its representatives. Let me quote from Susan Sontag's "What's Happening in America?" of 1968: "The truth is that Mozart, Pascal, Boolean algebra, Shakespeare, parliamentary government, baroque churches, Newton, the emancipation of women, Kant, Marx, and Balanchine ballets don't redeem what this particular civilization has wrought upon the world. The white race *is* the cancer of human history. . . ." That grants everything that Tolstoy and Gandhi argued, at least if we add the all-but-inevitable exordium, "So let us turn away from this culture as well as away from this civilization, let us turn towards the life-giving alternatives."

Of course we don't react as strongly, as stubbornly, against Susan Sontag's judgment because we believe she cannot so turn, any more than we can. We know that she has been deeply involved with all that culture all her life, and we assume that she will be again tomorrow, whatever she says today. We know that she is trapped, like us, and we can merely sympathize with her cries of protest. Perhaps then we should approach Gandhi by way of *his* involvement, his engagement in the arts, by temperament and aptitude; even though that engagement was so different in him, was tributary to his disengagement, still he was in his way, as Tolstoy was in his way, one of us.

In 1925, apropos of Tagore, Gandhi said, "There is nothing of the poet about me. . . . The poet lives in a magnificent world of his own creation, his world of ideas. I am a slave of somebody else's creation, the spinning wheel. The poet makes his gopis dance to the tune of his flute. I wander after my beloved Sita—the charkha—and seek to deliver her from the ten-headed monster from Japan, Manchester, Paris, etc." Sita is the heroine of the *Ramayana*, and its villain is a many-headed monster, Ravana, here representing foreign cloth. Tagore, Gandhi said, was an inventor, he an explorer: "The world easily finds an honorable place for the magician who produces new and dazzling things. I have to struggle laboriously to find a corner for my worn out things."

But the very phrasing of his denial must confirm us in resisting him. It must remain one of the major attractions of the Mahatma that he *was* in some sense a poet. How else can one describe the man who made such metaphors?

Even as a cup of milk which is full up to the brim does not overflow when sugar is gently added to it, the sugar accommodating itself in the milk, and enriching its taste; in the same way I would like you to live . . . so as not to become interlopers, so as to enrich the life of the people in whose midst you may be living. . . . The Himalayas are spotlessly snow-white in virtue of the spotless glory of the countless sages who laid down their lives performing penance in the caves. . . . The cities, which are not India, but the blotting paper sheets of London.

It is true that Gandhi did not write poems, nor did he speak of feeling any creative or shaping impulse in regard to any of the arts. Indeed, he once said, "God gave me a sense of art, but not the means to put it into effect." But on the other hand he also said, "If I had not taken the vow of a Satyagrahi for the deliverance of my country, I would probably have occupied myself only with songs. But now there is no help for it: I have taken upon myself this mission."

Clearly the decision to be a man of religion and not of art took place very early in him—too early to be a decision— before there was any formal resistance or contrary impulse; and of course that decision was repeated rigorously again and again throughout his life. But I think one can detect in his rich metaphors the raw material for that other, aesthetic, impulse. One of the very few glimpses we get of any esemplastic drive in Gandhi is an episode of 1921, recorded by Krishnadas. Gandhi called out to his secretary to come and admire something he had written: "Krishnadas, see what a beautiful article I have written! It is indeed a piece of beauty! See how I have described the condition of present-day India." It was an article entitled "Death-Dance," and it ended:

The Councillors want their fares and extras, the ministers their salaries, the lawyers their fees, the suitors their decrees, the parents such education for their boys as would give them status in the present life, the millionaires want facilities for multiplying their millions, and the rest their unmanly peace. The whole revolves beautifully around the central corporation. It is a giddy dance from which no one cares to free himself, and so, as the speed increases, the exhilaration is the greater. But it is a death-dance, and the exhilaration is induced by the heartbeat of a patient who is about to expire.

There the brilliance of the execution and even more the euphoria that accompanied it surely announce what we call the artist.

But the challenge of the Mahatma is that he turned away from that aesthetic option so completely. (The case of Tolstoy is of course even more dramatic, but the two are so different in their dimensions that it seems best to describe and analyze each separately.) Gandhi attracted poets and men of sensibility to him. They formed one of the main groups among his disciples and coworkers. But he was always calling on them to be more than poets.

An interesting case is Mahadev Desai, long his principal secretary, whom he saw as a poet, meaning, among other things, that he was hypersensitive and fragile. Thus he wrote to Esther Ferring in 1919, "I felt keenly for you and poor Mahadev. Both of you are so sensitive, almost cast in the same mold." He says he almost shuddered to see Mahadev in a situation of stress. He had taken Desai on in 1918 (indeed, Gandhi took the initiative and summoned the young man, whom he had only just met, to work for him). The letter he wrote him on that occasion shows something of what Gandhi meant by "poet":

> You are extremely pliant, and this I point out not as a merit in you, but as a defect. You succumb completely to the atmosphere around you. You do not display the mettle to resist and rise above a debasing environment. . . . You are like a painter who cannot help depicting obscenity in his portrait, if he chanced to see an indecent scene. Instead of completely detaching yourself from an unclean surrounding, you take an interest in it, are even tickled at it.

And we gather from other biographical sources that Mahadev was indeed an attractive, warm, responsive, somewhat unstable personality, often seduced or on the point of it, literally and metaphorically. He replied to Gandhi, he tells us, that though he always knew the close relationship between art and ethics, it was his nature to enjoy unhealthy literature for the sake of its attractive style or its gripping subject matter. The two of them took it as a joint task to save Mahadev from being merely a poet, Gandhi himself having long before turned away from that option in his own fate.

Curiously enough, there is a parallel in Gandhi's attitude to science and technology. He saw himself as called and attracted in that direction as well as to the arts. In 1918 he said to Desai that it was *his* nature always to look at structures and machines—they had just boarded a train—and to see how they worked and how they might be improved; that he might have been an engineer. And his disciple, J. C. Kumarappa, tells a story of Gandhi acting as doctor in 1938, which illustrates his "scientific" character quite vividly. Kumarappa had high blood pressure, of which the Bombay doctors could tell him only that it must be caused by nervous strain. Gandhi had him engage in a fifteen-minute discussion of various difficulties that were exercising him, and had his blood pressure taken before and after; there was a fifteen-point rise. Then he had him do a piece of carpentry, with the same measurements of blood pressure; there was a twenty-point rise. And then a furlong run, which resulted in a fifteen-point fall. With that evidence before him, he prescribed that Kumarappa should work until 11 or 12 A.M., each day, but should then relax for two hours, and should do a lot of walking. The whole procedure, clearly, is scientific. Indeed, Gandhi's many writings on diet and health are full of percentages and tables, and use the scientific vocabulary of carbohydrates and fats, vitamins, acids and alkalis, and so on.

It is, moreover, notable how much use he made of the image of the satyagrahi as a sort of scientist. The title of his autobiography, *Experiments with Truth,* is most seriously meant, and he consistently invoked the standards and methods of the scientist as a model for his coworkers: "A scientific experimenter has profound confidence in himself and is therefore never downhearted. At the same time he is so humble that he is never satisfied with his own work, and is not guilty of drawing hasty conclusions. . . . Our workers are generally lacking in this humility of the real man of science" (1932).

Thus we should take more seriously than we otherwise might his general use of scientific images, such as this of 1937:

An infinitesimal fraction of godhead, when it becomes active within us, can work wonders. The sun in the heavens fills the whole universe with its life-giving warmth. But if one went too near it, it would consume him to ashes. . . . Nonviolence is like the radium in its action. An infinitesimal quantity of it, imbedded in a malignant growth, acts continuously, silently, and ceaselessly, until it has transformed the whole mass of the diseased tissue into a healthy one.

Among Gandhi's followers there was considerable work on the spinning wheel, on diet, on agricultural methods. We might mention Maganlal Gandhi, Maurice Frydman, and C. Dasgupta as examples. But the theoretical side of Gandhian science was the province of J. C. Kumarappa, whose *Science and Progress* is a very interesting little book in a rather Orwellian manner. Pyarelal, often the closest to Gandhi in intellectual style among his followers, has referred to Tolstoy as the Einstein of Atman, Thoreau as its Bohr or Fermi, and Gandhi as its Oppenheimer. And the fact that Vinoba is a mathematician is an important part of his intellectual identity. In clarity and energy of thought, in all we tend to call "pure mind," he stands beyond Gandhi himself.

So there is no obscurantism in the depths of Gandhi's attitude to the arts and sciences. (Nor is there in Tolstoy's

depths, I believe, but that would be harder to demonstrate.)
I would not claim that their *policies* toward the arts and
sciences cannot be called obscurantist, but those policies
derive from the special features of modern art and science,
and from the special circumstances of the Western political
and religious crisis. (The same sense of both can be found
in Susan Sontag, as we have seen.) Setting those special
circumstances aside, the arts and sciences are recognizably
the natural "living space" for both Mahatmas' minds.

In Gandhi's attitude to Nature, moreover, there was
something of both scientific and artistic practice—together
with something of mystical religion. As V. Y. Kontali says,
"A peculiar mystique of Nature informed Gandhi's experiments in health." His use of sunbaths, homeopathic cures,
mudpacks, water-treatments, and so forth, all aimed at re-
capturing a consonance with the base rhythms of nature.
Here one sees a difference between him and Tolstoy, who
made a cult of Nature in his unregenerate days, but after his
conversion aimed merely at simplifying his demands. His
life became in one sense more natural thereby, but his identification with Nature was over, because Tolstoy's cult of
Nature had carried with it an intensified and excited consciousness of his own physique and personal strength, a
consciousness he later sought to reduce. In this as in many
matters, Gandhi developed and harmonized the ideas they
shared. The contrast is between Tolstoy hanging upside
down from his parallel bars every morning, developing his
body as the medium of a hypertrophied self, and Gandhi
lying on his cot in the sun and being massaged, recharging
his physical machine.

There seems to be a similar contrast between their two
attitudes to science. The unregenerate Tolstoy, though not
much interested in "hard" science, was certainly infected
by the scientific or scientistic enthusiasms of his age. As
examples of that infection, we might cite the reductive

rationalism of his approach to religion—and to art; his analysis of history in terms like "parallelogram of forces" and "differential of history"; his Benjamin Franklin notebooks, with the projects of self-improvement they contained; and the dividing up of his day into hours, each with its assigned activity and virtue. But after his conversion he was mostly concerned to warn people against science, and certainly did not incorporate scientism into his program and style, as Gandhi did.

But both art and science were acceptable to Gandhi only in subdued and limited forms, subdued to larger purposes, and at all times quiet. We can find an interesting case of how this applied to literary style in Chandrashaklar Shukla's remarks, introducing a book in 1951:

> The reader will forgive me if he finds the style of this book to be "insipid." Gandhiji insisted on understatement, avoidance of adjectives, and what he termed "delicacy" in writing. . . . In February, 1947 . . . he administered to me a withering rebuke for . . . what he called a "declamation," and for having in that letter used the adjective "brilliant" in respect of an article of Shri Jawarhalal Nehru, which he considered to be a "certificate" I had given to Jawarhalalji.

Similarly, and in the same year, Vinoba praised his coworker Mashruwala's style as "savorless-clear." He meant that it was like the cotton plant (symbolic to Indians for its clear and juiceless fibers). Mashruwala's style, Vinoba says, has, like cotton, fiber without juice; this is a pun, for guna (the word for fiber) can also mean quality, and rasa (the word for juice) can also mean passion. Guna without rasa is the ideal Gandhian style.

As for the other arts, Gandhi was, as already indicated, interested mostly in architecture and all that goes with it, decoration and furniture, and his taste favored folk tradition and local materials. He persuaded Nandalal Bose, a teacher of art at Tagore's Shantiniketan, to take charge of the buildings erected for various Congress meetings, and was very appreciative and commendatory of what he did. For instance, at the Lucknow Congress of 1936, he urged the delegates, "Go and see how the soul of man, even in an impoverished body, can breathe life into lifeless horns and metals. . . ." He was referring to an exhibition of local crafts Bose had arranged. "The exhibition is thus not a spectacular show, but a kind of fairyland. But our tastes have been so debased that the miracles happening before our very eyes appear like so much dust or clay, and mere trifles coming from abroad become exquisite works of art. . . . I should like to spend weeks at the exhibition and fill my soul with the atmosphere of the past." And at the Gauhati Congress he praised Bose's use of local materials: "Assam bamboo, Assam mud, Assam straw, Assam khaddar and Assam labor were responsible for the very simple but artistic huts erected. . . ."

Bose has some interesting reminiscences of Gandhi and describes the ashram and Gandhi's own hut: the floor and ceiling plastered with cow-dung; a mat in one corner with sheet and pillow for sitting or resting; a few packing cases of letters or files; another case covered with khaddar for a writing desk; a bottle of water; a bamboo basket; and a Gujarati lota with a cover of iron sheeting molded like a pipal leaf. "Is it not beautiful?" Gandhi said to him about the last, "It bears the impress of Nature; moreover a blacksmith of this very village has made it and given it to me as a token of his love. It is very precious to me." Bose adds that Gandhi himself, in his loincloth, looked like a sword of fine temper, kept unsheathed.

He said to Bose, "I know that I have earned notoriety as a philistine in art," and it is undeniable that he was the enemy of various freedoms that artists, especially those in the tradition of modernism, have claimed for themselves. On the other hand, he was not rabidly angry with, or destructive of, the arts. An anecdote that seems to be representative is told by Mulk Raj Anand, an Indian-writer-in-English who has written some quite modernist novels of Indian life, with a Marxist ideology. In 1929, in order to prepare himself to write his novel *Untouchable,* he went to Sabarmati to get Gandhi's advice. He was no Gandhian, so he declared himself immediately an atheist and a socialist, and refused to use Gandhi's term for the Untouchables, Harijans, on the grounds that Indian society did not grant them that status. Gandhi listened to his project, and said, "It is important to write about this question. But why not write a straightforward book attacking caste? The straight book is truthful and you can reform people by saying things frankly." Anand replied, "I wish to write a novel and not a propaganda tract. . . . Though I do want to reform people, I believe in posing the question, rather than answering it." Gandhi: "People are not likely to read your book in the English language—so it is for your own glory that you may wish to write this novel." Anand: "Perhaps you are right. Because in Europe the artist has tended to become a hero. But I have come to you because I wish to curb my egoism and learn from you to love the Untouchables. . . . Have I your permission to stay in the ashram?" And Gandhi replied, "You can stay . . . and we shall not be too hard on you." Having received something like a submission from the artist, something like a self-subordination of the claims of the aesthetic to the moral, Gandhi was tender rather than severe.

XII

TALK SIX

Teaching the Literature of Empire

I HAVE SOMETIMES said that the Gandhian cultural criticism I'm interested in would be only another kind of Brahminism—"being a good Brahmin." Naturally, I really mean it to be more than that. I could not claim it to be what Gandhi implicitly asks of us, and so I exaggerated and said that it amounted to a rejection of his calling. But in fact I believe it to be something between a rejection and an obedience—a reinterpretation of that calling in the light of other beliefs and knowledge to which Gandhi had no access, and a response that I expect, in some ideal sense, Gandhi to approve.

This response is teaching the literature of empire, for the other Gandhian activities to be added to that must necessarily be subordinate to it in the plan of the critic's life work. The basic idea is obvious enough: to look at what has been written in English to see what it has to say about the imperialist enterprise of its times, what it has to say through its forms as well as through its content. It seems that the major category of what has been written is the tale of adventure— adventure meaning challenges, encountered in environs remote from civilization or at least domesticity, in meeting which the hero defines or achieves his manhood, that is, his courage, resource, endurance, force. We will of course look for forms of adventure, and of manhood, appropriate to the modern world system, as distinct from those appropriate to feudalism and to other forms of imperialism.

But the adventure form is the crucial criterion, as opposed to the subject-matter of empire, whether that is present as setting or as theme. The latter has been more evident in the serious literature that sets out to be antiimperialist—take perhaps the most distinguished example, E. M. Forster's *Passage to India*. In the books that carry the myth of imperialism, the facts of empire are likely to be disguised or displaced. And these books are also likely to occupy a lowly place in most histories of the novel. But from my point of view they are vital parts of that history, because these are the tales English book-buyers wanted to hear told; the tales England told itself, to generate the courage needed for the imperialist adventure. The writing of them was one major force in the dialectic of the novel's career, and even those writers who set themselves in opposition to that force, who set themselves to produce opposite kinds of books, were still conditioned by it, and dependent on it, insofar as they were phenomena of "literature." To teach literature by concentrating exclusively on the "serious books" is in some ways a distortion of the subject—and an evasion of the truth—for "literature" is a dialectical phenomenon.

It is well known that we do find a major development in

fiction in seventeenth-century England, as the modern world system makes itself felt as altering the conditions of life in England, and that our subject first assumes major proportions in the work of Defoe. His very realistic narratives of adventure—I'm thinking of *Robinson Crusoe* and *Captain Singleton* primarily—render into myth the prudent, rational, trading spirit of the system Wallerstein describes. *Crusoe* stands in the same relation to modern empire as the chivalric romances, like that of *Amadis de Gaul*, stood to the premodern imperialism of Cortes and his Conquistadores. Wallerstein tells us that the modern world system began when the center of Europe's power moved from Seville and Madrid to Amsterdam and London. The literary and imaginative equivalent of that political and economic fact is the movement of fiction from the style of *Amadis de Gaul* to the style of Defoe. Behind the chivalric romance stood the knightly and Christian heroics of the Reconquista of Spain from the Moors; behind Defoe stood the trading and exploring voyages so painstakingly recorded in the collections of Hakluyt and Purchas. And ahead of Defoe's work, pointing the way for innumerable future writers, stood the figurehead of Crusoe, all do-it-yourself homeliness, as opposed to the fanciful extravagance of Amadis.

Well, there is nothing new in saying that Defoe is an important initiatory figure in our literary history. Perhaps I should do better to talk about a crucial choice to be made between *Robinson Crusoe* and *The Tempest* as myths of imperialism. (Defoe and Shakespeare both drew on the same source, the early history of Bermuda.) Quite a lot has been written about *The Tempest* from this point of view over the last twenty years, by literary critics but also by historians and psychologists. Caliban can obviously be taken as representing the indigenous race—and seen, therefore, as ugly and primitive—from the point of view of the paternalist Prospero, whose magic represents European know-how;

Caliban's attempted rape of Miranda represents the typical mythic fear of the oppressed race; Miranda's cry "O brave new world, that has such creatures in it" is ironically related to the men she sees, who are the dregs of the old world, exploiters, who make Caliban drunk and incite him to colonial rebellion; Prospero is typical of colonial administrators, in his jealous clinging to power—his reluctance to let Miranda or Ariel go—and in surrounding himself with subordinates and dependents and half-men; and so on. You can find this analysis in Leslie Fiedler, Leo Marx, and Frank Kermode, in Mannoni, a French psychiatrist writing about Madagascar, in Franz Fanon, in Aimé Césaire, who has re-written the play, in George Lamming, a West Indian writer who identifies himself with Caliban, and most interestingly in Philip Mason, a retired administrator of India, who frankly accepts the identification of men like himself with Prospero.

I have no objection to any of those interpretations on their own terms, but I do object to the terms, or at least I want to change them. I think there is a much more interesting meaning of myth, and that, applying that meaning, we shall find *Robinson Crusoe* rather than *The Tempest* to be the true myth of imperialism. (In formal terms, following Frye's scheme, *Robinson Crusoe* is not a myth but a romance. But Frye admits that romance always projects the values of the contemporary ruling class in ideal form, so romance is the form in literary terms whose content is myth in the social sense.) Crusoe ends as *mock* governor of his island. He pretends to be governor, and to have official forces at his disposal, in order to bluff the mutineers who land there. But he is only playing at it—Defoe could not ask us to identify with a real governor, like Prospero, much less with a magician—for when we take Crusoe most seriously is when we see him coping with the practical problems of solitary life, when we see him rebuilding by hand, in reason and prudence, all European technology, and thus proving himself worthy to be its heir and incarnation.

This is not only a different myth, but a different sense of myth, because it is energizing. To respond to *Robinson Crusoe* as Defoe intends us to is to want to go out and do likewise—prove ourselves worthy to be the heirs and incarnations of European technology and, as such, worthy to rule subject peoples. *The Tempest* is not energizing in that way. It is purely imaginative, purely literary, static and not kinetic, in the terms of Stephen Dedalus' aesthetics.

In *Regeneration through Violence* Slotkin describes three stages of development a myth goes through. The first is when it is full of energizing social meaning, what I have just described of *Crusoe*. The second or romantic stage is when it has become a literary formula that artists can elaborate in various ways, its social meaning being respected but not deeply or energetically responded to. Slotkin's example of this is Longfellow's "Hiawatha." (In the case of the Crusoe myth there were hundreds of adaptations; I'll just mention Marryatt's *Masterman Ready* [1841] and Ballantyne's *Coral Island* [1858].) And the third, the consummatory stage, as Slotkin calls it, is when a great artist renews a myth by taking it with full imaginative seriousness again, but transvalues it. His example is Joyce's *Ulysses*, and he points out that such versions of myth have no socially energizing power. In the case of *Robinson Crusoe*, one might point to Golding's *Lord of the Flies*, except that Golding is far from being a great artist. But he does renew the story by transvaluing it. (*Lord of the Flies* retells *Coral Island*, which retells *Robinson Crusoe*.)

My point is that *The Tempest* is a myth in its consummatory stage, and that is the kind of myth toward which men of letters have directed their attention—no doubt because, by Slotkin's theory, writers can renew a myth by literary means. (It is of course a paradox that the play should have appeared *before Robinson Crusoe*—when there was nothing to consummate—but then literary history is full of such paradoxes, like Sterne's appearing *before* many great traditional novelists.) Consummatory is probably not the right word, if no writer, however great, can renew a myth in its social vigor, only in its literary charm—but that is Slotkin's responsibility, not mine.

Obviously I cannot afford to go into detail about myth, or Defoe, or anything else, here. I shall have to make my points, or statements of intention, quite schematically. A Gandhian critic would read literature looking for its energizing myths as well as for quality in writing. And the main such myth he would find embodied in what is called the adventure story. The adventure story, by means of its landscape, its language, its hero, his antagonists, its hierarchy of other characters, shaped men's imaginations and sent them out on the adventure of imperialism. And if these are the books such a critic will study, his reading will differ from ours in two ways. One, it will not focus on the Great Tradition. Two, it will include many books barely mentioned even in the big histories of literature.

To develop the first point for just a moment, consider Jane Austen, George Eliot, Henry James, D. H. Lawrence—in none of these authors' works do either adventure or imperialism figure. And we find adventure only marginally in Hardy or Dickens. You could read those authors and barely know that England *had* an empire. You certainly wouldn't know it if you read them in a Great Tradition way. There is a split in the literature and the consciousness of the modern world system, which the criticism follows. Everything on the Great Tradition side of the split is in resistance to adventure and imperialism, because they are on the other side, and part of the resistance is a silent ignoring of them.

Here is a mid-nineteenth century American definition of the split, which I came across recently:

> There are those who rejoice in our Anglo-Saxon inheritance of the love of conquest, and the desire for boundless territory—who exult in the "manifest destiny" of the race, to plant the standard of the eagle, or the lion, in every soil, and every zone of the earth's surface. We rejoice much more in the love of country life, the enjoyment of nature, and the taste for rural beauty, which we also inherit from our Anglo-Saxon forefathers, and to which, more than all else, they owe so many of the peculiar virtues of the race.

If we add, by no extravagant extrapolation, the virtues of love and marriage and children and domesticity to the love of country life, then we have a fair description of the value-bearing subject matter of the Great Tradition. The split between that and the adventure myth that teaches the other Anglo-Saxon virtues means that the Gandhian critic would not only teach different books, but would have a different view of literary history as a whole. The Great Tradition would now look, in an honorable sense, reactionary.

As for the second point—that the new books are only briefly mentioned even in inclusive histories of literature—that means that the Gandhian critic would deal with the phenomena of popular literature and boys' literature, which means that he must develop new methods of study. I do not need to argue that it is in such books that energizing myths are always transmitted. The books an English department normally studies at best *deal with* social myths. And the methods by which we study—linguistic analysis, historical comparison—sterilize myth. It is popular books and children's books—or any books read as if they were popular—that carry the great subliminal messages of culture. So the Gandhian critic must deal also with the problems of reading they bring. It is not appropriate to bear down on such texts in the way one does on *Middlemarch* or *Women in Love*. But it is appropriate to study publication and distribution figures, author incomes and careers, translations and adaptations, reputations and testimonies of response to them. Out of such techniques must be developed a somewhat new way to read.

Among other authors we should of course read Kipling and Conrad, and we should find reason to change the division of respect and enthusiasm customarily made between the two, as between other such pairs of authors, when looked at from this point of view. After Kipling, after 1918, the adventure myth became barely viable in England, but that did not mean that the theme of empire was unimportant in the period to follow. It became important satirically. (This was a transition from the mode of romance to that of satire, as Frye defines those—from Summer to Winter.) Somerset Maugham was, in terms of popularity and subject matter, the Kipling of the 1920s and 1930s, an immensely popular writer read by the middle-class public, who wrote about imperial locations and types, but wrote cynically about them. (In fact, the contrast between him and Kipling is not simply a contrast between cynicism and enthusiasm, but it was seen that way at the time.) It is not many steps in mood or in story material from Maugham to Graham Greene; as soon as we put those two authors together in our minds we see how immediately that mood derives from, and finds an objective correlative in, the decay of empire. That is their value-bearing subject matter. Decaying imperial places, degenerating imperialist types, provide the material for much of their work, and indeed for a lot of quite brilliant work by Evelyn Waugh, Anthony Burgess, George Orwell, Joyce Cary, and others. In them we see the myth of adventure and of empire turned back upon itself in self-destruction.

But the range from Defoe to Kipling corresponds to the expansive history of the British empire, and we should find that many novelists writing in that period, besides those

obviously in the Defoe tradition, wrote out of the consciousness of empire in some degree. We should find, for instance,
that that immensely popular form, the historical novel as
popularized by Scott, is a disguised form of imperialist
adventure. That genre works essentially by contrasting two
cultures, which are characterized as being at different stages
of development. To the more primitive culture are allotted
all the traits of personal nobility, of epic adventure, of elevated speech, passion, loyalty, poetry. To the more advanced
culture go the virtues of prudence, responsibility, calcula-
tion, justice, and commercial viability—imaginatively a
much more meager style, but historically the style destined
to triumph. Waverley, representing the more advanced commercial culture of Hanoverian England, encounters the
splendors and miseries of the Highland clansmen in the
Stuart rising in 1745, recognizes their superiority, acquires
something of their virtue, and returns to modernity personally benefited. And the reader of such novels repeats that
experience in reading about it.

One might describe the development of the adventure
story in Scott's hands as the substitution of a historical axis
for the geographical axis it had in Defoe's hands. The representative of European civilization is confronted by "the
other," by contrastive forms of personal and social organization, doomed to defeat at his hands. This time "the other"
is defined as belonging to the past of his own race instead of
to other races in the present. (It is an incidental but very
important point that history and geography themselves, as
disciplines taught in school, bear the imprint of this myth—
as I can remember from what I was taught in school.)
Because of that stress on the past, there is in Scott much
more use of literary epic and romance, much more reference
to Homer and Shakespeare, as ways to define "the other." In
Fenimore Cooper you get some reversion to the Defoe
model. Natty Bumppo is, like Crusoe, a do-it-yourself hero,

and the books express more anxiety about the fate of the Indians, so that they feel more contemporary than Scott's do. But by and large Cooper followed Scott's pattern, as of course a dozen other novelists did in nineteenth-century England, America, France, Italy, Russia, and other countries.

As one last example of the development and transformations of the adventure myth, let me offer Twain and the humorous novel. In *A Connecticut Yankee in King Arthur's Court* the axis of subject matter is rotated yet again, away from history into satire. The Yankee as hero is easily recognizable as a version of Crusoe—indeed, he compares himself to Crusoe—while King Arthur's England is a satirical version of Malory and the other adventure myths of medieval chivalry, though it is also —at least the ending suggests this—a version of those primitive African kingdoms just then being modernized by explorer-administrators like Stanley. Stanley had appeared on the same lecture platforms with Twain, but he was a man of action, and had gone on to subdue a giant kingdom in Africa for King Leopold of the Belgians—for such purposes as to build a railway linking the loops of the Congo River and thus make it a navigable artery of commerce. But the Congo Free State became an international scandal at the end of the nineteenth century, a case onto which everyone agreed to discharge the increasing uneasiness over what *all* the European countries—England and France as well as Belgium—were doing in Africa. Through most of *Connecticut Yankee* Twain is of course wholly on the side of the Yankee and modernization. He is rendering in humorous form just the same energizing myth as Scott in historical form and Defoe in what I called the geographical. The case is particularly interesting because Twain's conscious motive was to refute Scott's romanticism about the past—which shows how spacious the myth was, how much room it included for variety and difference. And it is above all interesting because in the last part of the book the myth suddenly becomes disgusting to the narrator, its values are all horribly distorted, its hero and narrative tone retrospectively repudiated. Twain could no longer believe in adventure or empire, and so could no longer delight in the thought of modernizing a primitive culture.

That's all the time I can afford to devote to the books and their interpretation. I want to pass on to the argument that this topic, "the literature of empire," is the natural successor to the topic that so long sustained the work of Leavis and *Scrutiny* and those critics like Raymond Williams who in some sense developed Leavis' work. Their topic, I suggest, could be labeled "the literature of the people," for their concern was to rescue English literature for the people as a whole—seen as predominantly a rural and working-class people—from the clutches of the rich and socially privileged. The latter, as I've said before, always tend to absorb the country's literature as a class privilege or luxury, and also tend to fall prey to sophistication or perversity of taste. Literature, Leavis says in his most recent book, is a crystallization of language, and language is a creation of the people —an immemorial human collaborative creativity—and even the poets themselves can claim only a participatory right of property in it.

A characteristic activity of critics of this school was teaching in adult education, in Workers' Education or University Extension classes, bringing the classics of English literature to those who might otherwise never meet them—who might otherwise feel them to be the cultural property of the ruling class—and conversely bringing the challenge of those students' life experience to bear on the books generally given the status of classics. That was the social-political situation that implicitly surrounded and supported the literary criticism of that school, and gave their criticism an exhilarating extension of reference without adulterating its quality as criticism. Like any other idea, however, the idea of this school had a natural lifespan, after which it ceased to develop and bear fruit in readers' minds. For some time now, in my judgment, the criticism written from out of that implicit situation has been unexciting, and its extended reference has seemed theoretical. It is difficult to resist the judgment that the working-class reader these critics write for is no longer there—or no longer to be reached by them. If he is still there, then the obstacles between him and these critics are now so much subtler, so recalcitrant to their persuasions, that they amount to a resistance in him.

The natural successor to that social situation, I want to suggest, is the situation of the young immigrants in England today, many of them industrious and upwardly mobile as the native working class was in the nineteenth century, and most of them bewildered or bored by—generally out of touch with—the great monuments of culture referred to on official occasions. These are the people one sees in the public libraries nowadays, the hand reaching up for those large books, so familiar to us, so strange to them. And if they are to constitute our social situation, the extended reference of the Gandhian critic's writing, then our topic must be the part played by empire and adventure in England's development and England's literature.

Those novels will tell the immigrants, who are the hope of England now, the story of how they come to be where they are. That story is told, mythically told, from the native Englishman's point of view. But if the novels are discussed from this Gandhian point of view, sympathetic both to the novels and to these readers, then it will be clear why the process of colonization and imperialism looked to Englishmen as it did. And indeed, many of the authors of these stories, like Captain Marryatt and Captain Mayne Reid, were courageous liberals who risked their lives for others' freedom more than once. I would not expect immigrants wholly to like the England they would see revealed in these books. But then, liking England is hardly in question now. They could come to understand it better this way than by reading *Middlemarch.*

But the situation I foresee is not one of immigrant readers exclusively. Native Englishmen would read these books together with the immigrants and would discover, from the books and from the others' responses, how different the adventure looked to those among whom the English went adventuring. And besides this obvious moral-political point, there will be the literary point of discovering all these new books, and the new contours that the literature of each century will take on when seen from this point of entry.

The possession of empire made itself felt in so many ways, often quite implicitly, in the margin of freedom surrounding the life styles of almost all Englishmen, because one could always go to the colonies if one found England cramping. (One could always teach the English language, for instance.) And a charge of exhilaration must have touched almost every Englishman at some point, at the thought of how, in those colonies, he would be a lord, by birthright of being English. Stories like the military triumph of Clive's handful against enormous odds in India, and even more those of Cortes' incredible exploits in Mexico, were extraordinary myths as well as facts. Such stories burn deep into people's minds, European as well as colonial, and ever since 1600 Europeans have felt—could not but feel—that they were worth ten black men, that they were ten times as manly. That is the feeling that has to be faced and explored today, as class feeling had to be faced two generations ago in England. It is not explored by talking about racial prejudice.

Finally, it is worth realizing that Tolstoy and Gandhi themselves were powerfully affected by the adventure story and imperialist history. Like their feeling for the arts and sciences, their feeling for adventure makes their recoil from it more interesting and impressive. Tolstoy read *Robinson Crusoe* and listed Prescott's *Conquest of Mexico* among the powerful influences on his youth. His relation to that myth passed through a series of stages, typical of Tolstoy in many ways, beginning with a powerful identification, followed by an opting for an alternative, and finally an espousing of the opposite. Gandhi, also typically, apprenticed himself to those values, but transvalued them.

Tolstoy's first novel, after the autobiographical narratives of *Childhood, Boyhood, and Youth*, was *The Cossacks*, which is an adventure story of the pattern that combined Scott with Cooper. Olenin, an overcivilized young man like Waverley, leaves Moscow for the Caucasus, where he is involved in the war waged by the Cossacks, on imperial Russia's behalf, against the tribes on that border. Just like Waverley, he participates in a more primitive life, encounters the heroic and the epic in the character and customs of the Cossacks, in their modes of love and war, and returns to civilization renewed in manhood. He is complex, they are simple. He and his kind are bound to win, bound to inherit the earth. But they are larger, nobler, grander human possibilities.

Tolstoy wrote other stories in that vein, many of which could have been written by Kipling himself. One of them was *Hadji Murad*, a marvelous story published only posthumously and probably finished not long before his death. But of course long before that he had turned away from the adventure novel to the novel of marriage and domesticity. That, after all, is the ethical scheme of *War and Peace*, a contrast between the false heroics of Napoleon and the true values of the love between Natasha and Pierre and the children to be born to them. (Perhaps one should say that the ultimate contrast to Napoleon is Karataev, but Pierre is said somehow to combine the values of Karataev with those of Natasha.) The same is true of the contrast in *Anna Karenina*. Levin and Kitty succeed while Vronsky and Anna fail because the first pair have chosen the values of domesticity and country life—the values set in opposition to those of adventure in that passage I quoted. By what I have called the dialectic of literature, the two great serious novels seem to be antithetical to the tales of adventure, but to Tolstoy, once he stepped outside that dialectic, both genres seemed twin fruits of the same tree. They were all novels.

It is of interest to note that, biographically, Tolstoy may be said to have become a major novelist by grace of his marriage. I mean that his wife devoted herself quite extraordinarily to his writing. She organized family life to make it possible; she participated in the writing, copying, and criticizing; and it was her story, her sister's and family's story, that Tolstoy embodied in Natasha and the Rostovs. Indeed, she regarded the idea and experience of family love as hers, and not his—it is a case, in other words, quite like Frieda and Lawrence. And therefore, when Tolstoy began to withdraw from that phase of his career, Sonya felt abandoned and betrayed. Their marriage depended on his being a novelist, just as his novels depended on his being a married man.

But as we know, Tolstoy came to feel that marriage and novels both were a sad mistake, that they stood together with imperialism and adventure; those two options complemented each other rather than stood in opposition to each other. He passed on to the third stage of his career, spirituality. In stories like "The Death of Ivan Ilyich" and novels like *Resurrection* you find the condemnation and rejection of everything that began with *The Cossacks*.

As for Gandhi, he was not a reader of novels, much less a writer of them, but of course he was sensitive to the ideals of adventure and to the values borne by that myth, which were in the air around him. Take an image like this, from an article of 1920: "How much stronger must be the lungs of that man who scales a peak of the Himalayas without a stick or a carrier than of one who has to depend upon either? When the former reaches the top he will laugh aloud at the whole of India. . . ." And he defended fasting, sometimes, by a comparison between that and making an expedition to the North Pole. He made his body into a kind of Inner Space, a microcosm in which he could stage displays of heroism that mirrored in purer form the dramas of the great world; indeed, he did the same for the life style of the satyagrahi, so quiet and yet so intense. He was zealous for personal and national honor, saying that the humiliation of the Indians at Amritsar—their being forced to crawl where an Englishwoman had been attacked—was much worse than their being shot and killed.

For him those values crystallized in the idea of manliness. At school he formed an admiring friendship with the Muslim Sheikh Mehtab, who embodied manliness much more successfully than Gandhi, and who persuaded him to eat meat, and to go to a brothel, and to be unfaithful to his wife. These were all major means of acquiring manliness. And this was quite specifically linked to the cultural and political dominance of the English, for there was a Gujarati poem (which Gandhi cites in explaining all this) saying something like:

> See the mighty Englishman
> Who stands five cubits tall
> Because by eating meat
> He rules the Indian small.

And so Gandhi set himself to acquire the strengths of manliness, but soon repented and rebelled, and found even legal marriage too deeply tainted with animal lust. He devoted himself to spirituality and found happiness therein.

But he still held by a transvalued version of the English manly adventure ideal. He always recommended manliness, courage, duty, and so on, and even such specifically nineteenth-century English components of manliness as cold baths, early rising, punctuality, frugality, daily accounts, keeping a diary, and so on. Just before the struggle of 1931 he said, "No one will accuse me of any anti-English tendency. I have thankfully copied many things from them. Punctuality, reticence, public hygiene, independent thinking and exercise of judgment, and several other things I owe to my association with them." And Lloyd and Suzanne Rudolph have pointed out how similar Gandhi's daily schedule, and his list of virtues, was to Ben Franklin's. (Incidentally, Tolstoy's early diaries are full of such lists and schedules. And you may remember the fun D. H. Lawrence has with Franklin's virtue of humility, with its direction, "Imitate Jesus and Socrates." But that is exactly what Gandhi and Tolstoy did, and told others to do, as flatly as that.)

In South Africa Gandhi recommended to his followers Samuel Smiles' books, *Character*, *Duty*, and *Self-Help*, classics of modern world system morality. And Pyarelal's biography begins with a quotation from Kipling's "If," and a long exposition of how Gandhi corresponded, point for point, with that idea of character:

"If the poet had had for his pattern the man whom it was my privilege to serve and follow till the end of his days, the picture could not have been truer to life. Calm in the midst of storm, awake when others were lulled into false security . . . by the alchemy of his detachment he transmuted his anguish into a relentless drive for self-denial, self-purification, and self-surrender. . . . His iron will made every faculty of his body and mind obey its least command as an expert horseman does the animal under him."

In all such ways it was Gandhi who inherited Kipling's mantle. It was Indians who were taught the Kipling virtues in the generation when in England everyone was unlearning them, while Joseph Doke's admirable biography of Gandhi, the very first and written with Gandhi's cooperation, was to have been entitled *The Pathfinder* or *The Jungle-Breaker*, assimilating him to figures like Stanley, only transvalued.

Thus the values of the adventure myth and the myth of imperialism are intricately entangled with the values of spirituality, and to study English literature from this point of view—and in the sociopolitical situation I have described—could be an enterprise worthy of Gandhi's blessing.

XIII

Romain Rolland

and the Mahatmas

To BE A BRAHMIN, to aim at being a good Brahmin, was the fate most of my audience saw before them—more than their fate, their dharma. So what could be more instructive to consider than the case of a man of letters who was converted to, and then turned or fell away from, each of the Mahatmas in turn?

Romain Rolland (1866–1944) was one of those naturally Gandhian temperaments I described before, averse from all violence, averse, largely, from the body, concentrated in the mind, devoted to the spirit. In a letter of Nov. 13/14, 1889, to his mother (to whom he was unusually close, emotionally and spiritually), he says:

Pour les gens timides et concentrés comme moi, il est tout-à-fait nécessaire d'être seuls, pour sentir franchement et complètement; je ne me livre qu'à moi-même; c'est pour cela que mes lettres sont si souvent enthousiastes, et mes paroles, en général, si froides. Tout au plus, quand je parle, j'exprime aux autres le sens de mes idées;

jamais je ne dis qu'à moi-même, dans mes notes ou dans mes lettres, les véritables émotions que j'éprouve; encore un reste de honte m'empêche-t-il de les écrire souvent . . . for timid and concentrated men like me, it is absolutely necessary to be alone, in order freely and completely to feel; I can express myself only to myself; that is why my letters are so often enthusiastic, and my speech, often, so cold. When I am talking I at best convey to others the sense of my ideas; I never say, except to myself, in notes or in letters, what I am actually feeling; often a residue of shame prevents me from even writing them down.

(A self-description that suggests also the characteristic weakness of his books—the overemotionalism, the inauthentic organ-voice that comes from confusing the private with the public arenas of speech.) Physically not strong and emotionally not robust, his tastes were austere and ascetic. He attached himself, in imagination, to the great men of culture, wrote lives of such as Tolstoy, Beethoven, Michelangelo, in compensation for feeling himself feeble. In all this he resembled Krishnadas or Shriman Narayan.

But if we turn from physical temperament to intellectual endowment, we find him highly privileged; his mind was trained at the summit of the highly hierarchical French intellectual system, at the Lycée Louis-le-Grand and the Ecole Normale Supérieure. He was given the training of the intellectual elite of the Third Republic, when the French cultural establishment was an empire of the mind, and though he rebelled against his class, remained recognizably a member. This was true even in his acts of self-submission to the Mahatmas.

Romain Rolland wrote to Tolstoy in 1887, while still a student at the Ecole Normale Supérieure. Tolstoy was for Rolland and his friends then both Europe's greatest novelist and their personal hero of thought. He belonged to them, and not to their elders, by his "terrible accusations of the lies of civilization," by his "savor of nature," by his "sense of invisible forces," and by his "vertigo in the face of the infinite." But Rolland was troubled, being greatly gifted in several branches of art and thought, by Tolstoy's call to people like himself to take up manual rather than intellectual work.

Tolstoy replied with an emotional greeting to a fellow-spirit, but also with a stern explanation that manual work was necessary because the great sin of their day's depraved society was that it had liberated itself from such tasks and relied on the slave labor of the poor. Men like Rolland could only prove the sincerity of their repudiation of that society by doing such work—in particular by serving their own bodily needs: "Je ne croirai jamais à la sincérité des convictions chrétiennes, philosophiques, ou humanitaires d'une personne qui fait vider son pot à chambre par une servante." (Rolland was to come under pressure on just this point from Gandhi thirty years later, though indirectly. He records indignantly in his journal the excretory and sexual disciplines that Gandhi imposed on Edmond Privat, Rolland's friend, when the latter visited the ashram.)

Works of culture, Tolstoy said, *may* be useful (though more likely they are harmful), whereas to carry the burden of a tired traveler, to plough a field for a sick peasant, and so on, these things *must* be useful. And one is only happy doing what is useful. Our society's men of culture are its privileged caste, like a priesthood. They represent, and rely on our faith in, a social priesthood, an established religion. And like all priesthoods, by that reliance they degrade the principles they stand for. So a man like Rolland *must* prove his sincerity by sacrificing his comfort and his well-being.

The religion of culture, Tolstoy said, is an impediment even to thought: "There is faith in religion, there is faith in our civilization. They are absolutely analogous. . . . A believer in civilization says 'my power to reason stops short at the revealed truths of civilization, science and art.'" But we, men like Tolstoy and Rolland, must question even science and art, must put ourselves in the position of a child or of Descartes, and ask what would really make us happy. Certainly not culture, or any other construct of human nature. The grimly paradoxical answer is that since our unhappiness derives from the fact that others will never love us more than they love themselves, we must create an unnatural order within which *we* love *others* more than ourselves.

As the year after 1887 went by, however, Rolland himself became a famous writer, famous especially for his novel-sequence, *Jean-Christophe*. He was a humanist in literary taste and disapproved of the incipient modernism of Rimbaud, Verlaine, and Mallarmé. He described their work and them as "un art stérile, une poèsie qui méprise la vie et s'en détourne, une humanité atrophiée et desséchée. . . ." Later, he was similarly to condemn Joyce and Proust—and to be reciprocally condemned by the latter, who became the great novelistic alternative to Rolland, the hero of literary modernism vs. the hero of literary humanism. But before 1914 Rolland reigned supreme—he was known as "le prince de la jeunesse." And besides being a novelist, he was a famous playwright and pamphleteer, a famous critic and scholar of music—in short, culture incarnate, one of the princes or cardinals of the European mind. He still admired Tolstoy, and after the latter's death in 1910 published a very admiring short biography, but he was clearly no longer a Tolstoyan. His ideas were by then more Goethean. "Il faut fonder un Weimar nouveau et agrandi, une patrie intellectuelle et morale où se crée enfin l'âme européenne," he wrote in 1901.

But the outbreak of war in 1914 reradicalized him. He lost faith in the European civilization that could turn to mutual slaughter with such enthusiasm. He became differently famous, as a pacifist and an antiimperialist. In 1914 he appealed to the artists and intellectuals of Europe to withdraw from all participation in the war, but in vain. He moved from France to Switzerland, and was of course much abused for doing so. And in 1915 he decided to make himself the spokesman for India, and for Asia in general, in Europe. He could find in the East, he thought, the contemplative truths that the West had sacrificed in its search for material power, and for lack of which the West was committing suicide.

Rolland's journal about India begins in 1915 with his receiving an offprint from Ananda Coomaraswamy, the Indian art critic, after which Rolland read the latter's two-volume work, *The Arts and Crafts of India and Ceylon*. After finishing these books, Rolland wrote in his journal, "Ma poitrine éclate. . . . Si 10 ou 20 ans de vie me sont encore accordés, je voudrais mener la pensée de ma race sur les hauts plâteaux du monde. . . . On meurt, quand on tient la clef qui ouvre la porte du jardin—du jardin d'où furent chassés Eve et Adam tout nus." But he was granted those twenty years, and he devoted them to doing all that high culture could do for India and, later, for the Mahatma.

Rolland and Thomas Mann (himself much concerned with Tolstoy) were perhaps Europe's two greatest Brahmins, or at least the greatest contemplatives among the European intellectuals, each one a university in himself. (England's best effort in that direction may have been Aldous Huxley, and his failure to make much of Gandhi, even during a visit to India in 1930, may perhaps be the measure of his inferiority to the other two.) They were "good Brahmins" in excelsis. And in Rolland's relations with Gandhi one sees how much a good Brahmin may achieve. It may be enough to aim at.

However, among Indian intellectuals it was Tagore whom Rolland first came to know and admire, and the alternation of the two figures in Rolland's favor is very interesting. Tagore was already famous for having won a Nobel Prize for Literature in 1913—the first one to be awarded to an Asian—but Rolland admired him also as a pacifist. In 1916 he read an account of Tagore's antimilitarist and anti-European speeches in Japan, and in 1919 Tagore signed Rolland's *Déclaration pour l'Indépendence de l'Espirit*. Rolland proposed to him their setting up a *Revue de l'Europe et d'Asie*. And in April 1921 Tagore arrived in Villeneuve to visit Rolland.

The latter noted in his journal, already with a certain irony, "He is extremely handsome—almost too much so," and "He has a little the look of a magus." He remarks, after a boat trip on the lake, "No need to say that he created a sensation. (With his long forked beard and his long white hair, he has the air of God the Father. One woman said she thought she'd seen our Lord come in.)" The two men discussed Gandhi, and with great admiration, but Rolland was then more inclined to find Tagore a brother spirit, rather than Gandhi. He was much struck by an aestheticism in the former that he recognized from the Upanishads as Indian, and found very sympathetic personally. He quotes the Taittiriya Upanishad as saying, "Revelation occurs in the aesthetic. . . . Salvation comes only in knowledge of the Brahma . . ." and, "The worst acts are annulled by the possession of true knowledge."

In 1922 he published his book, *Mahatma Gandhi*, in which he contrasted Gandhi with Tagore as an apostle contrasted with a sage, or as a St. Paul with a Plato, or as the genius of faith with that of intelligence. After quoting Tagore's criticisms of Gandhi he says, "Thus would speak an Indian Goethe," and he implies some agreement with Tagore's protest against Gandhi's antiaestheticism. He quotes Gandhi and adds, "Something here, some *sileat poeta*, justifies Tagore's fears." Moreover, Rolland was anxious about the lesser men, Gandhi's disciples, who would be given the power to impose Gandhian disciplines on others.

But by 1925 Rolland's sympathies had changed. He had a pessimistic sense of great world conflicts soon to come, and was moreover disillusioned by Tagore's undependability and vanity—his willingness to go anywhere that he would be applauded and listened to—which Rolland encountered in attempting to arrange official appearances for Tagore in Europe and to guide him in European politics. He detected more clearly, and judged more sharply, the fundamental antipathy Tagore felt for Gandhi, the antipathy of the free spirit, in love with all the forms of life (and to some degree, he adds, a dilettante), for the puritan, disciplining his followers into a militia ready for battle and sacrifice. He noted that Gandhi's indifference to suffering revolted Tagore to the point of making him unjust; and in general he began to separate himself from Tagore's judgments.

In 1926 he was shocked to hear Tagore defend Italian Fascism, for Rolland was already deeply committed to arousing world opinion against Mussolini. And he connected Tagore's political frivolity with a general diffuseness in his thought: "Always a bit diffuse, vague, lacking in precise facts, and complacently indulging himself in flights of rhetoric (he is an orator in his very soul, and feels, I fear, a need to speak, even more than to listen.) Discussion is difficult. He prefers long discourses, with no interruptions." Moreover, Rolland decided that Tagore was obsessed by the sides of Gandhi that he disliked. He was finding India an uncomfortable place, now that he was out of harmony with Gandhi. When he lectured there, he found the crowd icily silent, and felt that only his former prestige saved him from outright hostile demonstrations.

Rolland arranged for a liberal French journalist to interview Tagore, to give him the chance to condemn Fascism, and so undo the harm done by his participation in official events during his visit to Italy. But what Tagore said, in a statement he prepared for this purpose, was even worse. By this time Rolland was deeply irritated, and impatient, with him. "I love him tenderly," Rolland wrote. "I revere him; and yet (should I admit it?) there has not been one interview when I have not felt a devilish, irritated desire to jump up and walk out—to break the constraint of that solemn courtesy and that etiquette."

The journal makes it clear that Rolland was making his choice and was turning decisively to Gandhi. He wrote to the latter in 1926, "All self-love dies in your presence; because you have shown us how. And he who writes, like me, bows down before him who acts, like you." And he wrote to Mira Behn, "When one has the luck to find oneself facing the Holy Spirit, it would be really despicable to think about oneself and one's own vanity." Mira was in some sense Rolland's gift to Gandhi. Reading Rolland's book on Gandhi, she had turned herself toward *him*, and had gone to India and assumed a new identity there as Gandhi's disciple. (Several other Europeans were also led to Gandhi by Rolland's book.)

In 1928, after Rolland had ventured to disagree with Gandhi and to write critically of him, Gandhi became eager to come to Europe, to meet him. When he wrote proposing the journey, however, Rolland replied in agitation that so much effort would not be justified, merely to meet him. He was, he said, devoted to the cause of peace:

But I am not consecrated uniquely to the cause of peace and social action. I am, on the one hand, a religious man, in my own way, which is a free way. On the other hand I am a European intellectual, an artist, whose main effort is aimed at being creative, at the living penetration of every human possibility. I believe it to be my main job to understand and to illuminate—to be a sort of bridge linking the minds of men and women, of peoples and races.

Tout comprendre, pour tout aimer. One example, to explain my situation. I have a profound respect for, I make an intellectual cult of, Goethe. Can Gandhi accept an attitude like that? So I fear that if Gandhi comes to Europe for my sake, I shall cause him great disappointment.

This he wrote to Mira, for Gandhi to read. And a little later he wrote to Gandhi directly:

I am not, like you, a man whose inner strength realizes itself in deeds (although what I do always keeps faith with what I think). But the essence of my life lies in what I think. Thinking truthfully, thinking freely, is an imperious need in me, a life-necessity, and the role which has been given me to play . . . a very deep religious instinct, long hidden, but half-awake, and which has become ever more alert . . . the man of pure thought (pure in the intellectual sense) exerts only a feeble influence over contemporary events. . . . But you, a man of active faith, you are the direct intermediary between the Eternal Powers and the present moment. I know my moral inferiority. I am not worthy to touch your feet. But I know the anxiety and the doubts that are besieging the better parts of Europe, and I bring you its voice.

In November 1931 Rolland wrote to Mira to tell Gandhi that the new enemy was International Finance, an invisible conspiracy of industrialists and financiers whose tools were the press and governments. It was against them that the resistance must organize. This was the new consciousness of Europe that Rolland felt he could and must transmit to Gandhi. It was the political version of what I call the second mode of cultural resistance. Rolland had been a defender of the Russian Revolution in Europe since 1917, though he was no party member.

When Gandhi came to Villeneuve at the end of that year, Rolland told him about the demise of the old liberal politics, and about the need to organize the workers of Europe—the only force left—against the octopus Finance. The means would have to be violent as well as nonviolent, he warned. Russia needed to be defended against the capitalist West. Soviet justice, Rolland assured Gandhi, was harsh but impersonal, and Lenin had no personal hatreds. Gandhi replied that he knew nothing of history, but he distrusted Russia because of the violence it employed. Moreover, Rolland was upset that Gandhi allowed English policemen to accompany him everywhere, and to see and hear everything. Rolland wanted him to be more militant, more suspicious, more angry. Gandhi told him he didn't mind if newspapers misreported him. Rolland said perhaps it didn't matter to Gandhi, but to others it did.

Gandhi said that in England at least—the only country he'd seen in Europe—the unemployed ought *not* to hate the capitalists, because the latter were equally victims of the Depression. And he was against any dictatorship of the proletariat. When he went to Italy, though he kept a much sharper control of both his judgments and his behavior than Tagore had (as Rolland admitted), still he wrote back that behind Mussolini's implacability lay a wish to serve his people, and that he thought most Italians *liked* the iron hand of fascist rule. It is not surprising that Rolland noted in his journal, even while Gandhi was still at Villeneuve, that he felt there was very little for them to say to each other, because each had chosen his path, and it was so far from the other's. Being respectively Brahmin and Mahatma, they were alien to each other. But they continued to talk and to correspond, and with no such failure of respect as occurred between Rolland and Tagore.

That encounter seems to me emblematic of all that can pass between a Brahmin and a Mahatma, and Rolland's achievement was perhaps great enough for an intellectual to take as a model. To be the man that Gandhi came to Europe to meet, and to be that man by virtue of one's criticism, one's disagreement with him; to be able to offer him, when he came, the new consciousness of the European intellectual; all this is a mode of action that might be called heroic. It was, after all, no mean feat merely to *know* Gandhi, to understand him, recognize him, distinguish between him and Tagore; and to give him that acknowledgement, generously and fully; and to make him known to others. But that encounter at Villeneuve was on a higher level, which I would call heroic.

There is much in Rolland's life and writing that I find unattractive. He seems to have treated himself—and called on others to treat him—with a kind of hushed awe, and a valetudinarian solicitude. And even intellectually and artistically, that overinflated rhetoric is self-defeating. He writes like a man out of date after 1918—in his books he sounds like a man in love with his own image, distracted by his mirror from the windows through which there were important things to be seen. But the comparatively undressed prose of his journal proves that he *was* looking out of the windows. His style was a decadent version of liberal humanism—the first mode of cultural resistance—but the content of his journal is quite radical, in the second mode of radicalism.

Rolland does not impress me as a great radical, and I think I see a way—indicated by Ganghi himself—to avoid that kind of radicalism altogether. But he was remarkably well-informed for a man of 1931, in touch with all the best that was being thought and said, and remarkably clear-headed and unbiased. Above all, he was remarkably qualified to sustain the demands of being Gandhi's interlocutor. I cannot think—and I have no impulse to think—of anything better that a European intellectual could have done with his time.

XIV

Tolstoy, Gandhi, and Literary Critics

I HAD THOUGHT of calling this chapter "Gandhi and Leavis," to imply both a contrast and a transition from one guru to the other. What I want to do is to cite passages from the life or work of teacher-critics I have admired—I shall use Orwell as much as Leavis to represent their point of view—in which the feasibility of such a contrast, and the distance to be covered in such a transition, becomes apparent.

I use Orwell because Leavis' writing is so oblique and tangential in method, especially in its relation to ideology, that to cite him is a very long-winded process, and to make any reply is equally difficult, whereas Orwell has written on both Gandhi and the late Tolstoy, and in marvelously simple and clear and self-committing fashion. Anyway Orwell is, in my eyes, a twin brother to Leavis in this matter, as in many others; they are twin representatives of that movement of cultural resistance to empire that I called the first, associated in the nineteenth century with critics like Carlyle and Ruskin, and novels like *Middlemarch* and *War and Peace*.

But since a contrast between Leavis and Gandhi could only make sense within a context of similarity, I'll first remark on some likenesses between the two. In many ways it is not an abrupt transition to make, even in the physical aspects of the two gurus. My images of the two men physically are similar—those small, lean, agile presences, so low-voiced on the platform, so fast-moving on the ground, so formidable in encounter, despite great simplicity. And that similarity in physique is clearly related to life style. Both men lived ascetically in matters of food, and strenuously in matters of exercise. Since Gandhi is famous in this way, I will just say that Leavis, at least for some years, would receive invitations to dine in other Cambridge colleges with the warning that he would probably embarrass the other diners because he only ate once a day, and not at dinner time; he has all his life been a long-distance runner as notable as Gandhi was a long-distance walker; and Leavis' tieless and unbuttoned shirt, and later his poncho, was as incisive a self-characterization in Cambridge as Gandhi's loincloth. Such traits of bodily discipline are of course crucial to spirituality.

One might also point to the crucial importance to both men's thought of the village—the organic society, as Leavis called it. Gandhi deplored the alienation of the city dweller from the villages: "He does not know them, he will not live in them, and if he finds himself in a village, he will want to reproduce the city life there." And as he says in his letter to Nehru as his heir, on the achievement of independence,

"We can realize truth and nonviolence only in the simplicity of village life and this simplicity can best be found in the charkha and all that the charkha connotes." Both men are anarchists, in the Kropotkin sense of anarchy, highly suspicious of and averse from central governments and their branches: armies, aristocracies, ruling classes, and the sophistications and worldlinesses of thought and feeling that develop at such centers. This is the equivalent in political thought for their asceticism in personal behavior, and equally important in energizing all their attitudes to more particular problems.

And finally I would point to a quality in both of them that I am tempted to call tragic, but could equally well be called nontragic. In the case of Gandhi, it is easy to specify. Gandhi lived in expectation and acceptance of death; even in the matter of vegetarianism, he was ready to die rather than drink beef tea; and I have given other examples before —death was the constant test of his sincerity. It is nontragic because his gaiety, dry humor, and charm all grew out of this day-by-day, repeated acceptance of the ultimate. In the case of Leavis it is perhaps impertinent to speak so freely, but surely his face and manner offer similar intimations of a tragic inner life, successfully transformed into intellectual and aesthetic urgencies.

He has been a great nay-sayer—both his admirers and his adversaries would agree about that. And I think they might and should agree also that what he has denied has been in some cases arbitrarily chosen. Where they differ is that the admirers—like me—have felt that even in those cases the nay-saying was in its way an act of spiritual protest directed ultimately, like Gandhi's, against the modern world system. The element of excess in his criticism, and in his personality, has worked as a gage of commitment, of intellectual honor —as *his* proof of sincerity.

Something in the line of these three traits can be detected

in Orwell. In his case the asceticism was less flamboyant, because it did not suit Orwell's idea of manliness, but it was there. He refers somewhere to a "secret teetotaler," with "leanings towards vegetarianism," and one might suspect him of similarly shame-faced cravings for self-punishment himself. The "village" feeling he also distrusted and mocked, but his life demonstrates that he shared it. He did, after all, go to live in a village and keep the village shop in the 1930s. And the depths of his sensibility were dark with suffering, as his novels make plain. Of course I am ignoring other traits that mark differences between these men, but one need only think of contrasting human types, like Churchill, or Nehru, or Evelyn Waugh, to see the point of grouping them together.

However, it is in fact the differences I am most concerned with, and I will begin with Orwell and his essay on Gandhi. This essay, which was published in 1949, at the end of Orwell's life, begins "Saints should always be judged guilty until they are proved innocent," and in fact saints—seen as being unlike "human beings"—were much on Orwell's mind during these years. He talks about Tolstoy as a saint in his essay on *King Lear*, published in 1947. So one external referent for this concept was the kind of spirituality I have been talking about. But he also says, in this essay, that this is a yogi-ridden age, which I think is more likely to refer to a different kind of spirituality. What was most in the air of that kind in 1949 was the Roman Catholic spirituality of Evelyn Waugh's *Brideshead Revisited* and T. S. Eliot's *Cocktail Party*. In any case, Orwell had attacked Tolstoy's sanctity as a form of spiritual bullying, and he now asked how much Gandhi was moved by vanity, and how much did he compromise to win political success. He was reviewing Gandhi's autobiography, and the evidence *that* presented was, he decided, in Gandhi's favor. Nevertheless, he had never felt much liking for Gandhi, and this is an idea he repeats—he feels "a sort of aesthetic distaste" for him. And I think we will see the source of this feeling—which is not trivial but a large part of Orwell's serious judgment—if we turn to *The Road to Wigan Pier*, and to Orwell's attack on the typology of English socialists. One type, for instance, he defines as "the outer-suburban creeping Jesus, a hangover from the William Morris period, but still surprisingly common, who goes about saying, 'Why must we level *down*? Why not level *up*?' and proposes to level the working class 'up' (up to his own standard) by means of hygiene, fruit-juice, birth-control, poetry, etc." I think that Gandhi looked to Orwell like an outer suburban creeping Jesus. A few pages later he says, "One sometimes gets the impression that the mere words Socialism and Communism draw towards them with magnetic force every fruit-juice drinker, nudist, sandal-wearer, sex-maniac, Quaker, 'Nature Cure' quack, pacifist, and feminist, in England." Every item in that list fits Gandhi. Orwell attacks those traits because they corrupt and vitiate the psychic normality that he regards as vital to English socialism. The English socialist must be a heartily manly man—and the way Orwell defines that is implicitly backward looking—if England is to vote a socialist government into power. And note also that all those traits are related more or less directly to spirituality—as ways for men to disengage themselves from modern materialism, and from that past to which Orwell looked back for his model of English manhood. These are the traits of what I called noncomformist meekness, or the idealistic socialism of Wilfred Wellock, driven out of English politics during World War I.

But to return to the essay on Gandhi, Orwell's main argument is that Gandhi's teachings cannot be squared with those of the Western left-wing movement because they are antihumanist, and allow for no exclusive love for individuals. "To an ordinary human being," says Orwell, "love means nothing if it does not mean loving some people more than others. [On this point Erikson implicitly agrees with Orwell, and condemns Gandhi] . . . The essence of being human is that one does not seek perfection . . . that one is prepared to be defeated and broken up by life, which is the inevitable price of fastening one's love upon other human individuals." The main motive for nonattachment, he suggests, is a desire to escape from the pain of living and above all from love, which, sexual or nonsexual, is hard work. (This charge, incidentally, is very similar to that which Leavis made against Eliot, apropos of *The Cocktail Party*— as I have said, a contemporary phenomenon—the charge that he has since developed as his major criticism of Eliot. I think it is fair to take that as evidence of the alignment of the two men in relation to spirituality of which I spoke.) Politically, nevertheless, Gandhi's pacifism may have been right, Orwell says, and, if it could be linked to a different ideology, might be of great value to us. In any case, regarded simply as a politician and compared with other leading political figures of our time, how clean a smell Gandhi has managed to leave behind. That is how he ends the essay, which I think is a classic statement on Gandhi, but a classic of unsympathetic scrutiny. That unsympathy does not extend to injustice, and his final judgment may be called generous. But it is, implicitly as well as explicitly, a firm repudiation of Gandhi.

His 1947 essay, "Lear, Tolstoy, and the Fool," is equally firm against the late Tolstoy. At the same time, it shows an equally intense engagement with him; what do you see, he asks, if you shut your eyes and say "Lear"? What Orwell sees is a majestic old man in a long black robe, with flowing white hair and beard—someone curiously like Tolstoy. And the play "Lear" is about a renunciation that fails to bring the renouncer happiness, which was Tolstoy's history, Orwell says, while Tolstoy's death was a phantom reminiscence of Lear's.

Nevertheless, Orwell repudiates Tolstoy's teaching. "A sort of doubt has always hung around the character of Tolstoy, as round the character of Gandhi," he says. (It is clear, by the way, that Orwell sees the two men, and their relation to himself, in exactly the way that I am presenting them.) In the case of Tolstoy, that doubt becomes the accusation that he really wanted to coerce others. The distinction that matters, Orwell says, is not that between violence and nonviolence, but that between having and not having the appetite for power. Creeds like anarchism and pacifism encourage the desire to get inside other people's brains and to dictate their thoughts. In Tolstoy's essay on Shakespeare, from which Orwell starts, he is out to prevent anyone else from enjoying Shakespeare. He wants to get inside their minds and do dirt on Shakespeare. (I am reminded that that phrase "do dirt on" is one Leavis uses about a writer he dislikes who "does dirt on life," just as "creeping Jesus" is a phrase Lawrence uses about a type he dislikes; both are vulgar and slightly old-fashioned phrases, and show us these men making alliance with "the people" against the enemies of normality.)

Orwell again sets up an antithesis between the saint and the human being. The saint tries to bring earthly life to an end, and put something different in its place. A normal human being does not want the Kingdom of Heaven; he wants life on earth to continue, even though life is suffering. There can be no reconciliation between the two. One must choose between this world and the next.

Shakespeare, Orwell tells us, was no saint, but a human being, and thus on Orwell's side—indeed he was in some ways not a very good human being. He was a flatterer of the powerful and a coward about expressing his social and political insights. He had a streak of worldliness in him, and his sympathies in *Lear* probably lay with the ignoble realism of the Fool. But at least he could see the whole issue, and could treat it at the level of tragedy, which Tolstoy could not. The Fool, Orwell tells us, is integral to the play, and is a trickle of sanity running all through it. The Fool reminds us that "somewhere or other, in spite of the injustices, cruelties, intrigues, deceptions and misunderstandings that are being enacted here, life is going on much as usual." Orwell and Shakespeare are on the side of life, which is taken to mean "as usual." In Tolstoy's impatience with the Fool one "gets a glimpse of his deeper quarrel with Shakespeare . . . [which is with] Shakespeare's tendency to take—not so much a pleasure as simply an interest in the actual process of life." This is the crucial point of Orwell's argument, and he aligns himself with Shakespeare and the Fool against Tolstoy. The latter's main aim in his later years, Orwell tells us, was to narrow the range of human consciousness, and he was incapable of tolerance or humility.

This self-alignment with the Fool is very characteristic of Orwell. It is parallel with his self-alignment with Sancho Panza in the essay on comic postcards, and elsewhere, with George Bowling in *Coming Up for Air* and with Dobbin in *Animal Farm*. And in "Why I Write," also published in 1947, he says that writers are great egotists, like all the top crust of humanity, but the great mass of mankind are not selfish. At about the age of thirty, Orwell says, most men abandon individual ambition and begin to live chiefly for others, or to be smothered in drudgery. For many years I found this aspect of Orwell's thought admirable as well as likable, but nowadays I read it as expressing a concealed resentment of greatness, artistic, religious, or whatever it may be. He made himself Sancho Panza because he wanted to destroy the Don Quixote in himself. If Orwell really thought that the mass of mankind lived for others in a way that

Gandhi and Tolstoy did not, then I think he was culpably deceiving himself. Putting it another way, I think that he declined the challenge of spirituality in the name of sentimental populism.

(It may be of interest, by the way, that in the essay that Orwell is attacking, Tolstoy is dealing with the cult of Shakespeare built up by German Romantic critics. He complains that they mythify and mystify Shakespeare [and all poetry, because they regard that as represented by Shakespeare] and that they chose him to represent poetry because Shakespeare habitually exaggerates—in language, in feeling, and in form. He avoids the simple and natural. That is why ineffable meanings can be ascribed to him, and these Germans wanted to make art out to be ineffable. They were mythifying culture as a whole. This seems to me a plausible proposition, which certainly makes Tolstoy's argument more interesting than it first sounds, but it is interesting to us for another reason also. Tolstoy is saying that this mythification of Shakespeare is an example of that second mode of cultural resistance I described to you before. It is a part of that German intellectual movement whose style has spread over the whole of the Western world, in modernism. Tolstoy, in attacking that, is like Gandhi attacking Marx. Though I don't mean to say that the essay isn't also a pretty shocking piece of philistinism, as Orwell says.)

As for Leavis, we have his essay on *Anna Karenina*, in the course of which he has some things to say about the late Tolstoy. He describes *Anna Karenina* as *the* European novel; it shows, from Leavis' point of view, what novels are for. And in that novel, he tells us, the principle of life is a lived question, or quest: "What Tolstoy has to guard against, is the intensity of his need for an answer. . . . The temptation in wait for Tolstoy is to relax the tension [a tension vital to his art] by reducing the question to one that *can* be answered, to simplify the challenge which life is for him, and deny the complexity of his total knowledge and need." And to take another key phrase, the essential mode of this book is antididactic.

You see that, for Leavis, to reduce your question to one that can be answered is to betray your seriousness. The only question you can seriously put to life is a rhetorical question. And of course Tolstoy was not asking rhetorical questions, so critic and novelist are bound to diverge, despite the critic's admiration.

The focal point of Tolstoy's temptation, Leavis tells us, is the figure of Levin. He and Kitty have, "for that crucial matter of the relations between men and women," a clear normative significance—that is, Leavis accepts them as an ideal pair. But at the end of the book Tolstoy undermines that normative significance, implicitly, by having Levin identify goodness with the peasants' way of life and their Christian beliefs. "In an ominous way," Leavis tells us, Levin (Tolstoy) begins to associate the peasants with the problem of the good life, and to solve his own problem of belief by imitating their faith.

Throughout his account of the book, Leavis lays a heavy stress on the inadequacy of various characters' efforts at sanctity—those of the Countess Lidia Ivanovna, of Madame Stahl, of Varenka, and of Karenin himself. Anna and Kitty, we are told, are right in their revulsion from such "saints." We feel directly the revulsion that Anna felt from her husband, and when we contrast Levin with his brother Koznyshev, we feel that the latter lacks—to use Kitty's word—"heart." And yet at the end we find Levin denying, or defying, such insights, which he had shared with Kitty and with his housekeeper Agafya Mihailovna, who had told him, when he worried about the peasants, that what he needed to do was marry. Levin defies these insights, and Leavis tells us that "the breakdown of Tolstoy into old Leo is here portended." (Old Leo is Lawrence's phrase for the late Tolstoy, and Leavis has all along worked with and through Lawrence's remarks about Tolstoy.)

I have pointed out that in writing his two great novels Tolstoy was peculiarly under the influence of his wife and his wife's family, and the myth of family happiness that that family had woven for and about themselves. This gives an extra interest to Leavis' analysis of what goes wrong at the end of *Anna Karenina*, for if Levin is rebelling against the teaching he had got from Kitty, a teaching full of domestic values, Tolstoy was rebelling against Sonya. Was *that* his mistake? Was Sonya right, in Leavis' judgment? In any case, Tolstoy was never wholly subdued to that idea, even as the novelist of *Anna Karenina*. To return to those characters who try to be saints, Leavis' stress on their failure is a little too heavy to be true to the novel. Tolstoy certainly asks us to see that Anna *could* not respond to her husband's embodiment of the Christian virtues. But he also asks us to see that Karenin, in making the attempt to embody them, did really move out beyond and above Anna.

The book is ambivalent all the way through, and it is not true to say, as Leavis does, "All the cogent force of the whole great work makes it plain that the answer he [Levin] threatens to commit himself to with all the force of his will is a desperately simplifying one . . . a rejection of life." It seems so to Leavis because he was not—at the time of writing the essay— asking real questions of life or looking for practical solutions of its problems. He had made up his mind that there were no answers, and so he asked only rhetorical questions. He was in Sonya's camp. But Tolstoy was still expecting answers, and so he went on, from being a novelist, to the spiritual quest that he handed on to Gandhi. Leavis says, "We, most of us, have to recognize a higher authority in the art, the creative power, of *Anna Karenina* than in the wisdom of the sage and the prophet."

And that is where one has to begin one's transition. Old Leo is to my mind a greater man than the author of *Anna Karenina*, and Gandhi is a greater man than Leavis.

(It may be worth pointing out that among Leavis' colleagues at Cambridge was one who notably derived inspiration from the late Tolstoy, and that was Wittgenstein. He did hold by the purest spiritual values, those of the third mode of cultural resistance, and indeed lived by them in his personal life, while in his professional life as a philosopher he was severely professional, esoteric, and remote from ordinary concerns—he worked in the spirit of the second mode. By virtue of his acceptance and rejection of philosophy as a discipline, as a career, Wittgenstein exemplified the life style I was recommending for the Gandhian culture critic.)

It seems to me demonstrable that Leavis' reading of *Anna Karenina* just won't do, and that the source of the inadequacy is in his blindness to Tolstoyan and Gandhian values. It is sad to see, even in India, men trained in the school of Leavis using literary parameters to circumscribe Gandhi, or using Tolstoy the novelist, or Lawrence the novelist, to represent a wholeness of vision next to which Gandhi or the late Tolstoy are partial or fragmentary. You can find two or three examples of that in the volume I mentioned before, *Gandhi and the West*, edited by the Mysore professor, Narasimhaiah. One can call that "sad to see" because the spectacle is pathetic rather than tragic; they are failing by their own professions of imagination and logic. One need not become a Gandhian to see their blindness.

But if one does become a Gandhian, must one not sacrifice sight altogether? There are anecdotes to give one pause. For instance, there is one told by Ronald Duncan, the English author of the play *This Way to the Tomb*. In 1937 he was twenty-two and had, since leaving his university, worked in a Yorkshire mine, and then gone to organize a South Wales miners' strike. He was a pacifist and had tried to make the strike a nonviolent demonstration, but his efforts were frustrated by communist leaders. He wrote a pamphlet about the experience, and sent a copy to Gandhi. Gandhi replied, and when Duncan asked if he could meet him, Gandhi wired, "Meet me in Wardha on the 23rd inst." When he got the wire, Duncan was playing chess with Dick Sheppard, the leader of the Peace Pledge Union; he was accompanied on his way to India, as far as Paris, by Benjamin Britten; that will help place him in the English social-intellectual milieu.

Well, his whole account of his visit to Wardha is very interesting, but I will confine myself to one anecdote, which relates to Gandhi's attitude to art—something that turned out to be crucial as far as Duncan was concerned. Duncan's model for the relation of art to religious and political causes was then Le Jongleur de Notre Dame. This is a medieval legend of which people like Chesterton made great use. The story is of the juggler who came to spend his declining years as a dependent of a great abbey and, being much impressed by a great festival in honor of Our Lady, wanted to make his own contribution but was too shy to do it publicly, so he crept into the abbey church at night and juggled before the statue of the Virgin, and in the morning was found dead of cold and exhaustion. And thus the novelist and the composer, too, should juggle away, and shyly offer their works—believing them to be worthless—at the feet of Mother Church. It's not a very convincing analogy, just a genial and picturesque fable, and apparently it didn't make much sense to Gandhi.

Duncan tells us that Gandhi once defined sin as attachment to the senses. "I remember I instantly asked him if he considered listening to Mozart was a sin. The question was all-important to me. 'All attachment to the senses is death,' he replied. It may seem strange, but I used Gandhi's light dismissal of Mozart as the reason for refusing his invitation, which he made later to me, to return to India again and live with him for a year." Well, it won't seem strange to any of us, I'm fairly sure, but then neither will it seem strange to hear that Duncan feels that he made a terrible mistake in deciding as he did.

To return to Leavis, and those characteristics he does share with Gandhi, I want to say a bit more about his concern for villages and the organic culture. In this he was of course at one with Morris and Ruskin, as was Gandhi. The thought of both Leavis and Gandhi, may be described, from this point of view, as twin fruit of one tree. But Gandhi went on to develop the Ruskin line of thought, most notably into practical political action, but also into a host of economic and cultural and educational enterprises. Must we say that Leavis, comparatively speaking, stood still?

My answer would be yes, so far as those large categories of Ruskinian thought go; the economic and political ideas may be said to have petrified and lost value, insofar as they are there to be glimpsed in Leavis' writings. But in his own line Leavis did something new, which amounted to a development of thought. He brought to literary criticism an intensity of moral and intellectual seriousness commensurate with that achieved by the poets and novelists he criticized. Though this seemed excessive to those used to older styles of criticism, it was in fact appropriate to the new intensity and elaboration of "culture." In other words, he fused the heritage of Ruskin and Morris with the spirit of modernism, combined the first with the second modes of cultural resistance. He committed himself to the modernism of T. S. Eliot and D. H. Lawrence, and the different modernism of Conrad and James; all of them were perhaps *semi*modern, but Leavis mastered the modernist elements in all four of them and brought them into a relation with his faith in the organic society that does service to both sides of the equation. Seen this way, his work was a development of the Ruskin inheritance, and parallel with Gandhi's in tendency.

But one cannot say that Leavis has done Gandhi's work in another sphere. The measure one uses to estimate Gandhi's work would make Leavis' seem very small. The two are incommensurate—and that means that Leavis is the smaller figure. But incommensurate means also that they presuppose different ideas of the world situation and its possibilities for action. *That* is why they cannot be measured in the same terms. Gandhi implies that the world can be saved from the violence of modern civilization and the centrifugality of modern culture. Leavis implies that it is too late for any salvation; he concentrates on finding reflected in one of the culture's fragments the wholeness there used to be. By 1895, after all, when he was born, England had no villages.

Putting it in that pictorial and descriptive way makes it seem that Leavis is the only practical model for us, since by 1978 there are still fewer villages. But there are prescriptive and exhortative ways of looking at the situation, too, which lead us to Gandhi. And there are other elements within it. During the last ten years we have seen a chaotic but powerful movement back to "organic" values, in the very heart of modern civilization. Above all, a model must be a hero, and Gandhi is a hero who will keep our minds alight even if or even as we finally go down in disaster.

XV

The Opposition to

the Mahatmas

THOUGH I have not, I believe, concealed the abrasive aspects of Tolstoy's and Gandhi's challenge, I must admit to having described it with a strong predisposition in their favor. So it seems appropriate to end this book by recording some of the striking things that have been said against them, not chosen this time with an eye to what the objections reveal about the objectors, but in order to face the opposition.

First of all I shall cite two modern critics of Tolstoy, who I think represent many others in what they say. On September 10, 1941, André Gide wrote in his notebook, "Tolstoy so arrogant, incapable of sincerity, ostentatious, *not* like St. Francis." And in 1953, concluding his *The Hedgehog and the Fox*, Isaiah Berlin wrote that the old Tolstoy was insanely proud and filled with self-hatred, omniscient and doubting everything, contemptuous and self-abasing, tormented and detached—"almost wholly isolated, the most tragic of great writers; a desperate old man, beyond human aid, wandering self-blinded at Colonus." These are representative judgments on a Mahatma when the latter is seen from the perspective of liberal humanists, who are dedicated to milder and more human (that is, consensual) values.

Another interesting witness, though less violent, is Aylmer Maude, Tolstoy's translator and editor, his biographer, and for a time his friend and disciple. His attack may be said to be on Tolstoy's doctrines rather than on his character. Maude supported a Tolstoy colony at Purleigh for a time, and he wrote about Tolstoyism out of his experience with that and out of his dealings with Chertkov, the leading spirit of that movement. And his criticism is interesting also because he makes his (very clear and explicit) points by reference to standard nineteenth-century liberalism. He compares Tolstoy as a moralist with Bagehot and Gladstone, he cites Lincoln and Lowell as models of that clarity of mind in which Tolstoy failed, and Jane Addams (whom Maude took to meet Tolstoy) as an example of the kind of social work in which we *should* invest our energies. Maude turned to liberalism *after* religious radicalism.

In his book on Tolstoy of 1918, Maude says that practical experience is against his teaching, and so is the example of the great Pym, Hampden, Lincoln, and Woodrow Wilson. He cites his experience of the disharmony at Tolstoy colonies, and says, "The real justification for that definiteness in making use of material objects which is the real essence of the so-called 'rights of property' lies in the fact that definiteness tends to facilitate harmony among men." And he praises the English sense of the *complexity* of life. Wherever men have tried "going naked," evil results have followed; even St. Francis' followers turned into sturdy beggars. We must therefore follow the moderate example of Lincoln and Jane Addams, and must do so *with conviction*: "To defend itself against the disintegrating forces of which Tolstoy is a striking example, human society must learn to recognize and respect what is noble, healthy, heroic in itself, and must cease to regard its baser elements as the cement that holds it together." Maude calls for a liberal-humanist moderation as a duty: "Surely the duty of man is not to do what he can't, but to do the best he can. . . . To speak, as Tolstoy sometimes does, of ceasing to do evil before we begin to do good, is . . . as if we insisted that a child cease to make mistakes before it continued to learn arithmetic." He concludes with cautious optimism: "I have tried to suggest reasons for believing that, however urgently the building may need repair, the foundations are as firm today as when they were first laid."

In his *Life of Tolstoy*, written in 1908 but revised in 1930, Maude makes some shrewd critical points:

> What Tolstoy does not show is what he does not know—the middle class world: the world of merchants, manufacturers, engineers, and men of business. . . . Of certain important types of humanity he had hardly any conception. Of the George Stephenson type, for instance, which masters the brute forces of nature and harnesses them to the service of man . . . the Sidney Webb type . . . evolving social order out of the partial chaos of modern civilization . . . the organizers in our great industrial undertakings; men whose hearts are set on getting much work well done with little friction and little waste. . . . The introduction of thought into methods of production, distribution, and exchange, which has during the last one hundred and fifty years revolutionized the Western world, should not be condemned as bad in itself. . . .

The modern world system is not as bad, and the human situation not as desperate, as Tolstoy made out.

Gorky and Lenin on the other hand, offer a criticism of Tolstoy couched in the terms of Russian history and of Marxist analysis. Gorky said he was repelled by Tolstoy's despotism and his "will to suffer, in order to vindicate his teachings and give them strength." Tolstoy's doctrine of anarchism was only the old Slav resistance to state-structure —"our desire to scatter, nomadically." This, Gorky says, is foolish and antihistorical. Tolstoy had been Russia's great man: "Yet men arose who realized that light must come to us not from the East but from the West; and now he, the crown of our ancient history, wishes, consciously or unconsciously, to stretch himself like a vast mountain across our nation's path to Europe, to the active life which sternly demands of man the supreme effort of his spiritual forces." And Lenin, foremost of those who turned to the West, wrote, "Tolstoyism, in its real historical context, is an ideology of an Oriental, an Asiatic order. Hence the asceticism, the non-resistance to evil, the profound note of pessimism." All of these criticisms are in their way true, it seems to me.

But we must above all listen to the voices of Tolstoy's wife and children, since it is his behavior in his family, I believe, that has most outraged us. Soon after that fatal quarrel with her husband of 1882, Sonya wrote to her sister, "He is a man ahead of his time, he marches in front of the crowd and shows the way it must follow. And I am one of the crowd, I live with it and, with it, I see the light in the men ahead of their time, like Leo, and I say yes, that is the light, but I cannot walk any faster than the crowd to which I am bound; I am held back by my environment, by my habits." And there is no need to doubt that this was sincere; such thoughts as these came from her best self. The tragedy was that she could not act out of that best self—especially in regard to him—that over the twenty-eight years still to follow she became the nay-sayer, the enemy, in some sense diabolically possessed by the drive to deny him, in proportion as he identified himself with the good. It is a terrible story, especially in the light of her 1865 journal entry, "I am so terribly afraid of being ugly, morally as well as physically." But that is not the story I have to tell in this book.

In 1881 she wrote, "It was all so different in the days when he was writing his chapters on the ball and hunting in *War and Peace*; he was so excited and joyful then, as though he himself were taking part in these entertainments." And it is natural that her disappointment in his change of subject, and of temperament, should infect her judgment of his gifts. In 1886, beginning to copy his play, *The Power of Darkness*, she asked, "Why is it that I have lost faith even in his literary power?" She no longer enjoyed the way he wrote, and was convinced he had ruined his talents.

But in fact the seeds of the conflict between them, and of her resistance to his larger ideas, were visible from the beginning of their marriage. In 1862 she wrote in her journal, "He disgusts me with his People. I feel he ought to choose between me, i.e., the representative of the family, and his beloved People. This is egoism, I know. But let it be. I have given my life to him, I live *through* him, and I expect him to do the same. . . . His influence is depressing because I begin to think in his way, to see things with his eyes, and I am afraid of losing my own self and yet not becoming like him. . . ." She determined to have a family in order to escape the feeling of being insignificant beside him: "If I could kill him and then make another man exactly like him, I should do it joyfully."

These remarks, intelligent and sincere and passionate enough to explain all that Tolstoy saw in her, become grimly predictive in the light of what followed. In 1890 she wrote, "He never knew how to love—it is something he never *learned* in his youth. . . . He had no family when he was young, and this lack of a family sense has lasted all through his life." She was appropriating the kingdom of love for herself, for the Behrs *had* been a family, and so were her children, by her grace. And in 1897, "He is indifferent to everyone around him and lives only for himself. . . . I do not believe in his goodness and love of humanity. I know the source of all his actions; glory and glory, insatiable, unlimited, feverish . . . he has no love for his own children and grandchildren."

What the children later wrote about their childhood—and what Tolstoy himself wrote—by and large confirms Sonya's claim that they were alienated from him. Ilya wrote, "As a boy of twelve, I felt that my father was getting more and more estranged from us . . . gloomy and irritable . . . a stern and censorious propagandist." And Tolstoy wrote, "My children do not even see fit to read my books. They think my literature is one thing and I another. But every inch of me is in what I write."

Ilya followed his mother's theory about his father's unlovingness: "All exhibitions of tenderness were entirely foreign to him—perhaps because he grew up without a Mother." But at times Ilya's description of those days is laden with reconsideration, and an implicit revaluation of his earlier sympathies: "We still had the same Nikolai the cook, the same Anke Pie, imported from the Behrs family and deeply rooted in the life of Yasnaya Polyana, the same tutors and governesses, the same lessons, the same succession of babies that my mother still nursed at her breast: all those foundations on which the life of our ant-heap rested were as unshaken as ever and as necessary for our selfish enjoyment." Ilya's tone varies considerably, even in this book, written long after his father's death. The children's sympathies were sharply divided.

But it is clear that at the time Tolstoy was defeated, both in his claim on his family's support and in his attempt to live according to his beliefs. What he had to settle for is indicated in a journal entry for July 2, 1908. He says that if he heard of a man who lived as inconsistently with his professed beliefs as he himself did, "I would never have hesitated to call him a cad. *That was what I needed to free me* from worldly things, and to enable me to live for my soul." Tolstoy had found a way to profit from, and so to accept, the situation in which he lived.

Turning to Gandhi, we might begin with the criticisms of men who had some reason to admire him—men who worked in the civil disobedience movement of America in the 1960s. Gene Sharp wrote in 1964:

> For a Westerner—and perhaps particularly for an American— Gandhi poses special problems [of evaluation]. Often his eccentricities get in the way so that it is difficult to get beyond them, or to take other aspects of his life seriously. Even for religious people in the West, his constant use of religious terminology and theological language in explanation or justification of a social or political act or policy more often confuses than clarifies. . . . "I claim," he once wrote, "to be no more than an average man with less than average ability." Indeed, in important respects, this was probably true. He only went to South Africa after having failed in his attempt to be a lawyer in India.

And W. R. Miller quotes Floyd Dell, saying in 1916 that nonresistance was then in its prescientific phase, and extends the application of that idea to include all Gandhi's work. We must move on, away from Gandhi's methods, toward something more scientific. He says that the first orders of priority in nonresistance today are historical, sociological, and psychological research; theology and ethics must take a second place. Men like Gandhi did not know what they were doing. Their successors will work with equipment designed by hardheaded men who have studied their achievements.

Gandhi, he says, inherited a pragmatic social movement and made it religious—made it semi-Christian. But he understood little of the pragmatic dimension of his move-

ment. He had no real sense of social dynamics and his
experiments with truth were not scientific. He was concerned with salvation, as remote from our condition as the
medieval mystics and rishis. He was a Mahatma, not a
modern man, and not sufficiently a universal man: "The
more we enter into an age of electronic technology, the
more he strikes us as a figure from the past."

Miller recommends overt anger and psychological violence to the black movement, and endorses Martin Luther
King over Gandhi. King was no Mahatma, and that was his
strength; he was a guide in a movement with many leaders.
He was a visionary but no Utopian, a man of God but no
saintly eccentric. He felt no need to give up smart attire,
good food, or sex, to be effectively nonviolent. And thus his
example was accessible to many today who would have been
awed by someone like Gandhi.

And there are some similarly severe judgments in Erik
Erikson's very sympathetic book on Gandhi—judgments on
Gandhi's cruelty, his hostility to love, and so on. Erikson
speaks of the barriers created between Gandhi and today's
and tomorrow's fighters for peace, by the "monotonous
references to lust" in his *Autobiography*. Gandhi refused to
admit that there could be mutuality in sex, and asked his
followers for sexual self-disarmament. His hatred of untruth
and uncleanness is displaced violence, and he is guilty at
times of both moralism and self-pity.

Two Indians who knew Gandhi well and admired him
deeply, Gokhale and Nirmal Kumar Bose, lend support to
Erikson's criticisms by their various testimonies. Gokhale
was an older man, Gandhi's political guru, and an intellectual of delicate health over whom Gandhi fussed posses-
sively. On one occasion, a visit to Gandhi's group in South
Africa, Gokhale burst out, "You all seem to think that you
have been born to suffer hardships and discomforts, and
people like myself have been born to be pampered by you.

You must suffer the punishment. . . . I will not let you touch me. Do you think that you will go out to attend to nature's needs and at the same time keep a commode for me? I will bear any amount of hardship but I will humble your pride." Obviously this protest was delivered humorously, but it is equally obvious that it had a serious meaning —a moral overweeningness in Gandhi.

Bose, who was Gandhi's secretary during his heroic pilgrimage to Noakhali in 1946–1947, resigned from the post in protest against some things Gandhi did, including his sleeping in the same bed with women coworkers. Bose did not accuse Gandhi of lust, but of secrecy, and of allowing the women to involve themselves in a psychological situation beyond their capacity to handle, which fostered a possessiveness in them toward him, and a hysteria. He said Gandhi first put men under strain and then indulged them —that he was, in this way, "possessive." This criticism came from one who was himself involved in the situation of possessiveness and hysteria, which was a reciprocal system. But Bose looks like a very reliable witness, very much on guard against himself and very much impressed by Gandhi. Above all, it seems undeniable that such a system existed around Gandhi, and although one can point to much in his behavior obviously calculated to diminish it, he must take the responsibility for however much of it flourished.

Perhaps the most hard-hitting of Gandhi's critics has been Arthur Koestler, who has clearly been interested and impressed, but who has come to an unqualified rejection. He calls Gandhi a paternal tyrant who deprived his sons of their manhood and sat on their shoulders like a djinn. And for his political and religious leadership he calls him a Stakhanovite, a Jacobin, a martyr, and inhuman. India is sicker, more estranged from a living faith, than the West, despite or because of Gandhism. Koestler traveled to the East in 1958–1959 "in the mood of a pilgrim," but "I came back rather proud of being a European." India, he declared, is *not* primarily concerned with the heart or the spirit: "Bapu still casts his saintly-sickly spell over it, but its power is waning as more and more people realize that, whether we like it or not, spinning wheels cannot compete with factories...."

In a later essay he defined Gandhi as being both yogi and commissar at once. He says Tagore recognized Gandhism's flaw, its use of magic formulas that flatter and feed a slave mentality. And Gandhi's attitude to sex was even more violent and bullying than Tolstoy's. He encouraged Hindu sex-guilt. The young women who came under his spell were seduced into chastity. And in political matters, "It would have taken a great deal of corpses to keep Bapu in non-violence." India would have achieved independence earlier without him.

And to parallel Sonya's testimony against Tolstoy, we should consult Kasturba's against Gandhi, though in this case we shall find no journal and no comparable articulated criticism. We shall have to look mostly at records of behavior—Gandhi's behavior toward his wife and his sons. In 1898 he forced her to clean the chamber pot of a Christian clerk who was living in their house. When she refused, or protested, he put her out of the house, until she said he was shaming them. He made her give up the gold and jewelry they were presented with on leaving South Africa. He persuaded her to reject a doctor's advice for herself, and later for their son, when there was real risk of death. He forced her to give up caste traditions she believed in—to accept Untouchables—and certain all-Hindu ways. Above all, perhaps, he left her behind, intellectually, morally, and spiritually.

Of the four sons, it was the eldest, Harilal, who was most luridly his father's victim. He wanted an education, which his father denied him, to prepare himself for a professional career. He married against his father's wishes, no doubt in part because he knew his father never would have agreed. In 1911, after having gone to jail for his father in South Africa, he ran away from home. His father sent him back to school in India, but he did badly, got into criminal activities, drank to excess, and finally became a convert to Islam, in a move clearly designed to wound and harm his father. He was a classic wastrel, destructive and self-destructive, with a sentimental devotion to his mother as his father's victim. He appeared at Gandhi's funeral, but disappeared again before his brothers could make contact with him, and died shortly after, a derelict, an outcaste, a habitual drunkard. He made himself everything his father hated—in something like the way Sonya Tolstoy made herself a monster. But Gandhi was not defeated by his wife and children, but by the political leaders of India, by Dr. Ambedkar, who led the Untouchables against him, by Nehru and Patel in his own Congress party, and above all by Jinnah, who insisted on a separated state for Indian Moslems, which split the country into hostile groups.

Jinnah was an opposite figure to Gandhi in most of his tendencies, though curiously parallel in certain circumstances. His parents came from Kathiawad, and his family had been Hindu before their conversion to Islam—had in fact tried to return to Hinduism, but had been refused. He was a lawyer, too, and had been in London to train, just after Gandhi. He had even been similarly devoted to Gokhale. But he was an intensely theatrical and rhetorical personality in every way. In fact, he had played Romeo in a touring company in England. And the style he adopted was intensely British. He wore a monocle, and stiff collars, and a buttonhole. He avoided physical contact, washed his hands every hour, and changed his underwear frequently. He addressed people as "My dear fellow," shook his forefinger at them to make a point, and used such characteristic locutions as "Failure is a word unknown to me" and "No, I cannot" in response to any "Can't you . . .?" He stood for constitutional methods, the debate, the party organization, the voting. He had belonged to the Congress until the changes Gandhi introduced made it so democratic that he felt out of place there. He had no hobbies but politics and no feeling for religion.

He became the great nay-sayer of Indian politics, refusing all Gandhi's attempts to carry the Muslims with the Hindus in various negotiations with the British. He manipulated all the traditional hostilities and irritations between the two religious groups at the crucial moment, and got a separate state set up, which was plagued with innumerable problems, economically and politically, from the beginning, partly just because it was so largely negative in inspiration. By his insistence India was divided, not only by the frontier but by huge transmigrations, and by vicious racial riots and persecutions. By these means it was demonstrated to the world that Gandhi's nonviolent movement had ended in violence, as its opponents had always said it would. Churchill, for instance, commented on the Moslim-Hindu riots with great satisfaction. Within that humiliation, Gandhi had to find his account, as Tolstoy had found his, within his defeat by Sonya. (Jinnah's demonstration of India's violence was like Sonya's demonstration of Tolstoy's vanity.) Gandhi's account was found in his pilgrimage to Noakhali, in his fasts, in his prayer meetings, and in his death, that he was able to die with He Ram on his lips.

INDEX

Abercrombie, Lascelles, 95
Academic values: cultural resistance to, 151; *see also* Education; Humanities; Teachers
Action: open to men of letters, 159–61; prior commitment to, 176
Addams, Jane, 234
Adventure myths: as energizing, 71, 193–94, 198; humorous and historical novels as, 197–98; satirical, 196; split between Great Tradition and, 194–95; Tolstoy and Gandhi and, 201–6
Aesthetics: Gandhi opposed to, 87, 101, 212; and politics, 104–26; in politics of Gandhi, 104–6, 110–26; *see also* Arts; Beauty
Alanahalli, Sriskrisna, 141
Ambedkar, Dr., 243
Anand, Mulk Raj, 188
Anarchism: of Bhave, 32; of Gandhi, 220; and Gandhi's theory of culture, 82–83; of Leavis, 220; of J.P. Narayan, 32; of Old Believers, 92; Orwell and, 224; of Tolstoy, 28, 55, 236
Andrews, C. F., 24–25, 48, 49, 99, 117
Anger: nonviolence and rejection of, 16, 18
Antihedonism, *see* Asceticism
Antiimperialism: in British Empire, 73–74; of Gandhi, 22–26; of modern art, 69–70; of Tolstoy, 26, 127, 132–33
Apte, Narayan, 29, 30
Architecture: Gandhi's interest in, 186–87
Arnold, Edwin, 90

Artaud, Antonin, 103
Arts: Gandhi and, 86–87, 115, 118–121, 174–84, 186–88; Gandhian approach to, 153–62; resistance heroes in, 92–95; Tolstoy and, 86–87, 127–30, 179–82, 184–85; utopian quality of, 116; *see also* Modern art; *and specific arts; for example*: Poetry
Asceticism: of Bhave, 32; diet and, 19–20; of Gandhi, xiii–xiv, 6, 38, 56; nonviolence and, 19 (*see also* Nonviolence); of Orwell, 221; in Rama cult, 10; and rejection of body, 101–2 (*see also* Sexuality); of Rolland, 208; spinning wheel as symbol of, 116; of Tolstoy, xiii–xiv, 236; *see also* Spirituality
Ashe, Geoffrey, 55
Atomic threat: Gandhism as only alternative to, 159
Aurobindo, Sri, 142
Austen, Jane, 95, 194

Bach, Johann Sebastian, 93
Bachelard, Gaston, 112
Bagehot, Walter, 234
Balanchine, George, 179
Ballantyne, Robert M., 193
Ballou, Adin, 92
Baptists, 92
Bates, Joshua, 77
Beauty: as source of inspiration, 118
Becharji, Swami, 10
Beckett, Samuel, 103
Beethoven, Ludwig van, 84, 86, 208

Index

Index

Index

Index

Index

Index